Lecture Notes in Computer Science 8563

Commenced Publication in 1973
Founding and Former Series Editors:
Gerhard Goos, Juris Hartmanis, and Jan van Leeu

Francisco José Perales
José Santos-Victor (Eds.)

Articulated Motion and Deformable Objects

8th International Conference, AMDO 2014
Palma de Mallorca, Spain, July 16-18, 2014
Proceedings

Springer

Volume Editors

Francisco José Perales
UIB – Universitat de les Illes Balears
Dept. Matemáticas e Informatica
Crta Valldemossa, Km 7.5, 07122 Palma de Mallorca, Spain
E-mail: paco.perales@uib.es

José Santos-Victor
Universidade de Lisboa
Instituto Superior Técnico
Av. Rovisco Pais 1, 1049-001 Lisboa, Portugal
E-mail: jasv@isr.tecnico.ulisboa.pt

ISSN 0302-9743   e-ISSN 1611-3349
ISBN 978-3-319-08848-8   e-ISBN 978-3-319-08849-5
DOI 10.1007/978-3-319-08849-5
Springer Cham Heidelberg New York Dordrecht London

Library of Congress Control Number: 2014942441

LNCS Sublibrary: SL 6 – Image Processing, Computer Vision, Pattern Recognition, and Graphics

Typesetting: Camera-ready by author, data conversion by Scientific Publishing Services, Chennai, India

Printed on acid-free paper

Springer is part of Springer Science+Business Media (www.springer.com)

Preface

The AMDO 2014 conference took place at Sa Riera Building (UIB), Palma de Mallorca, during July 16–18, 2014, institutionally sponsored the AERFAI (Spanish Association in Pattern Recognition and Artificial Intelligence) and the Mathematics and Computer Science Department of the UIB. Important commercial and research sponsors also collaborated, with the main contributors being: VICOM Tech, ANDROME Iberica, EDM (Expertise Cemtrum voor Digitale Media), iMinds.

The subject of the conference is the ongoing research in articulated motion on a sequence of images and sophisticated models for deformable objects. The goals of these areas are the understanding and interpretation of the motion of complex objects that can be found in sequences of images in the real world. The main topics considered as priority are: geometric and physical deformable models, motion analysis, articulated models and animation, modelling and visualization of deformable models, deformable model applications, motion analysis applications, single or multiple human motion analysis and synthesis, face modelling, tracking, recovering and recognition models, virtual and augmented reality, haptics devices, and biometrics techniques. The conference topics were grouped into these tracks: **Track 1**, Advanced Computer Graphics (Human Modelling and Animation); **Track 2**, Medical Deformable Models and Visualization; **Track 3**, Human Motion (Analysis, Tracking, 3D Reconstruction and Recognition); **Track 4**, Multimodal User Interaction and Applications.

The AMDO 2014 conference was the natural evolution of the seven previous editions and has been consolidated as a European reference for symposiums in the topics mentioned above. The main goal of this conference was to promote interaction and collaboration among researchers working directly in the areas covered by the main tracks. New perceptual user interfaces and the emerging technologies create new relationships between the areas involved in human—computer interactions. A new aim of the AMDO 2014 conference was the strengthening of the relationship between the areas that share as key point the study of the human body using computer technologies as the main tool. Also, the conference benefited from the collaboration of the invited speakers who dealt with various aspects of the main topics. These invited speakers were: Prof. João Manuel R.S. Tavares (University of Porto, Portugal). Prof. Maria Dolores Lozano, (University of Castilla-La Mancha, Spain), and Prof. Daniel Wickeroth (University of Cologne, Germany).

July 2014

F.J. Perales
S.V. Santos

Preface

Organization

AMDO 2014 was organized by the Computer Graphics, Vision and Artificial Intelligence team of the Department of Mathematics and Computer Science, Universitat de les Illes Balears (UIB) in cooperation with AERFAI (Spanish Association for Pattern Recognition and Image Analysis).

Executive Committee

General Conference Co-chairs

F.J. Perales	UIB, Spain
S.V. Santos	Instituto Superior Técnico; Universidade de Lisboa, Portugal

Organizing Chairs

Gonzalez M.	UIB, Spain
Mas R.	UIB, Spain
Jaume-Capó A.	UIB, Spain
Mascaró Oliver M.	UIB, Spain
Manresa-Yee C.	UIB, Spain
Varona X.	UIB, Spain
Buades, J.M.	UIB, Spain
Miró M.	UIB, Spain
Fiol G.	UIB, Spain
Moya-Alcover G.	UIB, Spain
Ramis S.	UIB, Spain
Amengual E.	UIB, Spain

Program Committee

Abasolo, M.	Universidad Nacional de La Plata, Argentina
Aloimonos, Y.	University of Maryland, USA
Bagdanov, A.D.	University of Florence, Italy
Baldassarri, S.	University of Zaragoza, Spain
Bartoli A.	CNRS_LASMEA, France
Baumela, L.	Technical University of Madrid, Spain
Brunet, P.	Polytechnic University of Catalonia, Spain
Bowden, R.	University of Surrey, UK
Campilho A.	University of Oporto, Portugal

Sponsoring Institutions

Commercial Sponsoring Enterprises

VICOM-Tech S.A., www.vicomtech.es
ANDROME Iberica S.A, www.androme.es
EDM (Expertise Cemtrum voor Digitale Media), http://www.uhasselt.be/edm
iMinds, www.iminds.be

Table of Contents

Video Segmentation of Life-Logging Videos

Marc Bolaños[1], Maite Garolera[2], and Petia Radeva[1,3]

[1] University of Barcelona, Barcelona, Spain
[2] Hospital de Terrassa-Consorci Sanitari de Terrassa, Terrassa, Spain
[3] Computer Vision Center of Barcelona, Bellaterra (Barcelona), Spain
mark.bs.1991@gmail.com, MGarolera@cst.cat, petia.ivanova@ub.edu

Abstract. Life-logging devices are characterized by easily collecting huge amount of images. One of the challenges of lifelogging is how to organize the big amount of image data acquired in semantically meaningful segments. In this paper, we propose an energy-based approach for motion-based event segmentation of life-logging sequences of low temporal resolution. The segmentation is reached integrating different kind of image features and classifiers into a graph-cut framework to assure consistent sequence treatment. The results show that the proposed method is promising to create summaries of everyday person's life.

Keywords: Life-logging, video segmentation.

1 Introduction

Recently, with the appearance of different LifeLogging (LL) devices (SenseCam [1], Looxcie [2], Narrative (previously called Memoto) [3], Autobiographer), people wearing them are getting eager for capturing details about their daily life. Capturing images along the whole day leads to a huge amount of data that should be organized and summarized in order to be able to store them and review later, being able to focus just on the most important aspects. On the other hand, LL data appear very promising to design new therapies for treating different diseases. LL data have been used to retain and recover memory abilities for patients with Alzheimer's disease [1] as well as to capture and display the healthy habits like nutrition, physical activities, emotions or social interaction. In [4] they are used as an aid for recording the everyday life in order to be able to detect and recognize elements that can measure persons' quality of life and, thus, to improve it [5,6].

LL devices being worn by a person the whole day, have the property to capture images for long periods of time. Depending on where the device is positioned (head-mounted, on glasses, camera with a pin, hung camera, ear-mounted, etc.) determines the field of view and the camera motion (usually, glass camera would be more stable and would give information, where the person is looking at, meanwhile camera hung on the person's neck moves more and lacks information on where the person is looking at). On the other hand, a hung up camera has the advantage that is considered more unobtrusive and thus, causes less repeal

F.J. Perales and J. Santos-Victor (Eds.): AMDO 2014, LNCS 8563, pp. 1–9, 2014.

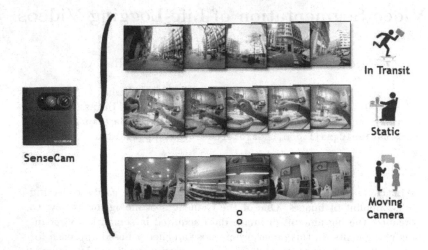

Fig. 1. Illustration of the three person movement-related events to be detected

from the persons around recorded by the camera [7]. Another important characteristic is the temporal resolution of the device. Meanwhile Looxcie has high temporal resolution and, thus, provides smooth continuous videos, many other LL devices like SenseCam has low temporal resolution (2-4 frames per minute) making difficult to consider consecutive frames as videos. Moreover, objects in consecutive images can appear in very different positions. On the other hand, low temporal resolution cameras have the advantages to acquire a reasonable amount of images in order to capture the whole day of the person and allow to process images covering long periods of time (weeks, months). Due to this reason, in this article, we focus on sequence segmentation with a SenseCam that is able to acquire and store images during the whole day activities of the person wearing the camera. Moreover, being hung on the neck, SenseCam is less obtrusive that head-mounted devices, but has low temporal resolution and significant free camera motion. Usually, a day captured by a SenseCam used to contain around 4000 images with no smooth transition between consecutive frames; in a month more than 100.000 images are generated.

Developing tools to reduce redundancy, organize data in events and ease LL review is of high interest. In [8], the authors proposed a method for segmenting and summarizing LL videos based on the detection of "important" objects [9]. Doherty et.al. proposed different methods like selecting specific keyframes [10], combining image descriptors [11] and using a dissimilarity score based on CombMIN [12] to segment and summarize also low-resolution LL data. The work in [13] reviews different techniques for extracting information from egocentric videos, like object recognition, activity detection, sports activities or video summarization.

Event segmentation in LL data is characterized by the action (movement) of the person wearing the device. The relation between scene and event depends on the person's action that is not always visible in the images; thus, standard event detection techniques in video are not useful. We group consecutive frames in three general event classes according to the human movement (see Figure 1): "Static" (person and camera are maintaining static), "In Transit" (person is moving or running) and "Moving Camera" (person is not changing his/her surroundings, but the camera is moving - e.g. person is interacting with another person, manipulating an object, etc.). Similar event classification has been proposed and addressed by video techniques in [8],where high-temporal resolution LL data are processed. Taking into account that in the case of low-temporal resolution data, video analysis techniques are not usable, we study a novel set of image features and integrate them in an energy-minimization approach for video segmentation[1]. In contrast to [8], we show that an optimal approach is achieved by combining a set of features (bluriness[14], colour, SIFT flow[15], HoG[16]) and classifiers integrated in a Graph Cut (GC) formulation for spatially coherent treatment of LL consecutive frames.

The paper is organized as follows: in section 2, we explain the design and implementation of our event extraction method. In Section 3, we discuss the results obtained and finish the paper with Conclusions.

2   Methodology

To address the event segmentation problem, our approach is based on two main steps: first, we extract motion, color and blurriness information from the images and apply a classifier to obtain a rough approximation of the class labels in single frames (Figure 2). Second, we apply an energy-minimization technique based on GC to achieve spatial coherence of labels assigned by the classifier and separate the sequences of consecutive images in events.

2.1   Feature Extraction of Life-Logging Data

Given that the three classes are basically distinguished by the motion of the camera or the person, as well as the big difference between frames, robust event segmentation needs motion features that do not assume smooth image transition. Hence, we propose to extract the folowing feature types:

SIFT flow data[15,17]: calculated as 8 components, which describe the motion on each cardinal direction scaled by its magnitude.

Blurriness [14]: calculated as 9 components representing the blurrines in each cell dividing the image in 3x3 equal rectangles.

Color difference: color histogram difference between the current image and the five previous ones. With the use of the SIFT flow features between each pair of consecutive images, we expect to find differences between sequences of images with label "Static", which should have a low magnitude and little resilient direction of the descriptors in a significant part of the images. Labels "Moving

---

[1] Although the low temporal resolution, we still speak about videos of data, refering to the consecutive image collection acquired during a day.

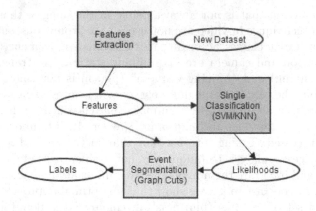

Fig. 2. Diagram of the main steps followed by our method

Camera" and "In Transit" should have a more clear movement. At the same time, the last two classes should be differentiated having vectors of flow with undefined and constantly changing direction (in the "Moving Camera" class) vs. those pointing from the center to the external part of the image due to the movement, when walking for the "In Transit" class. The advantage of SIFT flow is that it is able to find the correspondence of points almost independently of their difference in the image position. About the second descriptor, blurriness, we also expect different behaviour for distinguishing the "Static" from the other labels, which should have a more marked blur effect. Color differences is expected to be informative specially for the "Moving Camera" and "In Transit" classes.

2.2 GC-Based Event Segmentation of LL Data

Events are supposed to be sequences of frames with the same class label. In order to obtain such sequences, we apply a GC-based [18,19] energy-minimization technique to get a reliable event segmentation. GCs are based on the minimization of the energy resulting from the sum of two different terms:

$$E(f) = \sum_{i \in S} U_i(f_i) + W \sum_{\{i,n \in N_i\}} \frac{1}{N_i} P_{i,n}(f_i, f_n)$$

where f_i are the set of features used for the energy minimization, U_i is the unary term, $P_{i,n}$ is the pairwise term, which relates any image i in the sequence with each of its neighbours $n \in N_i$, and W is the weighting term for balancing the trade-off between the unary and the pairwise term. The **unary term**, U_i in our case, is set to $1 - L_H$, being L_H the result from a classifier output that represents the likelihood for each image to belong to one of the three defined classes. The **pairwise term** $P_{i,n}$ is a similarity measure for each sample on each cliqué (all neighbours of a given sample) with respect to the chosen image features that determines the likelihood for each neighbouring pair of images (with a neighbourhood length of 11 in our case) to have the same label. The GC

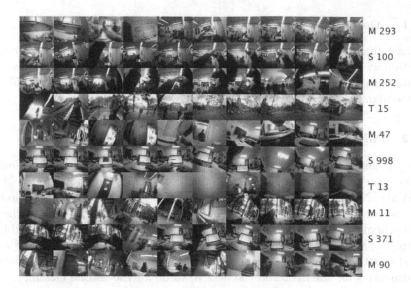

Fig. 3. Fraction of the total summary of events resulting from a dataset using KNN-based GC segmentation. Each row represents one of the 3 classes, with the total number of images and label belonging to each of them at the right.

algorithm [18,19] using a graph structure finds the optimal cut that minimizes the sum of energies $E(f)$ assigning a class label to each sample as a result of the energy minimization.

Taking into account that the pairwise term should "catch" the features relation between consecutive frames, it uses different features from the classifier ones, namely:

- **Color:** RGB color histograms with 9 bins (3 per color).
- **HoG [16]:** Histogram of oriented gradients with 81 components per image to capture changes in the image structures. The GC algorithm assigns all the consecutive images with the same label to the same class, and thus determines the final event division. Figure 3 illustrates different samples of the extracted events from the three classes. The length of each event is given on the right. For visualization purpose, each event is uniformly subsampled. Note that the "T" events represent image sequences with significant change of the scene (rows 4 and 7). "S" events are representing a static person although the images can differ due to hand manipulation (rows 2, 6 and 9), and "M" events suggest moving person's body (rows 1, 3, 5, 8, and 10).

3   Results

In this section, we review the datasets used in our experiments and the most relevant performed validation tests.

3.1   Datasets Description

Given that there is no public SenseCam dataset with event labels, for the validation we used the dataset from [6] that contains 31749 labeled images from 10 different days taken with a SenseCam. For the purpose of the article, 553 events were manually annotated with 57.41 images per event, on average.

3.2   Parameter Optimization

Regarding the GC unary term, we performed different tests using the output of two of the most popular classifiers in the bibliography: Support Vector Machines (SVM) [20] and K-Nearest Neighbour (KNN). Nevertheless, the method allows to use any classifier that provides a score or likelihood to be used in the graph-cut scheme. In pursuance of obtaining the most generalized result possible, when applying the Radial Basis Function SVM and the KNN, we designed a nested fold cross-validation for obtaining the best regularizing (λ) and deviation (σ) parameters for the first, and the best K value for the second classifier. We used a 10-fold cross validation selecting randomly the balanced training samples. The optimal parameters obtained were: $\lambda = 3$ and $\sigma = 3$, $K = 11$ on KNN with Euclidean distance metric and $K = 21$ on KNN with cosine distance metric.

With these tests, our purpose was to test the weighting GC parameter and to prove the importance of using the GC scheme compared to the frame classification obtained by the SVM/KNN classifiers. Regarding the weight value W, we used a range from 0 to 3.75 in intervals of 0.15 points. We can see in Figure 4 the difference in accuracy between the KNN and the GC for different W values. Note that for $W = 1.75$, the classification of frames improved from 0.72 to 0.86. It resulted that in this case, we obtained 108 events compared to the 56 events in the groundtruth of test set 10. Note that in this case the accuracy is 0.86 representing 15% of improvement regarding the baseline classification result, although the automatic approach tends to oversegment the events.

3.3   GC Performance for Event Segmentation

A summary of the average improvement of using frame classifier (the SVM/KNN) versus integrating it in the GC scheme can be seen in Figure 4. Here, KNNe stands for KNN using Euclidean metrics and KNNc stands for KNN with Cosine metrics. Analysing the results, we can observe that the KNN obtains higher accuracy than the SVM, and that adding the GC "label smoothing" after it, the results are widely improved. The only aspect to take into account, specially, when using the KNN with Euclidean distance is that the performance on all the classes is far from the balanced one (the accuracy of class "S" is much higher than that of the other classes). In this case, a KNN with cosine metrics is a good compromise of overall accuracy as well as accuracy of each class, separately. Regarding the result using SVM, GC has not been able to improve the results of the SVM (on average). However, it still has two advantages: 1) obtaining an average number of events more suitable and realistic with respect to each dataset and

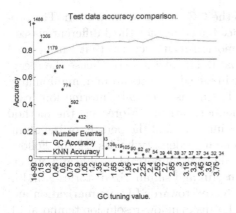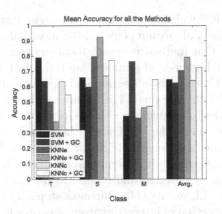

Fig. 4. Improvement in accuracy using different weights for the GC with respect to the KNN with cosine metrics; tests on the 10th dataset (left). Accuracy for each class (T,S,M) and average accuracy for the classifiers (SVM,KNN) and the GC (right).

2) having more similar average of accuracy for each class (without any negative peack of performance like class "M" in case of SVM).

In order to seek redundant image features, we applied a Feature Selection (FS) based on the Student's t-test. We tested the gain obtained by the FS method and the best p-value for it not using the less relevant features neither for the classifier (SVM/KNN) nor for the GC. Comparing the accuracy results, we obtained no statistical difference in performance of the method with and without feature selection. Very similar results were obtained by the Sequential Forward Floating Search method [21].

Once we have applied the GC video segmentation, we have the final sequence divided into events and classified with the respective labels. Events with a very low number of images, would correspond to too short events i.e. with less than 8 images (less than 2 minutes in real time). Since such sequences will not be enough to extract information in the future, neither for obtaining a summary nor for detecting actions of interest of the user, they are deleted.

The limitations of the method are related to the ambiguity between the "T" and "M" labels, due to their motion similarity, that make difficult to classify. Moreover, the "free" motion of the camera is difficult to differentiate (for any of the classifiers used), and this, added to the fact that we use the HOGs without any previous image orientation (that might be a problem when the camera is rotated), are some aspects that might be improved in future work.

4   Conclusions

In this work, we proposed a new method for motion-based segmentation of sequences produced by LL devices with low temporal resolution. The most remarkable results are represented by integrating a wide set of image features and a KNN classifier with cosine metrics into the GC energy-minimization. The proposed algorithm achieved the most balanced accuracy for the 3 different classes.

Our method proposes tools to detect motion-related events that can be used for higher-level semantic analysis of LL data. The method could ease the recognition of person's action and the elements involved (objects around, manipulated objects, persons). The events can be used as a base to create information "capsules" for memory enhancement of Alzheimer patients. Moreover, the method can relate the "In Transit" label to exercising action of the person, or the abundance and length of "Static" events evidencing sedentary habits [22,23]. Following works on high-temporal resolution LL data [9], important people and objects can be detected and related to the most useful and summarized stories found in the LL events [24]. Our next steps are directed towards LL summarization and detection of interesting events, people and objects in low-resolution temporal LL for either improving the memory of the user or visualizing summarized lifestyle data to ease the management of the user's healthy habits (sedentary lifestyles [22], nutritional activity of obese people, etc.).

Acknowledgments. This work was partially founded by the projects TIN2012-38187-C03-01, Fundació "Jaume Casademont" - Girona and SGR 1219.

References

1. Hodges, S., Williams, L., Berry, E., Izadi, S., Srinivasan, J., Butler, A., Smyth, G., Kapur, N., Wood, K.: Sensecam: A retrospective memory aid. In: Dourish, P., Friday, A. (eds.) UbiComp 2006. LNCS, vol. 4206, pp. 177–193. Springer, Heidelberg (2006)
2. Eisenberg, A.: When a Camcorder becomes a life partner, vol. 6. New York Times (2010)
3. Bowers, D.: Lifelogging: Both advancing and hindering personal information management (2013)
4. Sellen, A.J., Whittaker, S.: Beyond total capture: a constructive critique of lifelogging. Communications of the ACM 53(5), 70–77 (2010)
5. Hoashi, H., Joutou, T., Yanai, K.: Image recognition of 85 food categories by feature fusion. In: 2010 IEEE International Symposium on Multimedia (ISM), pp. 296–301. IEEE (2010)
6. Bolaños, M., Garolera, M., Radeva, P.: Active labeling application applied to food-related object recognition. In: Proceedings of the 5th International Workshop on Multimedia for Cooking & Eating Activities, pp. 45–50. ACM (2013)
7. Vondrick, C., Hayden, D.S., Landa, Y., Jia, S.X., Torralba, A., Miller, R.C., Teller, S.: The accuracy-obtrusiveness tradeoff for wearable vision platforms. In: Second IEEE Workshop on Egocentric Vision, CVPR (2012)
8. Lu, Z., Grauman, K.: Story-driven summarization for egocentric video. In: 2013 IEEE Conference on Computer Vision and Pattern Recognition (CVPR), pp. 2714–2721. IEEE (2013)
9. Lee, Y.J., Ghosh, J., Grauman, K.: Discovering important people and objects for egocentric video summarization. In: IEEE Conference on Computer Vision and Pattern Recognition (CVPR 2012), pp. 1346–1353. IEEE (2012)

10. Doherty, A.R., Byrne, D., Smeaton, A.F., Jones, G.J.F., Hughes, M.: Investigating keyframe selection methods in the novel domain of passively captured visual lifelogs. In: Proceedings of the 2008 International Conference on Content-Based Image and Video Retrieval, pp. 259–268. ACM (2008)

11. Doherty, A.R., Ó Conaire, C., Blighe, M., Smeaton, A.F., O'Connor, N.E.: Combining image descriptors to effectively retrieve events from visual lifelogs. In: Proceedings of the 1st ACM International Conference on Multimedia Information Retrieval, pp. 10–17. ACM (2008)

12. Doherty, A.R., Smeaton, A.F.: Automatically segmenting lifelog data into events. In: Image Analysis for Multimedia Interactive Services, WIAMIS 2008, pp. 20–23. IEEE (2008)

13. Bambach, S.: A survey on recent advances of computer vision algorithms for egocentric video (2013)

14. Crete, F., Dolmiere, T., Ladret, P., Nicolas, M.: The blur effect: Perception and estimation with a new no-reference perceptual blur metric. Human Vision and Electronic Imaging XII 6492, 64920 (2007)

15. Liu, C., Yuen, J., Torralba, A., Sivic, J., Freeman, W.T.: SIFT flow: Dense correspondence across different scenes. In: Forsyth, D., Torr, P., Zisserman, A. (eds.) ECCV 2008, Part III. LNCS, vol. 5304, pp. 28–42. Springer, Heidelberg (2008)

16. Dalal, N., Triggs, B.: Histograms of oriented gradients for human detection. In: IEEE Computer Society Conference on Computer Vision and Pattern Recognition (CVPR 2005), vol. 1, pp. 886–893 (2005)

17. Liu, C.: Beyond pixels: exploring new representations and applications for motion analysis, Ph.D. thesis, Massachusetts Institute of Technology (2009)

18. Boykov, Y., Veksler, O., Zabih, R.: Fast approximate energy minimization via graph cuts. IEEE Transactions on Pattern Analysis and Machine Intelligence 23(11), 1222–1239 (2001)

19. Delong, A., Osokin, A., Isack, H.N., Boykov, Y.: Fast approximate energy minimization with label costs. International Journal of Computer Vision 96(1), 1–27 (2012)

20. Cortes, C., Vapnik, V.: Support-vector networks. Machine Learning 20(3), 273–297 (1995)

21. Pudil, P., Novovičová, J., Kittler, J.: Floating search methods in feature selection. Pattern Recognition Letters 15(11), 1119–1125 (1994)

22. Kelly, P., Doherty, A., Berry, E., Hodges, S., Batterham, A.M., Foster, C.: Can we use digital life-log images to investigate active and sedentary travel behaviour? results from a pilot study. International Journal on Behavioral Nutrition and Physical Activities 8(44), 44 (2011)

23. Kerr, J., Marshall, S.J., Godbole, S., Chen, J., Legge, A., Doherty, A.R., Kelly, P., Oliver, M., Badland, H.M., Foster, C.: Using the sensecam to improve classifications of sedentary behavior in free-living settings. American Journal of Preventive Medicine 44(3), 290–296 (2013)

24. Shahaf, D., Guestrin, C.: Connecting the dots between news articles. In: Proceedings of the 16th ACM SIGKDD International Conference on Knowledge Discovery and Data Mining, pp. 623–632. ACM (2010)

Human Pose Estimation in Stereo Images

Joe Lallemand[1,2], Magdalena Szczot[1], and Slobodan Ilic[2]

[1] BMW Group, Munich, Germany
{joe.lallemand,magdalena.szczot}@bmw.de
http://www.bmw.de

[2] Computer Aided Medical Procedures, Technische Universität München, Germany
slobodan.ilic@in.tum.de
http://campar.in.tum.de

Abstract. In this paper, we address the problem of 3D human body pose estimation from depth images acquired by a stereo camera. Compared to the Kinect sensor, stereo cameras work outdoors having a much higher operational range, but produce noisier data. In order to deal with such data, we propose a framework for 3D human pose estimation that relies on random forests. The first contribution is a novel grid-based shape descriptor robust to noisy stereo data that can be used by any classifier. The second contribution is a two step classification procedure, first classifying the body orientation, then proceeding with determining the full 3D pose within this orientation cluster. To validate our method, we introduce a dataset recorded with a stereo camera synchronized with an optical motion capture system that provides ground truth human body poses.

Keywords: Human Pose Estimation, Machine Learning, Depth Data.

1 Introduction

Human body pose estimation in depth images has seen tremendous progress in the last few years. The introduction of Kinect and other similar devices has resulted in a number of new algorithms addressing the problem of 3D human body pose estimation [1,2,3,4].

Although these Kinect-like sensors work in real-time and usually provide depth images of a good quality with a small amount of noise and depth errors as depicted in Fig.1, they also have the disadvantages of only working indoors and at a very limited depth range. For these reasons, human pose estimation using Kinect has extensively been used for generic indoor scenarios. Many other applications however, especially automotive driver assistance, imply the use of outdoor-suitable sensors as e.g. stereo cameras. Since stereo camera systems are becoming standard in modern cars, there is a need for 3D human pose estimation from stereo data. For that reason, we propose a new algorithm using a stereo camera which provides real time depth images at a range of up to 50 meters, which is about 5 times higher than indoor sensors. As can be seen in Fig.1, real-time stereo algorithms integrated in vehicles generally produce noisy images,

F.J. Perales and J. Santos-Victor (Eds.): AMDO 2014, LNCS 8563, pp. 10–19, 2014.
© Springer International Publishing Switzerland 2014

where some regions are erroneously fused together (red circles) and the boundaries of the objects can be effected by a high number of artifacts (green and blue circles). These reconstruction artifacts introduced by stereo reconstruction affect the results of state-of-the-art methods, like the one of Grishick et al. [2], which we reimplemented and applied to these data. This is because of the two main reasons. Firstly, it is very difficult to perform 360 degree pose estimation using a single forest as there is a high confusion between front and back. Secondly the feature vector proposed in [1] seems to perform poorly on the stereo data. Therefore we present a new method for human pose estimation, adapting random forest classification and regression methodology into a two step pipeline to reliably estimate 3D human body pose. The first step consists in classifying the shape of a person into a cluster which represents its orientation with respect to the camera. In the second step, the skeleton pose of the person is estimated using a regression random forest trained only on the poses of the detected orientation. In order to make this pipeline operational we introduce a novel grid-based feature. This feature overcomes several disadvantages that appear when using the depth comparison feature introduced by Shotton et al. [1] on the stereo data as shown in the result section.

To verify and validate our method, we introduce a dataset which is recorded with a stereo camera synchronized with the ART marker based system for human motion capture [1]. The orientation classification is also evaluated on the publicly available pedestrian stereo data set introduced in [5].

2   Related Work

Many algorithms for human pose estimation from depth images have emerged in the last years. Shotton et al. [1] propose to use a classification random forest to classify each pixel of a foreground mask to a given body part, then infer the joint locations from the predicted body parts. Girshick et al. [2] extended this work by learning a regression model to directly predict the joint locations. This approach considerably improved the performance of the previous algorithm especially for occluded joints. Both works rely on a large synthetic training dataset in order to achieve good results and target good quality depth images.

In [3], Taylor et al. train a regression random forest to create a mapping from each pixel of a segmented foreground depth image to a human body model. Taking into account the forest predictions, physical constraints and visibility constraints, they use an energy minimization function to predict the pose of the model and the attached skeleton. This approach improves prediction accuracy compared to previous works and is able to predict poses in the 360 degree range, but still relies on the tree structures trained using the classification approach of [1].

Sun et al. [6] introduce a conditional regression forest learning a global latent variable during the forest training step that incorporates dependency relationships of the output variables, e.g. torso orientation or height.

---

[1] www.ar-tracking.com

A simple depth comparison feature is common to all these methods. Each dimension of it consists of the difference in depth computed at two random offsets from the reference pixel at which the feature is computed. As the foreground masks in stereo data contain many erroneous boundaries, the feature cannot be consistently extracted for the same pose. The proposed grid-based feature is robust to these errors because it consists of cells where depth and occupancy distribution are averaged over the whole cell.

Plänkers and Fua [7] use an articulated soft object model to describe the human body and track it in a system of calibrated video cameras, making use of stereo and silhouette data. Urtasun and Fua [8] additionally introduce a temporal motion models based on Principal Component Analysis. Bernier et al. [9] propose a 3D body tracking algorithm on stereo data. The human body is represented using a graphical model and tracking is performed using non-parametric belief propagation to get a frame by frame pose. Unlike the three previously mentioned works, which require initialization and track the human pose, our proposed method works on single frames and performs discriminative pose estimation. Up to the best of our knowledge, this problem has not yet been addressed for the kind of noisy input data as produced by stereo cameras or similar devices.

Keskin et al. [10] use a two-layer random forest for hand pose estimation. First, the hand is classified based on the shape, then the skeleton is determined for the given shape cluster using a regression forest. Though similar to [10], we introduce a novel grid-based feature and a two stage classification method for human pose estimation in noisy stereo data.

In [11], Enzweiler and Gavrila propose an algorithm for single-frame pedestrian detection and orientation estimation based on a monocular camera, where orientation is divided into 4 directions. In contrast to this, the proposed method is based on the depth information from the stereo camera and the orientation clusters are encoding direction as well as different poses within this direction.

3 Method

This section introduces the grid-based feature vector which is used both, for the classification of human body orientations and the human pose estimation per determined orientation and describes the two step classification pipeline. The first step involves determining the human body orientation. While the second computes the 3D pose of a skeleton choosing from poses of the estimated orientation cluster. Finally, we describe how the classification and pose prediction step are combined.

3.1 Grid-Based Feature

The proposed grid-based feature divides the shape of a person into arbitrary cells, then averages over depth values and occupancy distributions.

Let $\Omega \subset \mathbb{R}^2$ be a segmented foreground mask in a given image. The construction of the feature vector consist of 4 consecutive steps. The first step determines the bounding box around the foreground mask. In the second step, the bounding box is divided into an $n \times m$ grid of cells $c_{i,j}$. Note that this division is scale invariant, as the bounding box, regardless of its actual size, is divided into the same number of cells. In the third step, we attribute each pixel of the foreground to its corresponding cell and determine the median position, $x_{c_{i,j}} \in \mathbb{R}$ and $y_{c_{i,j}} \in \mathbb{R}$ and median depth $z_{c_{i,j}} \in \mathbb{R}$ in each cell. This cell structure now represents a very simple encoding of the shape of a person. If a cell is left unoccupied, it is assigned a very high value. Finally, the pixel-wise grid-based feature is given by:

$$f_{p_k} = \{x_k - x_{c_{1,1}}, y_k - y_{c_{1,1}}, z_k - z_{c_{1,1}}, \ldots, x_k - x_{c_{n,m}}, y_k - y_{c_{n,m}}, z_k - z_{c_{n,m}}\} \quad (1)$$

for a pixel $p_k = \{x_k, y_k, z_k\}$. Figure 1 shows the different steps of generating the feature vector. In this way, the feature vector is able to ignore small errors of the stereo algorithm especially around borders and systematic errors of the algorithm are taken into consideration as shown in Fig. 1 (b). The result section provides analysis of the influence of the feature dimension on the performance of the classifier.

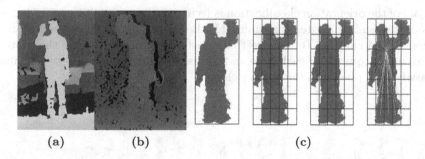

(a)   (b)   (c)

Fig. 1. (a,b): Comparison between the data quality acquired with Kinect(a) and with the stereo camera(b). (c) Different stages of creating the feature vector here for 5×7 cells from left to right: the bounding box tightly laid around the foreground mask, the subdivision of the bounding box into a grid of cells, the computed median in each cell in red, the feature vector for a randomly chosen pixel in green and the connection to each cell median in yellow.

3.2   General Theory on Training Random Forests

A random forest is an ensemble of decorrelated binary decision trees. It is trained on a dataset Δ, consisting of pairs $\psi_i = \{f_i, l_i\}$ of feature vectors f and the labels l, learning the mapping from the features to the labels. Each tree is trained on a subset of the training data ensuring that the trees are randomized. At each node of the tree, a decision function $g_{\nu,\tau}(f) \equiv \nu * f < \tau$ is trained sending samples to the left child node if this condition is verified else to the right child node, where ν chooses exactly one feature dimension thus creating axis aligned splits. In order to train this decision function, at each node, a subset of all feature dimensions is randomly chosen and for each feature, n thresholds are generated, separating the incoming samples Δ into left and right subsets Δ_l and Δ_r. For each of these splits, an information gain is computed:

$$\mathbf{I}_{\nu,\tau} = -\frac{|\Delta_l|}{|\Delta|} H\left(\Delta_l\right) - \frac{|\Delta_r|}{|\Delta|} H\left(\Delta_r\right) \tag{2}$$

where H is an entropy function depending on the kind of random forest and $|\cdot|$ denotes the number of elements in a set. The final decision function g_{ν^*,τ^*} is given by finding $argmax_{\nu,\tau}\left(I_{\nu,\tau}\right)$. This process is repeated iteratively until a leaf node is reached, which is defined by the following criteria: (i) the maximum depth is reached, (ii) a minimum number of samples is undercut or (iii) the information gain falls below a certain threshold. In the leaf nodes, all incoming samples are used to compute a posterior distribution which depends directly on the kind of forest trained.

3.3   Orientation Classification

The goal of the orientation classification is to assign the current foreground mask to its corresponding cluster containing all the poses of a specific orientation in relation to the camera. To achieve this, clusters are created using the motion capture data acquired for each pose and a classification random forest is trained to classify each pixel into the correct cluster.

(a)   (b)

Fig. 2. (a)30 Orientation clusters obtained with k-means clustering. For such a large number of clusters, the poses are divided by orientation but also broadly into arm and leg movements. (b) Orientation classification results for different sizes of the grid like feature and different number of orientation cluster.

Generation of Orientation Clusters. The clusters are generated in an unsupervised manner, using the motion capture data from the training dataset. For each pose, the angles between all neighboring joints are computed. Clustering is done using the k-means approach on these joint angles. In case k-means is run on the euclidean distances of joint positions in 3D space, the algorithm not only separates poses in terms of joint angles but also people of different heights. By using only the joint angles and deliberately omitting limb lengths, we get consistent clusters for different poses with regard to the overall orientation of the person. K-means relies on initial seeds to create clusters and results can vary depending on those seeds. In order to achieve a certain level of independence from this, we run 100 instances of k-means and choose a cluster combination which is most often reached during this process. The influence of the number of clusters is analyzed in the Sec 4. Although other clustering algorithms, e.g. mean shift [12] were tested, they didn't give satisfactory results. Since fixing the bandwidth of mean shift by hand is not trivial. K-means was the final choice for clustering.

Classification of Orientation Clusters. The classification random forest is trained using the grid-based feature to classify each pixel to the correct cluster. Shannon's entropy is used for the information gain. Additionally, we use the random field based reweighting function described in [13]. This reweighting scheme takes into account the class distribution of the full training dataset, instead of reweighting only the samples in the current node, which was shown to yield more accurate results. The information gain I is rewritten as:

$$I_{\nu,\tau} = - \sum_{i \in \{l,r\}} Z\left(\Delta_i\right) \sum_{c \in C} n\left(c, \Delta_i\right) \log \left(\frac{w_c n\left(c, \Delta_i\right)}{Z\left(\Delta_i\right)} \right) \tag{3}$$

where Δ_0 is the total training set, $n\left(c, \Delta_i\right)$ is the number of occurrences of class c in the subset Δ_i, and $w_c = \frac{\sum_{k \in C} n(k, \Delta_0)}{n(c, \Delta_0)}$ is the weight obtained by dividing the total number of samples k in the dataset Δ_0 by the number of occurrences of class c. It is lowest for the most represented class and vice versa. $Z\left(\Delta_i\right) = \sum_{k \in C} w_k n\left(k, \Delta_i\right)$ is analogous to the partition function in a random field and represents the weight of a given subset Δ_i. It replaces the weight $\frac{|\Delta_i|}{|\Delta|}$ in Equation 2. The detailed derivation of this formula from the standard Shannon's entropy is presented in the works of Kontschieder et al. [13] where this new information gain was first introduced. The leaf nodes store the distribution of classes of all incoming points as a histogram.

3.4 Pose Estimation Per Orientation Cluster

One regression forest is trained for the pose estimation of each cluster. For each tree, the training set consists of pixels obtained from a bootstrap of the training images belonging to a given cluster. The ground truth joint positions are provided by a motion capture system, as will be explained in Sec. 4.1. The training dataset consists of pairs of pixel-wise features as described in Sec. 3.1 and labels containing the offset from the given pixel to all joint positions. For a given pixel $p_i(x_i, y_i, z_i)$ and the pose $J = \{j_1, \ldots, j_N\}$ consisting of N joints, the label is given by $\Psi = \{\psi_1, \ldots, \psi_N\}$, with each $\psi_k = (j_{k,x} - x_i, j_{k,y} - y_i, j_{k,z} - z_i)$. During training we iteratively search for the optimal split in each node. As shown in [2], the body joints can be modeled using a multivariate gaussian distribution. Following this idea, we can model the information gain based on the differential entropy of gaussians and assume independence between the different joints. The entropy function H in the information gain function can thus be reduced to:

$$H\left(\Delta\right) = \frac{1}{2}\log\left((2\pi e)^{3N}\left|\Sigma^{(\Delta)}\right|\right) \tag{4}$$

where Σ is the diagonal of the covariance matrix of the joint positions and N is the number of joints. Once a leaf node criterion is fulfilled, the mean shift is computed on all incoming points for each joint and the main mode is stored with its weight, equal to the number of points voting for the main mode .

3.5   Prediction Pipeline

For each image with an unknown pose, the grid-based feature is computed for a random subset of pixels from the foreground mask. They are then sent through all trees of the orientation classification forest. The histograms, containing the distribution over orientation clusters, extracted from all leafs are averaged over all pixels and trees. We retain the three best orientations for the pose estimation. In the pose estimation step, all pixels are sent through the forests belonging to those three best orientation clusters. The final pose aggregation is done by applying mean shift to the predictions for each joint separately and choosing the main mode as the prediction outcome.

4   Experiments and Results

4.1   Data Acquisition

In order to be able to test our algorithm, we have created a new dataset, using a stereo camera and a motion capture system. Since the mocap system does not work outdoors, the training data was acquired indoors. The training set consists of sequences depicting 10 people performing various walking and arm movement motions. During the acquisition the actors were wearing 14 markers which reflect the infrared light emitted by 8 infrared cameras and are used to provide ground truth skeleton positions for each frame. The dataset consists of 25000 frames.

4.2   Orientation Classification

Proposed Dataset: In this paragraph, we analyze the orientation classification part, described in Section 3.3. The evaluation is twofold, first we analyze how the number of clusters affects the classification outcome, then we evaluate the influence of the number of cells of the feature vector and compare to the depth comparison feature. The number of clusters were set to 10 and 30 during the experiments. For the feature vector, we perform an evaluation progressively increasing the number of cells from 3×3 to 11×11 in steps of 2. The maximum allowed tree depth is set to 20, and each forest consists of 5 trees. All results are averaged over a cross validation. For each validation, the forests were trained on 8 people and tested on the remaining 2. Results can be seen in Fig.2 (b). The best results are achieved for 30 clusters. There are two important observations regarding the feature vector. Firstly, dividing the feature into too many cells, especially along the y-axis, decreases the overall performance of the feature. Especially for side views and poses where all limbs are close to the body, a fine grid along the y-axis negatively effects the noise reduction properties for which the feature was designed. Secondly, the feature vector seems to perform best if the ratio between the number of rows and columns is closer to the height versus width ratio of the human body.

In order to compare the grid-based feature to the feature used in [1,2,3], we trained a random forest sampling 500 feature candidates and 20 thresholds at each node with a maximum probe offset of 1.29 pixel-meters, identical to those proposed in [1]. All other parameters were kept identical to the other experiments. The grid-based feature achieved 81.4% and 89.9% for 10 and 30 clusters respectively compared to 64.6% and 72.3% for the depth comparison feature used in [1].

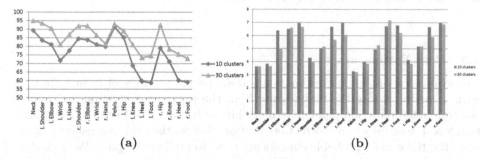

(a)   (b)

Fig. 3. Evaluation of the grid-based feature vector with regard to the number of clusters and the number of cells in the grid. (a): The accuracy per joint (b):error in cm per joint.

Daimler Pedestrian Segmentation Benchmark: In order to show that the approach also works outdoors, we evaluate the orientation classification on the publicly available dataset of Flohr and Gavrila [5], consisting of 785 single disparity images of pedestrians at various distances from the camera. This dataset contains annotated groundtruth for the foreground masks of the pedestrians but does not contain orientation information. To evaluate our approach, we separate the orientation clusters of our approach into 8 directions with regard to the camera {front, front-left, left, back-left, back, back-right, right and front-right}, choosing for each of the generated clusters the dominant torso orientation. Since the ground truth pose is not available for this dataset to determine the correct cluster, we choose visually the closest orientation used for the manually labeled clusters. Tests were run for the 30-cluster training setup using the best feature from the previous experiments, achieving 78% accuracy.

It is noteworthy that most of the disparity images provided by the dataset are much smaller in size than the training images. In only about half of the provided images, the height of the foreground mask is higher than 120 pixels, which is roughly half of the average height of the training images. This shows that our algorithm and especially the feature work well even if the size of testing images is a fraction of the size of the training images In Fig. 4, we show some example images from the dataset with the determined orientation.

Fig. 4. Example images from the dataset of [5]. The ground truth label is denoted in green and the prediction in red. The yellow number displays the percentage of foreground pixels voting for the predicted cluster. We show the original image instead of the depth image, as it is visually more helpful.

4.3   Pose Estimation

The evaluation of the pose estimation is done for cluster sizes of 10 and 30. For each scenario, we use the best feature from the previous evaluation and apply the complete prediction pipeline as described in Section 3.5. First the classification forest determines the correct orientation cluster, then the regression forests from the three most probable clusters are used to predict the pose. We consider a joint to be correctly estimated if it is within a radius of 10 centimeters of the ground truth joint position. This follows the evaluation criteria established by several related works [1,2]. Results are shown in Fig.3 (a). Fig.3 (b) shows the median error per joint. We explicitly use the median, as an error in the orientation classification is propagated to the pose estimation producing wrong poses with per joint errors of up to 1m. By displaying the median error, we can show that if the correct orientation has been determined, the pose prediction produces good results for all different orientations. Examples are shown in supplementary materials video. To compare our grid-based feature to the depth comparison feature of [1], we train regression forests for each cluster using the same parameters as have been described for the orientation classification. For a fair comparison between both features in terms of pose regression, we use the output of the classification forest trained with the grid-based feature. This way, we do not penalize errors of the depth comparison feature in the orientation classification step. The grid-based feature achieved 75.8% and 84.9% for 10 and 30 clusters, compared to 71.3% and 80.0% for the depth comparison feature.

The prediction pipeline including feature computation, orientation classification and the pose prediction run in real-time at 35 fps on an Intel(R) Core(TM) i5-2540 CPU.

5   Conclusion

We propose a new algorithm for human pose estimation in stereo images consisting of two stages procedure, where we first classify global orientation and then predict the pose. We introduced a new grid-based feature vector and proved its effectiveness compared to the commonly used depth comparison feature of [1]. This feature is also used in our two-stage procedure where first a classification forest was used for orientation prediction and then a regression forest is used for pose estimation. In the future, we want to include the color information provided by the stereo camera and consider temporal information to cope with isolated wrong predictions.

References

1. Shotton, J., Fitzgibbon, A., Cook, M., Finocchio, T.S.M., Moore, R., Kipman, A., Blake, A.: Real-time human pose recognition in parts from single depth images. In: CVPR (2011)
2. Girshick, R., Shotton, J., Kohli, P., Criminisi, A., Fitzgibbon, A.: Efficient regression of general-activity human poses from depth images. In: ICCV (2011)
3. Taylor, J., Shotton, J., Sharp, T., Fitzgibbon, A.: The vitruvian manifold: Inferring dense correspondences for one-shot human pose estimation. In: 2012 IEEE Conference on Computer Vision and Pattern Recognition (CVPR), pp. 103–110. IEEE (2012)
4. Pons-Moll, G., Taylor, J., Shotton, J., Hertzmann, A., Fitzgibbon, A.: Metric regression forests for human pose estimation. In: BMVC 2013 (2013)
5. Flohr, F., Gavrila, D.M.: Pedcut: An iterative framework for pedestrian segmentation combining shape models and multiple data cues. In: BMVC 2013 (2013)
6. Sun, M., Kohli, P., Shotton, J.: Conditional regression forests for human pose estimation. In: IEEE Computer Vision and Pattern Recognition (CVPR), pp. 3394–3401 (2012)
7. Plänkers, R., Fua, P.: Articulated soft objects for multi-view shape and motion capture. IEEE Trans. Pattern Anal. Mach. Intell. 25(10) (2003)
8. Urtasun, R., Fua, P.: 3d human body tracking using deterministic temporal motion models. In: Pajdla, T., Matas, J(G.) (eds.) ECCV 2004. LNCS, vol. 3023, pp. 92–106. Springer, Heidelberg (2004)
9. Bernier, O., Cheung-Mon-Chan, P., Bouguet, A.: Fast nonparametric belief propagation for real-time stereo articulated body tracking. Computer Vision and Image Understanding 113(1), 29–47 (2009)
10. Keskin, C., Kıraç, F., Kara, Y.E., Akarun, L.: Hand pose estimation and hand shape classification using multi-layered randomized decision forests. In: Fitzgibbon, A., Lazebnik, S., Perona, P., Sato, Y., Schmid, C. (eds.) ECCV 2012, Part VI. LNCS, vol. 7577, pp. 852–863. Springer, Heidelberg (2012)
11. Enzweiler, M., Gavrila, D.M.: Integrated pedestrian classification and orientation estimation. In: IEEE Computer Vision and Pattern Recognition, CVPR (2010)
12. Comaniciu, D., Meer, P.: Mean shift: A robust approach toward feature space analysis. IEEE Trans. Pattern Anal. Mach. Intell. 24(5) (2002)
13. Kontschieder, P., Kohli, P., Shotton, J., Criminisi, A.: Geof: Geodesic forests for learning coupled predictors. In: CVPR 2013 (2013)

Holistic Human Pose Estimation with Regression Forests

Vasileios Belagiannis, Christian Amann, Nassir Navab, and Slobodan Ilic

Computer Aided Medical Procedures, Technische Universität München, Germany
{belagian,christian.amann,navab,slobodan.ilic}@in.tum.de

Abstract. In this work, we address the problem of human pose estimation in still images by proposing a holistic model for learning the appearance of the human body from image patches. These patches, which are randomly chosen, are used for extracting features and training a regression forest. During training, a mapping between image features and human poses, defined by joint offsets, is learned; while during prediction, the body joints are estimated with an efficient mode-seeking algorithm. In comparison to other holistic approaches, we can recover body poses from occlusion or noisy data. We demonstrate the power of our method in two publicly available datasets and propose a third one. Finally, we achieve state-of-the-art results in comparison to other approaches.

1 Introduction

Human pose estimation from single images is a fundamental problem in Computer Vision [1]. It has a wide range of potential applications such as surveillance, health care and human computer interaction. Real life applications involve a huge amount of human appearance variations. Furthermore, out of studio environments usually include dynamic background and clutter. To address these challenges, most of the recent work relies on modelling the human body from an ensemble of parts [2,3].

There are two main categories of approaches in human pose estimation: holistic and part-based. In both categories, the human pose is defined in terms of a body skeleton which is composed of a number of connected joints. On one hand, the part-based approaches synthesise the body skeleton from a set of parts. The most acknowledged model of this category is pictorial structures [4,5,6]. Currently, most of the state-of-the-art approaches for human pose estimation rely on pictorial structures [7,8,2,3]. Those approaches have delivered promising results on standard evaluation datasets, but they build on complex appearance and body prior models.

On the other hand, the holistic approaches predict directly the body skeleton by learning a mapping between image features and skeletons [9,10,11,12]. These approaches usually face problems with occlusion or noise because they require complete data. They also generalize up to the level at which unknown poses start to appear. However, Random Forests [13] have been proven to generalize well with unknown poses [14,15].

F.J. Perales and J. Santos-Victor (Eds.): AMDO 2014, LNCS 8563, pp. 20–30, 2014.

In this work, we address the problem of human pose estimation in still images, by building on the holistic idea. We propose to learn the appearance of the human body from image patches. These patches, which are randomly chosen from a bounding box around the person, are used for extracting HOG features and training a regression forest [13]. During training, we learn a mapping between image features and human poses, defined by joint offsets. During prediction, we can recover the human pose even under occlusion or from noisy data (Figure 1). Moreover, we propose an efficient algorithm for estimating the mode of the joint density function from the aggregated leaf samples.

In the experimental section, we demonstrate that a holistic approach is not limited to complete data for performing accurate human pose estimation. To show this, we evaluate our model on two publicly available datasets which include self-occlusion, large appearance and pose variations. In addition, we propose a new challenging dataset which is different from the existing datasets because of its low resolution and noisy data. We have compared our method with the state-of-the-art approaches and achieved better or similar results.

| (a) | (b) | (c) | (d) |

Fig. 1. Human Poses: Qualitative results of our algorithm on different datasets. We can recover human poses with large appearance and motion variations. Furthermore, our method handles (b)-(c) self-occlusion or (d) noisy input data.

2   Related Work

There is a tremendous amount of approaches that tackle the problem of human pose estimation from still images [1]. We follow the categorization of the methods into holistic and part-based and review only the most related work.

Part-Based Approach. Starting from the part-based methods, pictorial structures models have become the current state-of-the-art in human pose estimation in the last decade. They have been introduced in the 70s [6], but got a lot of attention much later [4,5]. In the pictorial structures models, the human body is decomposed into a set of body parts, prior on the human pose. The goal is to infer the most plausible body configuration given the image likelihoods, usually estimated by body part detectors, and a prior. One idea for improving the model is by using better appearance models [16,17,18]. This has also been done by using Random Forests for body part classification [19] or regression [20]. Shape-based body parts generally achieved better performance [21]. The other direction of improvement is to introduce richer priors using a mixture of models [8,3] or fully connected graphical models [22]. Recently, the idea of modelling the body part templates jointly has been also explored [20,23]. In [20], two layers of Random Forests capture the information between different body parts, while in [23] the parts are sharing similar shape. Both directions of improving pictorial structures have resulted in strong local appearance and prior models. However, part-based models, such as pictorial structures, fail to capture the whole anatomy of the human body. Morever, they have evolved by building on computationally expensive and complex models.

Holistic Approach. Unlike part-based methods, the holistic approaches rely on learning and predicting the joint positions of the human skeleton at once. They usually rely on learning a mapping between image features and human poses. Mapping exemplars to human poses, in particular, became the standard way on holistic pose estimation [24,10,25]. The disadvantage of the exemplar-based approaches is the necessity for accurate matching of the whole body. To solve this problem, classification [9], regression [12] and segmentation-based [26] methods have been proposed. However, these methods can be sensitive to noisy input and cannot generalise to unknown poses. In order to cope with these problems, holistic approaches have relied on Random Forests [14,11,15]. In the depth domain, Random Forests have been used for classification [15] and regression [14]. In both cases, a holistic model has been proposed for classifying the body joints [15] or predicting their position [14] in the 3D space. In the image domain, Random Forests have been introduced for human body pose classification [11].

Finally, the combination of holistic and part-based methods has been explored by introducing the concept of Poselets [27] in the pictorial structures framework [2,28]. These approaches have proposed an intermediate representation but they still do not capture the whole anatomy of the human body.

In our work, we adapt the idea of regression forests to the image domain and learn to map image features to 2D human poses. To the best of our knowledge, we are the first ones who apply a regression forest to image data for estimating the body joints at once. The big advantage of our method in comparison to other holistic approaches is our ability to cope with incomplete data.

3   Method

Random Forests have become very popular for human pose estimation from depth data [29,14,15]. In this work, we build on a regression forest for extracting the human pose from image data. Below, we explain the basic principles of a regression forest and the way we apply it to our problem.

3.1 Regression Forest

A regression forest is an ensemble of regression trees T that estimates continuous output. The goal of training a regression forest is to learn a mapping between image patches and the parameter space. In our paradigm, the parameter space $\mathbb{R}^{2 \times N}$ consists of a set of N joints in the 2D space. The body skeleton is defined by the joints and the image patches are estimated using HOG features [30].

In the training phase, a pool of randomly extracted image patches P with associated skeleton joint offsets serves as input to each tree. The patches are extracted from random positions within a bounding box that localises the human. Then, a tree is built from a set of nodes which include binary split functions. Each node encloses a split function θ which is defined on the values of the HOG features of the patch. The HOG feature vector of the image patch is extracted as in [31]. The binary split function determines if a p sample image patch will go to the left P_l or right P_r subset of samples. In particular, the split function is a threshold on one dimension of the HOG feature vector. Among the dimensions of the HOG feature vector, the threshold that gained the best split defines the split function:

$$\theta^* = \arg\max_{\theta} g(\theta) \tag{1}$$

where $g(\theta)$ corresponds to the information gain. The information gain measures how well the split function divides the training data into two subsets P_l and P_r. Thus, the criterion for choosing the split function is to maximize the information gain $g(\theta)$ by optimally splitting the input training image patches of the current node. The information gain can be formulated as:

$$g(\theta) = H(P) - \sum_{i \in \{l,r\}} \frac{|P_i(\theta)|}{|P|} H(P_i(\theta)) \tag{2}$$

where $H(P)$ is the entropy. For estimating the entropy, the sum-of-squares-differences is used:

$$H(P) = \sum_{p \in P} \sum_{j} \|\mathbf{v}_{p,j} - \boldsymbol{\mu}_j\|_2^2 \tag{3}$$

where the vector $\mathbf{v}_{p,j}$ includes the offsets for each joint j from the image patch centre and $\boldsymbol{\mu}_j$ denotes the mean for each joint offset. In order to estimate the mean $\boldsymbol{\mu}_j$, we introduce a threshold ρ to consider only joints that are close to the sampled patch, similar to [14]. Finally, the tree grows until it reaches the maximum depth, the minimum number of samples per leaf or the information gain for the node drops below a threshold. The same process is a repeated for all the trees of the forest. Finally, we store the offsets of all body joints in the leaves.

3.2 Forest Parameters

In order to correctly train the regression forest, there is a number of parameters that has to be determined for the training data.

Image Patches: The size of all image patches is predefined during training and prediction. Thus, all the HOG feature vectors have the same size. We discretize the image gradients into 9 bins and follow the implementation from [31].

Scale Invariance: The training persons in different training images are apparently of different sizes, but they are all localized by a bounding box. We scale all the data with respect to the height of the bounding box which usually corresponds to the height of the person. This allows us to capture pose variations of different humans using a common scale. Since we assume a localized person, we scale at the prediction phase as well.

Threshold ρ: We argue that a split function has a more local than a global role. For that reason, samples having large offsets are penalized by a threshold. We set it experimentally to 0.8 of the human bounding box height and exclude the joints that are outside this radius.

3.3   Prediction

In the prediction phase, the human is localised with a bounding box which is also rescaled. Similar to training, random pixel positions are used as input to our algorithm. An image patch is extracted for each random position and the HOG feature vector is then estimated. In each tree, the split functions direct, left or right, the input image patch until it reaches the leaf in which we have stored the vectors that predict the joint positions. Thus, the next step is to aggregate the votes of the leaves of the different trees of the forest.

For a certain joint, finding the most probable location of the joint corresponds to estimating the mode of the density function. The most common algorithm for estimating the mode is Mean Shift [32]. However, Mean Shift is a computationally expensive algorithm and requires a significant amount of time to converge, given a plethora of samples at the leaves. To overcome this limitation, we propose the *dense-window* algorithm which is a greedy approach for estimating the mode of a density function from samples. The *dense-window* algorithm relies on a sliding window search in which convergence is deterministic. It only depends on the step of the sliding window and scales linearly with the number of the samples.

To enable fast estimation, the *dense-window* algorithm discretizes all the 2D predictions for every joint on a grid such that every grid cell stores the number of predictions that lie within this cell. The runtime is linear to the number of joint predictions s. Then, an integral matrix is generated for each cell in order to accumulate its votes. All the cells together form an integral image. Now, the window containing the maximum number of points can be found by sliding the window over the integral image. This can be done in $O(m^2)$ time where m is the resolution of the grid. We set experimentally the sliding window to 0.1 of the person's bounding box height and the grid resolution to 100x100 pixels. The complexity of this algorithm is $O(s + m^2)$ which is much faster than $O(Ts^2)$ of Mean Shift, where T is the number of iterations.

4   Experiments

The current state-of-the-art on human pose estimation, from still images, relies on part-based models [16,2,3]. Through our experimental evaluation, we stress that holistic human pose estimation leads to high performance as well. In this section, we analyse our model, evaluate on three datasets and compare it with the state-of-the-art approaches.

First, we present the results for estimating the parameters of the regression forest. We perform all the experiments only on the training images of the Image Parse [3] dataset to avoid parameter over-fitting. Then, we compare our method with an approach which relies on body part classification forests on the KTH Football dataset [19]. In order to show the power of our model in comparison to part-based methods, we evaluate on the Image Parse dataset. Finally, we propose the new and very challenging Volleyball dataset which has very noisy and low resolution data. We evaluate our approach on it and compare with a part-based method [3]. For all the experiments, we use the PCP evaluation score [17].

4.1   System Parameters

We first choose the parameters of the regression forest by evaluating on the Image Parse dataset [3]. We mainly focus on determining the number and depth of the trees, as well as the size of the window of the image patch. Figure 2 presents the results.

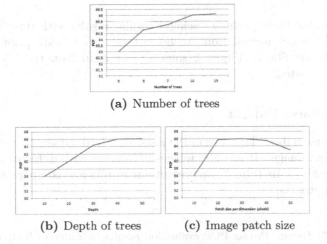

(a) Number of trees

(b) Depth of trees   (c) Image patch size

Fig. 2. Forest parameters: We have estimated the parameters of the regression forest on the training dataset of the Image Parse dataset [3]. The number and the depth of trees are explored, as well as the size of the image patch.

Based on the results of the Figure 2, we have chosen to use 15 trees with a depth of 40. The trees are very deep due to the high variation in terms of appearance and motion of the human poses. The patch size is set to 30 pixels per dimension.

Finally, we have evatluated the prediction step with the Mean Shift and *dense-window* algorithm and we ended up with almost identical results. In particular with the the *dense-window* algorithm, we achieved PCP 67.1 while with the Mean Shift algorithm PCP 67.0.

4.2 Football Dataset

In this experiment, we compare our method with the part-based method which relies on classification forests [19]. In this work the forest classifies each pixel in the image as a specific body joint. Afterwards, a body prior model (i.e. pictorial structures) helps to improve the final result. The results are summarized in Table 1. For the method of Yang and Ramanan [3], we have compiled and test their code that is available online.

Table 1. KTH Football: PCP evaluation results for different body parts

	Head	Torso	Upper Arms	Lower Arms	Upper Legs	Lower Legs	Avg.
Our method	0.86	**0.98**	0.88	0.57	0.92	0.80	0.84
Yang&Ramanan [3]	0.84	0.98	0.86	0.55	0.89	0.73	0.80
Kazemi et al. [19]	0.94	0.96	0.90	0.69	0.94	0.84	0.87
Kazemi et al. [19] + Prior	**0.96**	0.98	**0.93**	**0.71**	**0.97**	**0.88**	**0.89**

For most of the body parts, we achieve similar results with the classification forest of [19]. In our formulation, we do not rely on a body prior model for smoothing the results. In Figure 3 some of our results on the KTH football dataset are presented.

4.3 Image Parse Dataset

The Image Parse dataset [3] is one of the most standard datasets for human pose estimation from images. It includes images of humans with different appearance and pose (Figure 4). In Table 2, we present our results and compare with several part-based approaches.

Table 2. Image Parse: PCP evaluation results for different body parts

	Torso	Upper Legs	Lower Legs	Upper Arms	Lower Arms	Head	Avg.
Our method	88.8	**80.9**	**72.8**	58.2	27.5	74.1	67.1
Andriluka et al.[4]	86.3	66.3	60.0	54.6	35.6	72.7	59.2
Yang&Ramanan [3]	82.9	69.0	63.9	55.1	35.4	**77.6**	60.7
Pischulin et al. [2]	**92.2**	74.6	63.7	54.9	39.8	70.7	62.9
Pischulin et al. [33] + [2]	90.7	80.0	70.0	59.3	37.1	77.6	66.1
Johnson&Everingham [8]	87.6	74.7	67.1	**67.3**	**45.8**	76.8	**67.4**

Our method achieves similar results to the other approaches with the great difference that we use smaller amount of training data. We have used the set of 100 train images for our regression forest. This is significantly lower in contrast to Pischulin et al. ([2],[33]), where they train with 1000 images. Similarly, Johnson and Everingham [8] train with 10000 images. The reason for achieving similar results is that Random Forests can generalise to unknown poses. The only case where we have lower performance is at the lower arms due to the blurry input.

Fig. 3. KTH Football: Qualitative results of our algorithm on some samples. The main feature of the dataset is the motion variation.

4.4   Volleyball Dataset

We propose the Volleyball dataset for 2D human pose estimation. The dataset is composed of 800 training image of men and 205 testing images of women playing volleyball. We have used two different volleyball matches to create the dataset. The main feature of this dataset is the low quality and noisy image data. In Figure 5, we demonstrate some samples of the Volleyball dataset with the inferred pose. Evaluating on this type of data, we would like to highlight that our holistic model can cope with incomplete data. The dataset and our code will be made publicly available upon publication.

Table 3. Volleyball: PCP evaluation results for different body parts

	Head	Torso	Upper Arms	Lower Arms	Upper Legs	Lower Legs	Avg.
Our method	**97.5**	**81.4**	**54.4**	19.3	**65.1**	**81.2**	**63.8**
Yang&Ramanan[3]	76.1	80.5	40.7	**33.7**	52.4	70.5	59.0

We have evaluated our method on the Volleyball dataset using the PCP evaluation score. In order to compare with another approach, we have trained and tested the code of Yang and Ramanan [3]. The results are summarized in Table 3. We perform better for most of the body parts but we have achieved worse results for the lower arms. This happens because the lower arms are often fully occluded and then the forest predicts an average pose.

5   Conclusion

We have presented a holistic model for human pose estimation from 2D images. The model has been built on Random Forests and image patches. We have demonstrated that our formulation delivers state-of-the-art results by evaluating on two datasets and comparing with other approaches. We have also introduced a new challenging dataset which main feature is the noise and the low quality of image data. In all datasets, we have showed that our holistic approach can perform well and equally compete with the most recent part-based approaches.

Fig. 4. Image Parse: Qualitative results of our algorithm on some samples. The dataset has large appearance variation.

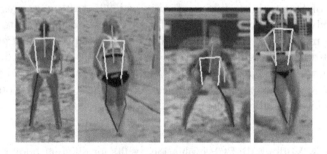

Fig. 5. Volleyball: Qualitative results of our algorithm on some samples. This is a new challenging dataset with low resolution and noisy images.

References

1. Moeslund, T.B., Hilton, A., Krüger, V., Sigal, L.: Visual Analysis of Humans. Springer (2011)
2. Pishchulin, L., Andriluka, M., Gehler, P., Schiele, B.: Poselet conditioned pictorial structures. In: IEEE CVPR, pp. 588–595 (2013)
3. Yang, Y., Ramanan, D.: Articulated pose estimation with flexible mixtures-of-parts. In: IEEE CVPR, pp. 1385–1392 (2011)

4. Andriluka, M., Roth, S., Schiele, B.: Pictorial structures revisited: People detection and articulated pose estimation. In: IEEE CVPR, pp. 1014–1021 (2009)
5. Felzenszwalb, P.F., Huttenlocher, D.P.: Pictorial structures for object recognition. IJCV 61(1), 55–79 (2005)
6. Fischler, M.A., Elschlager, R.A.: The representation and matching of pictorial structures. IEEE Transactions on Computers 22(1), 67–92 (1973)
7. Belagiannis, V., Amin, S., Andriluka, M., Schiele, B., Navab, N., Ilic, S.: 3d pictorial structures for multiple human pose estimation. In: IEEE CVPR (2014)
8. Johnson, S., Everingham, M.: Learning effective human pose estimation from inaccurate annotation. In: IEEE CVPR, pp. 1465–1472 (2011)
9. Agarwal, A., Triggs, B.: Recovering 3d human pose from monocular images. TPAMI 28(1), 44–58 (2006)
10. Mori, G., Malik, J.: Estimating human body configurations using shape context matching. In: Heyden, A., Sparr, G., Nielsen, M., Johansen, P. (eds.) ECCV 2002, Part III. LNCS, vol. 2352, pp. 666–680. Springer, Heidelberg (2002)
11. Rogez, G., Rihan, J., Ramalingam, S., Orrite, C., Torr, P.H.: Randomized trees for human pose detection. In: IEEE CVPR, pp. 1–8 (2008)
12. Urtasun, R., Darrell, T.: Sparse probabilistic regression for activity-independent human pose inference. In: IEEE CVPR, pp. 1–8 (2008)
13. Breiman, L.: Random forests. Machine Learning 45(1), 5–32 (2001)
14. Girshick, R., Shotton, J., Kohli, P., Criminisi, A., Fitzgibbon, A.: Efficient regression of general-activity human poses from depth images. In: IEEE ICCV, pp. 415–422 (2011)
15. Shotton, J., Sharp, T., Kipman, A., Fitzgibbon, A., Finocchio, M., Blake, A., Cook, M., Moore, R.: Real-time human pose recognition in parts from single depth images. Communications of the ACM 56(1), 116–124 (2013)
16. Andriluka, M., Roth, S., Schiele, B.: Discriminative appearance models for pictorial structures. IJCV 99(3), 259–280 (2012)
17. Eichner, M., Ferrari, V.: Better appearance models for pictorial structures (2009)
18. Sapp, B., Toshev, A., Taskar, B.: Cascaded models for articulated pose estimation. In: Daniilidis, K., Maragos, P., Paragios, N. (eds.) ECCV 2010, Part II. LNCS, vol. 6312, pp. 406–420. Springer, Heidelberg (2010)
19. Kazemi, V., Burenius, M., Azizpour, H., Sullivan, J.: Multi-view body part recognition with random forests. In: BMVC (2013)
20. Dantone, M., Gall, J., Leistner, C., Van Gool, L.: Human pose estimation using body parts dependent joint regressors. In: IEEE CVPR, pp. 3041–3048 (2013)
21. Zuffi, S., Freifeld, O., Black, M.J.: From pictorial structures to deformable structures. In: IEEE CVPR, pp. 3546–3553 (2012)
22. Bergtholdt, M., Kappes, J., Schmidt, S., Schnörr, C.: A study of parts-based object class detection using complete graphs. IJCV 87(1-2), 93–117 (2010)
23. Sun, M., Savarese, S.: Articulated part-based model for joint object detection and pose estimation. In: IEEE ICCV, pp. 723–730 (2011)
24. Gavrila, D.M.: A bayesian, exemplar-based approach to hierarchical shape matching. IEEE Transactions on Pattern Analysis and Machine Intelligence 29(8), 1408–1421 (2007)
25. Shakhnarovich, G., Viola, P., Darrell, T.: Fast pose estimation with parameter-sensitive hashing. In: IEEE ICCV, pp. 750–757 (2003)
26. Ionescu, C., Li, F., Sminchisescu, C.: Latent structured models for human pose estimation. In: IEEE ICCV, pp. 2220–2227 (2011)
27. Bourdev, L., Malik, J.: Poselets: Body part detectors trained using 3d human pose annotations. In: IEEE ICCV, pp. 1365–1372 (2009)

28. Wang, Y., Tran, D., Liao, Z.: Learning hierarchical poselets for human parsing. In: IEEE CVPR, pp. 1705–1712 (2011)
29. Criminisi, A., Shotton, J.: Decision forests for computer vision and medical image analysis. Springer (2013)
30. Dalal, N., Triggs, B.: Histograms of oriented gradients for human detection. In: IEEE CVPR, vol. 1, pp. 886–893 (2005)
31. Felzenszwalb, P.F., Girshick, R.B., McAllester, D., Ramanan, D.: Object detection with discriminatively trained part-based models. TPAMI 32(9), 1627–1645 (2010)
32. Comaniciu, D., Meer, P.: Mean shift: A robust approach toward feature space analysis. TPAMI 24(5), 603–619 (2002)
33. Pishchulin, L., Jain, A., Andriluka, M., Thormahlen, T., Schiele, B.: Articulated people detection and pose estimation: Reshaping the future. In: IEEE CVPR, pp. 3178–3185 (2012)

Mood and Its Mapping onto Facial Expressions

Diana Arellano[1], Francisco J. Perales[2], and Javier Varona[2]

[1] Institute of Animation, Filmakademie Baden-Württemberg, Germany,
diana.arellano@filmakademie.de
[2] Computer Graphics, Computer Vision and Artificial Intelligence Group, University
of Balearic Islands, Spain
{paco.perales,xavi.varona}@uib.es

Abstract. This paper presents a method for the representation of mood in FACS-based facial expressions. To achieve this, a mapping of FACS Action Units (AUs) into the Pleasure-Arousal-Dominance (PAD) space is done. The PAD space is used as our mood model. From this mapping a set of rules are obtained, which compute the activation areas and intensities of each AU in the PAD. To validate these rules, we conducted an experiment, shedding light on the AUs combinations that result in recognizable expressions of certain mood.

Keywords: Affect recognition, Facial Expressions, Mood, FACS.

1 Introduction

Non-verbal expressions of affect can be performed using voice, gestures, body positions, and above all, facial expressions.

The main focus of this work are facial expressions because they are one of the richer and more accurate ways of expressing affect [1]. Emotions in particular have been extensively studied in facial expressions. However, how mood can be represented in the face is still in it early stages.

According to Sedikides [2], mood states are defined as "frequent, relatively long and pervasive, but typically milder in intensity than emotions". Thus the main difference between emotions and moods is the temporal nature of the latter.

But when it comes to facial expressions, Faigin [4] sets the question: "to what extent are day-to-day moods visible on the face?". And moreover, how can be day-to-day moods represented on the face?

To answer these questions, we establish a correspondence between Facial Action Coding System (FACS) Action Units (AUs) [5] and a mood model, so it would be possible to know which set of AUs would describe moods. The mood model we have selected is the Pleasure-Arousal-Dominance model (PAD), proposed by Albert Mehrabian [6], which categorizes mood in eight octants: Exuberant, Bored, Disdainful, Dependent, Docile, Hostile, Anxious and Relaxed.

In the following we present a review of previous works on mood. Then, we explain the methodology to obtain a mapping between AUs and moods; and finally, we show the results of the experiment to validate the former mapping.

F.J. Perales and J. Santos-Victor (Eds.): AMDO 2014, LNCS 8563, pp. 31–40, 2014.

2   Previous Works

The extensive research on mood in the field of Psychology and the use of the PAD model in more computational, or artistic applications have resulted in a number of interesting works, which will be briefly referenced in this section.

An early example of the use of the PAD model is the work of Payne et al. [7]. They used the PAD as theory for mood representation in order to investigate the impact of leisure on mood that is produced by watching movies. In a more artistic field, "Ada: Intelligent Space exhibit" [8] was an "artificial organism, integrating a large number of sensory modalities". It perceived its environment and behaved coherently to achieve a set of behavioral goals. Whilst emotions in Ada were thought as categories (joy, surprise, sadness and anger), mood was expressed in terms of pleasure and arousal.

In the field of affective computing, especially for the generation and representation of affect in virtual characters there is an important number of works that have used the PAD model for mood simulation. Some examples are the works of Gebhard [9], Burkitt and Romano [10], Peña et al. [11], Santos et al. [12], Kasap et al. [13], Ben Moussa and Thalmann [14], and Courgeon et al. [15].

Various reasons can be attributed to the use of the PAD model for depiction of mood. For instance, Peña et al. [11] find it suitable for the representation of emotions at specific instants, and of emotional states (moods) as the emotional data collected over time. They used the PAD model because it shows the tendency of the emotional states when the emotional stimuli are weak or nonexistent; and the aggregation of emotions that change the emotional state (mood) of a person. Another property of the PAD model is that it integrates in a same framework the semantics of affective behavior together with temporal properties. The "emotional states" defined by Mehrabian are the transitory conditions of the organism (e.g. feeling alert vs. tired, happy vs. unhappy), which comply with the temporal characteristic associated with mood.

3   Action Units and the PAD Space

The Facial Action Coding System (FACS) [5] is a well known method introduced by Paul Ekman, Wallace V. Friesen, and Joseph C. Hager to measure facial behavior and to systematically categorize facial expressions.

The PAD Model is a framework for the definition and measurement of emotional states, emotional traits, and personality traits in terms of three nearly orthogonal dimensions: Pleasure (P), Arousal (A), and Dominance (D) [6].

The dimension Pleasure-displeasure distinguishes positive affective states from negative ones. Arousal-nonarousal is defined as a combination of mental alertness and physical activity. Dominance-submissiveness is defined in terms of control versus lack of control over events, one's surroundings, or other people.

From the intersection of the Pleasure, Arousal and Dominance axis eight octants can be derived, representing mood categories: Exuberant (+P +A +D), Bored (-P -A -D), Docile (+P -A -D), Hostile (-P +A +D), Dependent (+P +A -D), Disdainful (-P -A +D), Relaxed (+P -A +D) and Anxious (-P +A -D).

This section presents an approach to mapping Action Units (AUs) to octants in the PAD space, with the main objective of describing each of the eight moods in terms of AUs. This contribution represents a step forward in the representation of mood through facial expressions.

3.1   Definition of Rules Based on Examples

In a first step, we identified a subset of AUs that could be considered sufficient to potentially express in a readily recognizable manner a set of facial expressions [16]. These are: AU1 - Inner Brow Raiser, AU2 - Outer Brow Raiser, AU4 - Brow Lowerer, AU5 - Upper Lid Raiser, AU6 - Cheek Raiser, AU10 - Upper Lip Raiser, AU12 - Lip Corner Puller, AU14 - Dimpler, AU15 - Lip Corner Depressor, AU25 - Lips Part, AU26 - Jaw Drop and AU43 - Eye Closure.

In a second step, we considered previous works on mapping emotions into the PAD space. The mapping of emotions in the dimensions Pleasure, Arousal and Dominance was initially proposed by Russell and Mehrabian [18], and later refined in the ALMA model [17]. A part of this mapping is shown in Figure 1.

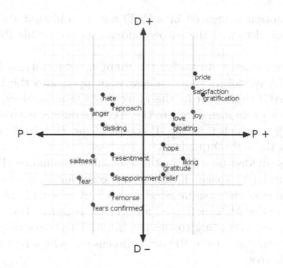

Fig. 1. Location of example emotions in PD space

We also took into account the AUs analysis of facial expressions of emotions to formulate the rules to map each AU into a region, or regions of the PAD space. The AUs analysis was based on annotated examples provided by the Facial Expression Repertoire (FER) [19]. It is an on-line database developed by the Filmakademie Baden-Württemberg that maps over 150 emotional expressions, both static and dynamic to FACS, and explains in detail which AUs are activated in each of them. The main reason for the use of FER is that it provides a greater number of facial expressions that, to the best of our knowledge, have not been

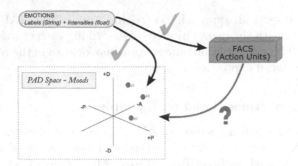

Fig. 2. Facial expressions for AU-based mood modeling

yet annotated by any other existent database. Figure 2 presents graphically all the elements taken into account for the AUs-PAD mapping.

3.2   Mapping AUs into the PAD Space

Given that an emotion is located in a PAD region, and that this emotion has a set of AUs, we need to find the correspondence between this PAD region and this set of AUs.

The methodology consists in taking the mapping of Emotions-PAD, which is done in the ALMA model [9] (e.g. *sadness* is mapped into the Bored octant), and identify the AUs that describe the movements in a facial expression of the emotion. This gives us an idea of where the AUs are mainly active. For example, AU1 is active in *fear*, which is in the -P -D quadrant. But AU1 is also active in other emotions in the +P -D quadrant.

The analysis is divided in: AUs in the Pleasure-Dominance (PD) space and AUs in the Arousal (A) space. It takes into consideration: (a) the values of P,A,D for each emotion (e.g. sadness: $P = -0.5$, $A = -0.42$, $D = -0.25$), (b) the emotions where the AU is activated and (c) the regions PD or A where those emotions are mapped according to the list in [9]. Then we can depict for each AU a function dependent on the PD or A dimension, which represents the area where the AU is active.

The reasons for this division in PD and A are that it facilitates the analysis of the dimensions where the AUs could be activated, and there are AUs that can be easily associated with arousal (e.g. opening of the mouth or the eyes).

– *AU1* - **Inner Brow Raiser**. It is activated in *sadness*, which is associated to low pleasure and low dominance (-P-D) [19] [20]. We use the values of *sadness* ($p = -0.5$, $d = -0.25$) to formulate a linear function that returns the area in the -P-D where $AU1$ is activated, see Equation 1.

$$AU1_{intensity} = \begin{cases} (-4.0)d & \text{if } d \in (-0.25, 0.0] \\ 1.0 & \text{if } d \in [-1.0, -0.25] \end{cases} \tag{1}$$

$AU1$ is also found in +P-D in emotions like *liking* and *relief* (*relief happiness* in FER). Using the values of *relief* ($p = 0.2$, $d = -0.4$), we formulated Equation 2, which is similar to Equation 1, but with an offset of -0.4 because *relief* is the point where $AU1$ begins to change from -P to +P.

$$AU1_{intensity} = \begin{cases} 0.0 & \text{if } d \in [-0.4, 0.0) \\ (-4.0)(d+0.4) & \text{if } d \in (-0.65, -0.4) \\ 1.0 & \text{if } d \in [-1.0, -0.65] \end{cases} \quad (2)$$

- $AU2$ - **Outer Brow Raiser**. It is activated in *sadness* and *fear*, which are in the -P-D quadrant. Using the P and D values of both emotions, we obtained a progression beginning at the location of *sadness* ($p = -0.5$, $d = -0.25$) and ending in *fear* ($p = -0.65$, $d = -0.45$), see Equation 3. This AU is also found in +P-D, thus we used the same analysis as for $AU1$, see Equation 4.

$$AU2_{intensity} = \begin{cases} 0.0 & d \in (-0.25, 0.0] \wedge p \in [-1.0, 0.0) \\ (-4.0)d & d \in (-0.45, -0.25] \wedge p \in [-1.0, 0.0) \\ 1.0 & d \in [-1.0, -0.45) \wedge p \in [-1.0, 0.0) \end{cases} \quad (3)$$

$$AU2_{intensity} = \begin{cases} 0.0; & d \in [-0.4, 0.0] \wedge p \in (0.0, 1.0] \\ (-4.0)(d+0.4); & d \in (-0.65, -0.4) \wedge p \in (0.0, 1.0] \\ 1.0; & d \in [-1.0, -0.65] \wedge p \in (0.0, 1.0] \end{cases} \quad (4)$$

- $AU4$ - **Brow Lowerer**. It is found in the -P+D and -P+D dimensions. To map this AU in -P+D we use *anger* ($p = -0.5$ and $d = 0.25$). In FER the expressions considered were: *enraged (compressed lips)* and *sternness*, which have about the same dominance value in the -P. Equation 5 depicts the area where $AU4$ is activated. For the -P-D quadrant we use *sadness* ($p = -0.5$ and $d = -0.25$), resulting in Equation 6.

$$AU4_{intensity} = \begin{cases} (4d)(-2p) & \text{if } P \in (-0.5, 0.0] \wedge D \in (0.0, 0.25) \\ (-2.0)p & \text{if } P \in (-0.5, 0.0] \wedge D \in [0.25, 1.0] \\ (4.0)d & \text{if } P \in [-1.0, -0.5] \wedge D \in (0.0, 0.25) \\ 1.0 & \text{if } P \in [-1.0, -0.5] \wedge D \in [0.25, 1.0] \end{cases} \quad (5)$$

$$AU4_{intensity} = \begin{cases} (-4d)(-2p) & \text{if } p \in (-0.5, 0.0] \wedge d \in (-0.25, 0.0] \\ (-2.0)p & \text{if } p \in (-0.5, 0.0] \wedge d \in (-1.0, -0.25] \\ (-4.0)d & \text{if } p \in [-1.0, -0.5] \wedge d \in (-0.25, 0.0] \\ 1.0 & \text{if } p \in [-1.0, -0.5] \wedge d \in [-1.0, -0.25] \end{cases} \quad (6)$$

- $AU6$ - **Cheek Raiser**. It is activated in displays of genuine positive emotions. To find the area of activation in +P-D, we used *liking* ($p = 0.4$ and

$d = -0.24$). For +P+D we used *joy* ($p = 0.5$ and $d = 0.25$) and *satisfaction* ($p = 0.5$ and $d = 0.47$), see Equation 7.

$$AU6_{intensity} = \begin{cases} (2.0)(d + 0.25) & \text{if } d \in (-0.25, 0.25) \\ (4.0)(0.5 - d) & \text{if } d \in [0.25, 0.5) \\ 1.0 & \text{if } d \in [0.5, 1.0] \end{cases} \quad (7)$$

- $AU10$ - **Upper Lip Raiser.** It is activated in -P+D, since it is a key feature of *contempt*. Similar emotions are *disdain* or *arrogance*. To compute its intensity we used *arrogance* ($p = 0.0$ and $d = 0.5$). Equation 8 computes the area of activation of $AU10$.

$$AU10_{intensity} = \begin{cases} (2.0)(d - 0.5) & \text{if } 0.5 \geq d \leq 1.0 \\ 0.0 & \text{if } 0.0 \geq d \leq 0.5 \end{cases} \quad (8)$$

- $AU12$ - **Lip Corner Puller.** It is also activated in positive emotions like *joy*, along the dominance dimension. In the +P-D space, FER expressions that can be associated are *qualifier smile*, the *coy smile* and the *embarrassment smile*. In +P+D, we find it in *joy* and its many variants. Equation 9 computes the activation area of $AU12$.

$$AU12_{intensity} = \begin{cases} 0.0; & p \in [-1.0, 0.0) \\ (2.0)p; & p \in [0.0, 0.5) \\ 1.0; & p \in [0.5, 1.0] \end{cases} \quad (9)$$

- $AU14$ - **Dimpler.** It appears in the smiling mouth as a key feature of positive Pleasure. In FER it is activated in *enjoyable contempt*. Therefore, it is activated in +P+D, see Equation 10.

$$AU14_{intensity} = \begin{cases} 2(0.5 - p)2(d - 0.5); & p \in [0.0, 0.5) \wedge d \in (0.5, 1.0] \\ 0.0; & else \end{cases} \quad (10)$$

- $AU15$ - **Lip Corner Depressor.** It is found in *sadness*, *fear* and *anger*. Therefore, $AU15$ is mapped into the -P dimension along the Dominance axis. Using the P and D values of *sadness*, we obtained Equation 11.

$$AU15_{intensity} = \begin{cases} 0.0; & p \in (0.0, 1.0] \\ (-2.0)p; & p \in (-0.5, 0.0] \\ 1.0; & p \in [-1.0, -0.5] \end{cases} \quad (11)$$

- $AU5$ - **Upper Lid Raiser.** It is found in emotions with high arousal such as *fear* ($a = 0.6$), *terror* ($a = 0.82$) or *worry* ($a = 0.14$). That is why we considered only the **positive Arousal** dimension (+A) to locate $AU5$. Equation 12 depicts a progression that begins at worry and ends terror.

$$AU5_{intensity} = \begin{cases} 0.0; & a \in [-1.0, 0.1] \\ \frac{a - 0.1}{0.7}; & a \in (0.1, 0.8) \\ 1.0; & a \in [0.8, 1.0] \end{cases} \quad (12)$$

- *AU*25 - **Lips Part**. According to FER, it is found in emotions like *rage*, *surprise*, *disgust*, or in "confused" expression. We use *confusion* ($a = 0.27$) and *rage* with $a = 0.72$ to map it into the +A dimension, see Equation 13.

$$AU25_{intensity} = \begin{cases} 0.0; & a \in [0.0, 0.3] \\ \frac{a-0.3}{0.4}; & a \in (0.3, 0.7) \\ 1.0; & a \in [0.7, 1.0] \end{cases} \qquad (13)$$

- *AU*26 - **Jaw Drop**. It is found in *surprise*, *fear* or *disgust*, among other FER expressions like *uproarious laughter* and *yawning*. We use the values of *fear* ($a = 0.6$) and *disgust*, ($a = 0.35$) to compute a progression beginning in disgust, and ending in fear. See Equation 14.

$$AU26_{intensity} = \begin{cases} 0.0; & a \in [0.0, 0.35] \\ \frac{a-0.35}{0.25}; & a \in (0.35, 0.6) \\ 1.0; & a \in [0.6, 1.0] \end{cases} \qquad (14)$$

- *AU*43 - **Eye Closure**. It is activated in emotions or states like *tiredness*, *disdain* or *relief happiness*. To compute the area where *AU*43 is activated we use *fatigued* ($a = -0.57$), see Equation 15.

$$AU43_{intensity} = \begin{cases} 0.0; & a \in [0.0, 1.0] \\ \frac{a}{-0.6}; & a \in (-0.6, 0.0) \\ 1.0; & a \in [-0.6, -1.0] \end{cases} \qquad (15)$$

As a result, we obtained a general mapping of AUs into regions of the PAD space. Nevertheless, a refinement and validation of these associations was carried on through a perceptual experiment that is explained in the following section.

4   Experimental Validation

We performed a perceptual evaluation with the intention of constraining the number of AUs, regarding the ones that were more representative of each mood.

Our hypothesis was to prove that all moods have associated expressions, which are described by the AUs activated in their corresponding PAD dimension.

The first step was to generate $3^3 = 27$ images of expressions corresponding to the combinations of {low, medium, high} $\cup$ {pleasure, arousal and dominance}, for each of the 8 moods. This gave a total of 216 images that were randomly evaluated. The virtual character used to generate the expressions was Alfred, from the Game Engine of the University of Augsburg [21] and a set of the evaluated expressions is shown in Figure 3.

A total of 109 subjects (59 male and 50 female) between 19 and 55 years old (mean = 29,2; SD = 7,1) took part on survey. To assess the images we used the Self-Assessment Manikin (SAM) questionnaire [22], which is a non-verbal, graphic representation of each of the three dimensions (P, A, D). It directly assesses the pleasure, arousal and dominance associated to an object or event.

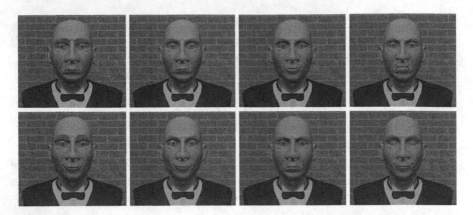

Fig. 3. Facial expressions in the mood quadrants of the PAD Space. Upper row: Anxious, Bored, Dependent, Disdainful. Lower row: Docile, Exuberant, Hostile, Relaxed.

The experimental stimuli consisted of 18 static images, randomly selected from the pool of 216 images. Each subject rated each of these 18 images using SAM, based on a 5-item Likert Scale, where 1 corresponded to the minimum value of the dimension and 5 to the maximum. For analysis purposes, this scale was normalized between -1 and 1. The questions were of the form: (1) How is Alfred feeling? (SAM items for pleasure). (2) How energetic seems Alfred? (SAM items for arousal). (3) How dominant is Alfred? (SAM items for dominance).

When analyzing the results, we observed that each image was evaluated in average 10 times. Then, for each mood we computed the average recognition rate (mean value) of all its 27 images. Table 1 contains the mean values and standard deviations of the identification of mood in the expressions.

Table 1. Mean analysis of recognition of mood in facial expressions

Mood		Pleasure		Arousal		Dominance	
		Mean	SD	Mean	SD	Mean	SD
Anxious	-P+A-D	-0.5	0.43	0.0	0.57	-0.3	0.61
Bored	-P-A-D	-0.4	0,50	-0,5	0,50	-0,5	0,50
Dependent	+P+A-D	0.5	0.37	0.3	0.44	0.3	0.48
Disdainful	-P-A+D	-0.4	0.45	-0.1	0.61	-0.1	0.61
Docile	+P-A-D	0.5	0.31	-0.1	0.49	0.0	0.56
Exuberant	+P+A+D	0.4	0.44	0.4	0.44	0.4	0.48
Hostile	-P+A+D	-0.5	0.44	0.4	0.54	0.2	0.62
Relaxed	+P-A+D	0.4	0.35	-0.2	0.52	0.1	0.52

The former results showed that not all the expressions for each mood were associated as such. However, we used this fact to constrain the set of expressions, and hence the set of AUs. The resultant set were indeed the expressions recog-

Table 2. AUs describing expressions of mood

Mood	(AUs)
Exuberant	$AU6, AU5, AU12, AU25, AU26$
Bored	$AU1, AU2, AU4, AU15, AU43$
Docile	$AU1, AU2, AU12, AU43$
Hostile	$AU4, AU10, AU5, AU15, AU25, AU26$
Anxious	$AU1, AU2, AU4, AU5, AU15, AU25, AU26$
Relaxed	$AU6, AU12, AU43$
Dependent	$AU1, AU2, AU5, AU12, AU25, AU26$
Disdainful	$AU4, AU15, AU43$

nized with the P, A and D values of the mood they described. Table 2 presents the AUs, which allowed us to generate the mood facial expressions.

5   Discussion

After the analysis of the results, we found that the expressions associated with a mood are indeed described by the AUs in the octant of that mood. Regarding the easiness of recognition, the results concluded that:
- Pleasure was correctly identified in the majority of the cases, except when P value was close to zero. It is the dimension that gives meaning to the expression.
- Arousal was also correctly identified in most of the cases, except when A was negative and most of the subjects did not know how to assess it.
- Dominance presented most of the perception problems. Subjects were not sure how to measure it or what to take into consideration to do it.

These results showed that pleasure and arousal are dimensions that can be represented in the expression, while dominance is a dimension that is manifested during interaction. Therefore, it was difficult to assess from an static image. Nevertheless, the use of SAM icons helped considerably to successfully perform the questionnaire, facilitating the understanding of the questionnaire.

Acknowledgments. This work was supported in part by the projects 28/2011 (Balearic Island competitive groups funds) granted by the Govern de les Illes Balears, and TIN2012-35427 and the Campus de Excelencia Internacional Program of the Spanish Government, with FEDER (European Regional Development Fund) support.

References

1. Ekman, P.: Darwin's contributions to our understanding of emotional expressions. Philos. T. Roy. Soc. B. 364(1535), 3449–3451 (2009)
2. Sedikides, C.: Changes in the Valence of the Self as a Function of Mood. Review of Personality and Social Psychology 14, 271–311 (1992)

3. Neumann, R., Seibt, B., Strack, F.: The influence of mood on the intensity of emotional responses: Disentangling feeling and knowing. Cogn. Emot. 15(6), 725–747 (2001), doi:10.1080/02699930143000266
4. Faigin, G.: The Artist's Complete Guide to Facial Expressions. Watson-Guptill, New York (1990)
5. Ekman, P., Friesen, W.V., Hager, J.C.: The Facial Action Coding System. Weidenfeld & Nicolson, London (2002)
6. Mehrabian, A.: Pleasure-arousal-dominance: A general framework for describing and measuring individual differences in temperament. Curr. Psychol. 14(4), 261–292 (1996)
7. Payne, L.L., Shaw, T., Caldwell, L.L.: Movies and Mood - An Exploration of the Critical Variables related to Mood States. In: Proceedings of the 1997 Northeastern Recreation Research Symposium, pp. 60–63 (1998)
8. Wassermann, K.C., Eng, K., Verschure, P., Manzolli, J.: Live Soundscape Composition Based on Synthetic Emotions. IEEE MultiMedia 10(4), 82–90 (2003)
9. Gebhard, P.: ALMA: A layered model of affect. In: AAMAS 2005, pp. 29–36 (2005)
10. Burkitt, M., Romano, D.M.: The Mood and Memory of Believable Adaptable Socially Intelligent Characters. In: Prendinger, H., Lester, J., Ishizuka, M. (eds.) IVA 2008. LNCS (LNAI), vol. 5208, pp. 372–379. Springer, Heidelberg (2008)
11. Peña, L., Peña, J.-M., Ossowski, S.: Representing emotion and mood states for virtual agents. In: Klügl, F., Ossowski, S. (eds.) MATES 2011. LNCS, vol. 6973, pp. 181–188. Springer, Heidelberg (2011)
12. Santos, R., Marreiros, G., Ramos, C., Neves, J., Bulas-Cruz, J.: Personality, Emotion, and Mood in Agent-Based Group Decision Making. IEEE Intell. Syst. 26(6), 58–66 (2011), doi:10.1109/MIS.2011.92
13. Kasap, Z., Ben Moussa, M., Chaudhuri, P., Magnenat-Thalmann, N.: Making Them Remember - Emotional Virtual Characters with Memory. IEEE Comput. Graph. Appl. 29(1), 20–29 (2009)
14. Ben Moussa, M., Magnenat-Thalmann, N.: Applying Affect Recognition in Serious Games: The PlayMancer Project. In: Egges, A., Geraerts, R., Overmars, M. (eds.) MIG 2009. LNCS, vol. 5884, pp. 53–62. Springer, Heidelberg (2009)
15. Courgeon, M., Clavel, C., Martin, J.C.: Appraising emotional events during a real-time interactive game. In: AFFINE 2009, pp. 7:1–7:5. ACM, New York (2009)
16. Fabri, M., Moore, D.J., Hobbs, D.J.: Designing Avatars for Social Interactions. In: Canamero, L., Aylett, R. (eds.) Animating Expressive Characters for Social Interaction. Advances in Consciousness Research Series, Benjamins Publishing (2008)
17. Gebhard, P.: Emotionalisierung interaktiver Virtueller Charaktere. Dissertation, Universität des Saarlandes (2007)
18. Russell, J.A., Mehrabian, A.: Evidence for a three-factor theory of emotions. J. Res. Pers. 11(3), 273–294 (1977)
19. Facial Expression Repertoire (FER), http://research.animationsinstitut.de/
20. Lance, B., Marsella, S.: Glances, glares, and glowering: How should a virtual human express emotion through gaze? In: AAMAS, vol. 20, pp. 50–69 (2010)
21. Bee, N., Falk, B., André, E.: Simplified Facial Animation Control Utilizing Novel Input Devices: A Comparative Study. In: IUI 2009, pp. 197–206 (2009)
22. Bradley, M.M., Lang, P.J.: Measuring emotion: The self-assessment manikin and the semantic differential. J. Behav. Ther. Exp. Psy. 25, 49–59 (1994)

Multimodal Interface Towards Smartphones: The Use of Pico Projector, Passive RGB Imaging and Active Infrared Imaging

Thitirat Siriborvornratanakul

Graduate School of Applied Statistics
National Institute of Development Administration (NIDA)
118 SeriThai Rd., Bangkapi, Bangkok 10240, Thailand
thitirat@as.nida.ac.th

Abstract. This paper proposes a study regarding smartphone-oriented mobile devices capable of simultaneous passive RGB imaging and active infrared imaging for both projection and image sensing. Using RGB and infrared wavelengths together enables foreground interactive projection and background vision-based analysis to be done without unwanted crosstalk between the two spectrums or visible interruption to audiences. Our proposal includes detachable and rotatable mobile configuration designs, general computing paradigm and multimodal interface strategy; all are presented in a smartphone-oriented manner. Experiments are conducted to clarify efficiency and limitation of our proposal using a proof-of-concept setup. Despite of internal optic and mechanism which requires cooperation from technologys owner to fully accomplish, we believe that our proposal is useful and sustainable, enabling easy compatibility and maintenance with future mobile devices.

Keywords: Projector-camera, infrared, multimodal interface, smartphone.

1   Introduction

It is likely to become a new norm that recent electronic devices are accompanied with smartphone applications. Projectors are another devices that have already set foot in this world overwhelming with the smartphone-oriented trend, particularly for pico projectors whose small form factors are perfect for being smartphone's future partners. Using a pico projector with a smartphone introduces a multimodal interface where there are at least one input and output each from smartphone, and one output from projector. In this paper, we focus on the interface that uses a smartphone with a mobile device; the mobile device mentioned here refers to a combination of pico projector, passive RGB imaging and active infrared imaging.

Our proposal can be divided into two parts: (1) smartphone-oriented ubiquitous configurations regarding the mobile device that is capable of real-time RGB

F.J. Perales and J. Santos-Victor (Eds.): AMDO 2014, LNCS 8563, pp. 41–50, 2014.

projection, near-infrared projection, passive RGB image sensing and active in-frared image sensing, and (2) a design of the multimodal interface that connects a smartphone and the mobile device together. The device and interface are de-signed for uses in ubiquitous environment-aware interactive projection systems where projected imagery can interactively respond to an arbitrary environment in an intelligent manner. In those interactive projection systems, smartphone and RGB projection are responsible for foreground interactions with users, whereas infrared projection, RGB image sensing and infrared image sensing do back-ground analysis regarding recognition of the ubiquitous environment.

For the rest of this paper, Section 2 explains difficulties and challenges of vision-based interactive projection through examples of previous researches. Sec-tion 3 presents smartphone-oriented configurations, general computing paradigm and multimodal interface regarding the proposed device. Section 4 then conducts quantitative experiments that observe efficiency and limitation of visual sensing based on our proof-of-concept setup. Finally, Section 5 concludes this paper together with possible future works suggested.

2 Related Works

Our work draws on previous researches in interactive projection systems, partic-ularly ubiquitous and mobile projection. To narrow down the scope, we will only discuss about works whose interactive projection involves difficulties or solutions regarding crosstalk between RGB projection and RGB image sensing as this is a fundamental challenge found in most vision-based interactive projection.

Perhaps the simplest solution for vision-based interactive projection is to use a predefined fiducial marker whose essential visibility when being seen by cam-era is barely degraded by overlaid projection imagery. Examples can be found in many proof-of-concept works like [6,8]. This solution is simple and effective; however, obtrusive nature of these markers violates the true spirit of ubiquity where projection target may be varied and unprepared. Avoiding overlap be-tween projected imagery and physical object by careful calculation as in [11,14], is another solution for a mobile system. Nevertheless, this solution limits area for projection and may not be suitable for projection in a cluttered area.

Many works utilize more complicated techniques to reduce visibility of pro-jected imagery to nearly invisible or imperceptible in camera feedback. For exam-ple, reengineering the internal mechanism of projection engine [10], and analyzing unique characteristics of micro-mirror flipping and color wheel in an off-the-shelf DLP (Digital Light Processing) projector [2,3]. Results of these techniques re-quire little effort during online computation; however, they depend on special cameras (high speed and externally triggered) and specific projection technol-ogy which may not be last long. Besides, it is not easy to reengineer or control internal projection mechanism without cooperation from technology's owner.

A cheaper and more independent alternative that makes projected imagery invisible in camera feedback, is to separate their working light spectrum. By letting projected imagery stay in the visible light spectrum and camera feed-back in the infrared light spectrum as in [9,13], there is no visual crosstalk to be concerned. Nonetheless, using active infrared imaging to assist interactive projection has already gone far beyond the crosstalk elimination. As proposed in [12], projecting one or more predefined markers in infrared enables M2M (machine-to-machine) visual communication among multiple projectors to be done in peer-to-peer (P2P) style.

In this paper, we focus on a concrete design of a mobile projector-camera device intended for smartphone-oriented vision-based interactive projection. Rather than creating a design that works for one specific interactive projection requirement like previous works, our proposal is more general and enables all previously proposed features like crosstalk elimination and invisible M2M communication.

3   Proposed System

This section explains key components of our proposed mobile device consisting of RGB projector, infrared projector, passive RGB camera, and active infrared camera. The explanation includes design and configuration, computing paradigm, and multimodal interface design. Combining the three parts not only solves general crosstalk problems between projection and camera but also facilitates invisible visual communication among multiple projectors in P2P style.

3.1   Smartphone-Oriented Mobile Configuration

For a fully developed design and configuration, our vision is a mobile device that consists of at least an IR-RGB dual-input projector and a multi-band camera, forming a self-contained compact module that can act as either a standalone environment-aware interactive projection device or a detachable accessory for smartphones. The IR-RGB dual-input projector is a projector capable of projecting two independent series of RGB and infrared images simultaneously. Unfortunately, this type of projectors is mostly found as research prototypes [1,4,5,12] or in some recent high-end non-mobile projectors. The multi-band camera refers to a camera or a set of cameras that is able to sense reflected light energy in different wavelengths at a time; in our context, this refers to a camera that can capture one RGB image (including ambient light and RGB projection) and one near-infrared image (including near-infrared projection only) at a time.

Combining the dual-input projector and the multi-band camera into a single device can be tricky. If all related optical axes in the device are coaligned, it can guarantee that everything the camera sees can be projected upon and there is no need for 3D recovery. However, this coaxial design refers to complicated mechanism that can only be fully accomplished by authorized manufacturers. To keep thing simple in term of mechanism, some may choose an alternative not to coaxialize but externally calibrate them instead. This is the same as implemented in Microsoft Kinect sensor for Xbox 360 where RGB camera, near-infrared camera, and infrared emitter are linearly fixed in a horizontal bar which can be programmatically tilted.

The remaining issue of optional detachable accessory is inspired by recent models of detachable pico projectors for smartphones; for example, Aiptek i55

Projector (2013), iPower Pro Projector (2013), and 3M sleeve projector (2012). Our proposed configuration refers to an integrated design that combines the IR-RGB dual-input projector, the multi-band camera, and an onboard battery, forming a compact device that can serve as a detachable accessory for smartphones. This design virtually fuses a smartphone and the proposed device into a single device convenient for mobile usages. Besides, with this detachable form factor, the device consumes no power from the detaching smartphone and allows easy development as well as maintenance in the future. For example, adding an external processing module for speeding up computation.

Regardless of complicated optic and mechanism that are beyond our scope, our proposed configurations are illustrated in Fig. 1. For the non-coaxialized design, we do not place the RGB camera next to the RGB projector and the same to the infrared projector and the infrared camera. This is done on purpose so that there is an adequate baseline distance between the two optics, allowing techniques like triangulation and 3D recovery to be carried on when required.

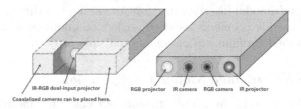

Fig. 1. Two proposed configurations of the self-contained mobile device. Left and right images show coaxialized and non-coaxialized designs respectively.

3.2   General Computing Paradigm

Fig. 2 shows a diagram illustrating four main computing modules that can be shared by any vision-based interactive projection system using our configurations proposed in Section 3.1. In this diagram, one arrow represents two piece of information regarding visual RGB and infrared wavelengths. Inputs to the system are one RGB image and one infrared image captured by the multi-band camera. Outputs from the system are two projected images—one visible RGB image for foreground interaction with users and one invisible infrared image for facilitating background analysis or M2M communication.

In detail, input images are sent to the first and second modules responsible for calibration and analysis respectively. The first module is crucial for non-coaxialized design and any design involving synchronization so that the two input images can be used correctly during further computation. The second module involves main tasks for interpreting the two input images and extracting required information. Results from the first two modules are then sent to the interaction manager where appropriate interactive projected images are computed based on incoming information (the third module) and may also be compensated or corrected (the fourth module) if required. The fourth module is often

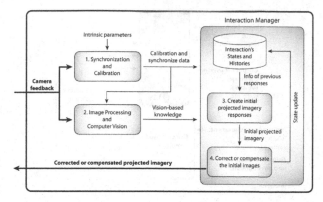

Fig. 2. Four computational modules to be used with the proposed mobile device.

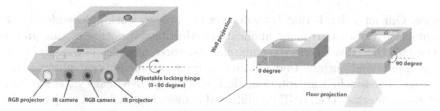

Fig. 3. Revised design of the proposed mobile device, including an adjustable locking hinge. Note that this revision can be applied for the coaxialized design as well.

found in smart projection systems where original images intended for projection are altered before actual projection. Generally this is referred to geometric and photometric (a.k.a., radiometric) compensation.

As for usages with a smartphone, our vision includes a basic remote-control application. This application allows basic controls of our proposed device to be done via the hosting smartphone's screen. Regarding this remote-control application, we propose a revised configuration including an adjustable locking hinge as illustrated in Fig. 3. This will allow a user holding the device to easily see and touch the smartphone's screen regardless of different projecting angles.

Last but not least, because our proposal is intended for interactive mobile usages, the key problem is the fact that real-time interactive projection in a mobile environment introduces huge computational loads that exceed capability of recent mobile devices. Hence, to accomplish this computing paradigm in practice, we strongly recommend using an additional processing unit to gear up the computation. Alternatively, specific hardware for image or graphic processing might be included for time-consuming frequently-used tasks.

3.3 Multimodal Interface Design

Fig. 4 shows the multimodal interface that connects our proposed mobile device and an attaching smartphone to users and environment. It can be seen that there are two separated devices working together—a smartphone and our proposed

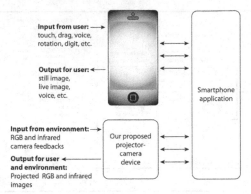

Fig. 4. Multimodal interface consists of many inputs and outputs sending among user, environment, smartphone and the proposed mobile device.

device. Our intension is that both devices are able to work independently or in conjunction via a smartphone application. Multimodal nature of this proposal is the fact that this interface (combining the three modules in Fig. 4) involves many inputs and outputs that fall into at least two obvious categories—tactile interface (i.e., touch, drag, rotation, digit, still image, live image via smartphone) and visual interface (i.e., RGB and infrared camera feedback and projection from the projector-camera device).

4   Proof-of-Concept Experiments

According to Section 3, it is obvious that to achieve our proposed design perfectly, master in hardware and optic as well as full authorization to projection's mechanism is crucial. For efficiency investigation of this section, we simulate the non-coaxialized design using one RGB pico projector (i.e., Brookstone HDMI 85-lumen pocket projector) and one Microsoft Kinect for Windows sensor as shown in Fig. 5. At a time, Kinect sensor acts as a passive RGB camera, an active infrared camera and a static non-programmable infrared light source. Kinect's infrared emitter is blocked by two layers of semi-transparent papers in order to diffuse Kinect's infrared pattern from dot to uniform light. Both RGB and infrared camera feedbacks are captured at resolution of 640x480 pixels.

In this section, we closely observe efficiency of vision-based recognition under actual active infrared circumstances. The goal is to quantitatively measure how well vision-based recognition can perform under infrared spectrum, comparing to the same recognition done under visible light spectrum. Section 4.1 observes efficiency of recognizing a physical object, referring to the ability of active infrared where the physical object can be seen by infrared camera without crosstalk from RGB projected imagery. Section 4.2 then observes efficiency of recognizing a projected imagery. This can convey to efficiency of recognizing the projected infrared imagery during infrared visual communication among projectors.

Our development software includes Microsoft Visual C++, Open Source Computer Vision Library (OpenCV) 2.4.6, and Kinect for Windows SDK 1.7,

Fig. 5. Proof-of-concept configuration using RGB pico projector and Kinect sensor.

executing on a Fujitsu Lifebook S Series laptop. Scale-Invariant Feature Transform (SIFT) [7] is used as a representative of vision-based recognition algorithm. In each experiment, four corners of the target object in camera feedbacks are identified by SIFT algorithm. Ground truth of each corner is manually located before it is used to compute an Euclidean distance error of the corner; average of the four Euclidean distance errors represents value plotted in graphs.

All experiments are conducted indoor in order not to intrude the onboard infrared light source with external infrared light. For comparative studies, four camera feedbacks are planned for each experiment—RGB camera feedback in a well-lit room, RGB camera feedback in a dark room, infrared camera feedback in a well-lit room, and infrared camera feedback in a dark room. Nevertheless, in our indoor environment, there is no difference between the two infrared images. Therefore, only one infrared image will be considered for both lighting conditions.

4.1   Visual Analysis of a Physical Object

In order to compare vision-based efficiency done under active infrared with those done under normal visible light, a 2D binary logo printed on a white A4 paper is used as the target of visual recognition. Because RGB camera feedbacks in a dark room are almost pitch black in this experiment, they are omitted from the experiment. Fig. 6 shows experimental results when the printed logo is placed at different distances from Kinect. Note that Kinect is projecting a uniform infrared light whereas the pico projector is projecting nothing in this experiment.

From Fig. 6, it can be seen that, for RGB camera feedbacks in a well-lit room, the printed logo is discovered by SIFT algorithm at almost every distance with errors below 3 pixels; this is equal to 95% of successful recognition. In contrast, only 60% of the same printed logo are recognized in infrared camera feedbacks with errors below 10 pixels; all successful recognitions fall in the distances of 25–95 cm before SIFT algorithm completely fails to recognize the printed logo at distances greater than 95 cm. From this experiment, we can conclude that efficiency of visual recognition in RGB camera feedbacks regarding a well-lit environment is more precise and stable whereas recognition in infrared spectrum introduces unpredictable instability and limited working distances. Inefficiency of recognition in infrared images is partly caused by noises and low contrast nature of infrared images themselves. Besides, because Kinect is the only infrared light

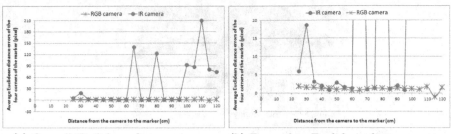

(a) Overall Euclidean distance errors.   (b) Zoomed in Euclidean distance errors.

Fig. 6. Average Euclidean distance errors of recognizing the physical object located at different distances to Kinect, where there is no RGB projection involved. Note that negative error values represent failure of SIFT algorithm to recognize the printed logo in that camera feedback; magnitude of the negative error conveys no meaning here.

source in this experiment, amount and distribution of light are not as good as visible light sources distributed all around the experimental room.

In conclusion, although systems using active infrared camera sensing and RGB real-time projection easily eliminate traditional crosstalk between projected imagery and camera feedback, efficiency of visual recognition and quality of camera feedbacks are not as precise and stable as visual sensing in visible light spectrum. Also, an onboard infrared light source must be chosen carefully so that its brightness can cover desired range of working distances.

4.2   Visual Analysis of a Projected Imagery

In this experiment, we observe scenarios when an arbitrary infrared image is projected for the purpose of invisible P2P visual communication among projectors. Because there is no commercial mobile infrared projector available for testing yet, we conduct an indirect experiment using RGB projected imagery in a dark room, pretending that it is an infrared projected imagery where the projector is the only infrared light source illuminating the room. Two controlled conditions are investigated—recognizing RGB projected imagery in a well-lit room, and recognizing RGB projected imagery in a dark room.

Fig. 7 (left) shows experimental results. Because the size of projected logo expands along the increasing distance, recognition errors should not significantly depend on distances until the distance is too great to reach by the limited brightness of the projector. Experimental results collected in a well-lit room support this assumption. Nevertheless, experimental results in a dark room intended for mimicking infrared projection, show interesting issues despite of the distance. *"Using a projector in a dark room"* is a quote that has been repeatedly stated, particular for a mobile projector with limited brightness. However, according to Fig. 7, it can be seen that recognizing the projected logo in a dark room is very unstable; only half of the experimental images are successfully recognized with errors less than 20 pixels. To investigate this issue more closely, Fig. 7 (right) shows comparison of RGB camera feedbacks captured at the same distance but

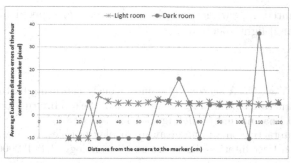

Fig. 7. Left image shows average Euclidean distance errors of recognizing the RGB imagery projected on a white paper located at different distances to Kinect. Note that negative error values represent failure of SIFT algorithm to recognize the printed logo in that camera feedback; magnitude of the negative error conveys no meaning here. Right image shows two RGB camera feedbacks at the distance of 50 cm in light and dark room corresponding to successful and failed SIFT recognition respectively.

in different ambient light. It is obvious that because of high brightness of the projected light in the dark room, some visual appearances of the projected imagery are burned out and contrast between black and white projection is low, causing failure in SIFT algorithm. In the light room, because brightness of the projected logo is diluted by ambient light, burning out is not happened.

Carrying these experimental results to cases of recognizing infrared projected imagery, we conclude that distances are still one of key factors; very small distances cause projected imagery to appear over saturated in camera feedbacks and very great distances mean inadequate amount of light is illuminating the surface. In addition, intensity of infrared projected imagery and its projected contents must be carefully considered as too-bright projection causes details burned out and too-dim projection may reduce the range of working distances. For projectors allowing projection of arbitrary infrared images, adapting techniques of real-time photometric compensation in RGB projected imagery should help ensure proper brightness of the projected imagery as seen by camera.

5   Conclusion and Future Works

This paper proposes configurations, computing paradigm and multimodal interface regarding a mobile projector-camera device utilizing active infrared and passive RGB image sensing. The device is designed in a way that will support easy maintenance and integration with future smartphones. Excluding optic and mechanism issues that are beyond our scope, experimental results show that adding active infrared mechanism to the projector-camera device does eliminate crosstalk problem between RGB projection and RGB camera, and enable sensing regardless of light or dark room. In exchange, visual sensing in infrared spectrum introduces unstable recognition results and limited working distances.

Extending from the current setup, our future works include developing an actual application running in smartphone platform as well as an interactive projection system whose printed appearances of physical objects are specifically designed for sensing in infrared light spectrum.

References

1. Akasaka, K., Sagawa, R., Yagi, Y.: A sensor for simultaneously capturing texture and shape by projecting structured infrared light. In: Procs. of the 6th International Conference on 3-D Digital Imaging and Modeling, pp. 375–381 (2007)
2. Cotting, D., Gross, M.: Interactive environment-aware display bubbles. In: Procs. of the ACM Symposium on User Interface Software and Technology (UIST 2006), pp. 245–254 (2006)
3. Cotting, D., Naef, M., Gross, M., Fuchs, H.: Embedding imperceptible patterns into projected images for simultaneous acquisition and display. In: Procs. of the 3rd IEEE/ACM International Symposium on Mixed and Augmented Reality (ISMAR 2004), pp. 100–109 (2004)
4. Follmer, S., Johnson, M., Adelson, E., Ishii, H.: deform: An interactive malleable surface for capturing 2.5d arbitrary objects, tools and touch. In: Procs. of the 24th Annual ACM Symposium on User Interface Software and Technology (UIST 2011), pp. 527–536 (2011)
5. Lee, J., Hudson, S., Dietz, P.: Hybrid infrared and visible light projection for location tracking. In: Procs. of the 20th Annual ACM Symposium on User Interface Software and Technology (UIST 2007), pp. 57–60 (2007)
6. Lochtefeld, M., Gehring, M., Schoning, J., Kruger, A.: Shelftorchlight: Augmenting a shelf using a camera projector unit. In: Internation Conference on Pervasive Computing, Workshop on Personal Projection (UbiProjection 2010), pp. 1–4 (2010)
7. Lowe, D.: Distinctive image features from scale-invariant keypoints. International Journal of Computer Vision 60(2), 91–110 (2004)
8. Mistry, P., Maes, P., Chang, L.: Wuw - wear ur world: A wearable gestural interface. In: Procs. of the CHI Extended Abstracts on Human Factors in Computing Systems (CHI 2009), pp. 4111–4116 (2009)
9. Molyneaux, D., Izadi, S., Kim, D., Hilliges, O., Hodges, S., Cao, X., Butler, A., Gellersen, H.: Interactive environment-aware handheld projectors for pervasive computing spaces. In: Kay, J., Lukowicz, P., Tokuda, H., Olivier, P., Krüger, A. (eds.) Pervasive 2012. LNCS, vol. 7319, pp. 197–215. Springer, Heidelberg (2012)
10. Raskar, R., Welch, G., Cutts, M., Lake, A., Stesin, L., Fuchs, H.: The office of the future: A unified approach to image-based modeling and spatially immersive displays. In: Procs. of the 25th Annual Conference on Computer Graphics and Interactive Techniques (SIGGRAPH 1998), pp. 179–188 (1998)
11. Siriborvornratanakul, T., Sugimoto, M.: Clutter-aware adaptive projection inside a dynamic environment. In: Procs. of the 15th ACM Symposium on Virtual Reality Software and Technology (VRST 2008), pp. 241–242 (2008)
12. Willis, K., Poupyrev, I., Hudson, S., Mahler, M.: Sidebyside: Ad-hoc multi-user interaction with handheld projectors. In: Procs. of the 24th Annual ACM Symposium on User Interface Software and Technology (UIST 2011), pp. 431–440 (2011)
13. Wilson, A.: Playanywhere: A compact interactive tabletop projection-vision system. In: Procs. of the 18th Annual ACM Symposium on User Interface Software and Technology (UIST 2005), pp. 83–92 (2005)
14. Yoshida, T., Hirobe, Y., Nii, H., Kawakami, N., Tachi, S.: Twinkle: Interacting with physical surfaces using handheld projector. In: Procs. of IEEE Virtual Reality Conference, VR 2010, pp. 87–90 (2010)

Using Webcam to Enhance Fingerprint Recognition

Bibek Behera, Akhil Lalwani, and Avinash Awate

Indian Institute of Technology, Bombay
Powai, Mumbai-400076, India
bibek@cse.iitb.ac.in,
lalwani.akhil@gmail.com,
awate_avinash@yahoo.com
http://www.cse.iitb.ac.in

Abstract. Fingerprint recognition has always played an important role in biometrics. Presently, biometric devices come with scanners that take images in a controlled manner. This paper studies how webcams can be used to take images in more or less uncontrolled manner to produce images that can be used for fingerprint matching. The idea is to take photo of a finger(preferably thumb) casually from a webcam either using a mobile device or tablet. The image is then preprocessed using techniques such as gamma normalisation, HDR (High Dynamic Range) toning and other tools from Photoshop softwares. The preprocessed image is then fed to the fingerprint enhancement algorithm. Our experimentation shows that inspite of lack of light or high quality cameras, our system is robust to change in brightness or quality of cameras.

Keywords: Gamma normalisation, HDR toning, ridge, local adjustment, fingerprint, webcam.

1 Introduction

This paper describes a simple webcam based approach for enhancing images for automatic fingerprint identification system (AFIS). The idea of a webcam based AFIS comes in the backdrop of conducting technical courses all over India across 300 institutes as a part of IIT-Bombay edX distant learning educational program. This software will be installed in local servers at distant learning centres. The software can be used for authorisation during test and quizzes to prevent unauthorised persons from taking test for others. These days biometric devices are used everywhere for fingerprint recognition. These devices have hardware as well as software componenets that could cost around Rs. 22,000 or 300 €. Installing these devices all over India would be an expensive process that severely limits the outreach of our program. We need to ensure that our webcam based approach meets the quality standards of existing biometric system. So in this paper, we have compared our techniques with Peter Kovesi's code which loosely follows the approach presented by Hong et al. [2], which is the present state of the art for fingerprint recognition.

F.J. Perales and J. Santos-Victor (Eds.): AMDO 2014, LNCS 8563, pp. 51–60, 2014.

This work is centered around various pre-processing techniques such as HDR toning. All these techniques are well-known in Photoshop®[1] world. They have been used to enhance quality of images such as human faces, natural scenery, etc. These methods can bring out darker aspects of images and make them visible. Sometimes when we take images in natural light, often the picture has patches of highlights and shadows. These regions are not suitable for fingerprint matching using webcam. In these cases, we need some advanced image processing techniques like gamma normalisation, HDR toning that can normalise the highlights and shadows of images. Highlights are over-illuminated regions and shadows are unlighted regions.

A very simple yet effective technique is gamma normalisation that darkens darker parts and lightens lighter parts. This technique has been shown by Islam et al. [3] to bring out ridges in a fingerprint to a level of clarity sufficient for fingerprint identification and has also improved the accuracy of fingerprint matching. Despite this fact, gamma resolution fails over the shadowed regions because they are darker but the requirement is extraction of ridges from darker regions. This leads to failure of such system in absence of enough light. Moreover even if we change the gamma value to reverse the effect of contrast i.e. make dark parts lighter and lighter parts darker, again we lose information from the lighter parts. Also the darker parts are not enhanced to a huge extent. This makes gamma normalisation an ineffective technique and there is scope for better techniques for producing better quality images.

Other works include Hong et al. [2] which describes the image enhancement algorithm on ridge extraction. We describe a novel approach that uses HDR toning to preprocess images before using the ridge extraction algorithm. Techniques like HDR toning work way better in adding light to darkened regions. In HDR toning, there are four techniques. In this paper, we investigate the role of each technique.

The rest of the paper is divided into 4 sections. In section 2, we describe HDR toning, various modes of HDR toning and comparison of these modes. In section 3, we discuss the algorithm used to develop the skeleton of fingerprint from the image of the finger. Section 4 describes our details of our experimental set-up along with results. Finally we conclude in section 5.

2   HDR-Toning

Before knowing about HDR toning, we need to understand the background and peculiarities of HDR.

2.1   Background of HDR

HDR means high dynamic range i.e. 32 bit images. Dynamic range in digital photography means ratio between maximum and minimum measurable intensity.

---

[1] Product is copyright of Adobe Systems.

Every device has its own fixed range. For example in print nothing can become brighter than the paper itself or in display nothing can become brighter than the maximum intensity pixel. Similarly our eyes also have their own dynamic range. 8 bit or 16 bit images are classified into LDR (Low dynamic range). HDR images use these extra bits to create an arbitrarily large scale to fit the requirements of any kind of scene.

2.2   Peculiarities of HDR

HDR empowers the photographer to enhance the range of tonal detail better than that provided by any camera. Merge to HDR is an option in Photoshop that integrates a number of bracketed exposures to one single image, which magically has the tonal detail of the entire variation of exposure[2]. But as we know there is nothing free of cost, expansion in tonal range comes at the expense of decreased contrast in some tones.

2.3   HDR Toning - An Understanding

HDR toning transforms 8 bit images to 32 bit images, processes it and then brings the pixel values back to 8 bit range. It is like stretching an image and then collapsing the image to produce a super clear image. Fig. 1 is the input image taken by a webcam using LED lights embedded in the webcam.

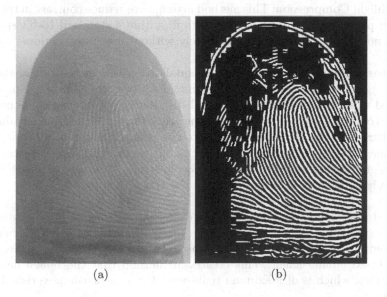

(a)   (b)

Fig. 1. (a) Image taken from a 5MP webcam (b) Skeleton of fingerprint

---

[2] http://www.cambridgeincolour.com/tutorials/high-dynamic-range.htm

As we can see this image has shadows on the left side because the source of light was placed towards the right. In such cases the fingerprint skeleton is totally darkened in the shadowed region as can be seen in Fig. 1. The skeleton is obtained using Peter Kovesi's code [3] which was rewritten by us in Python. Once we have obtained the skeleton, it is forwarded to the matching algorithm [2]. But if the image has darker segments or any relevant information is missing in the original image, the algorithm described by Hong et.al [2] is unable to enhance those segments. Techniques like HDR toning can introduce light in these darker regions and hence come handy to discover hidden ridges as we will show in this paper.

2.4   Various Modes of HDR

HDR toning has four modes of operation.

1. Exposure and Gamma
2. Highlight Compression
3. Histogram equalisation
4. Local adaptation

Fig. 2 shows all the images obtained with these modes.

1. Exposure and Gamma: This mode allows us to control the exposure and gamma which are pictorially equivalent to brightness and contrast adjustment, respectively.

2. Highlight Compression: This method attempts to reduce contrast in the highlight portions of the image to get it to fit within a standard 16-bit space. It has no controls, functioning completely without user intervention. [4]

3. Histogram equalisation: Histogram equalisation is a method of image processing of contrast adjustment using image's histogram. One of the problems faced while taking images is unequal distribution of intensities. Some portions of the images are bright and some are darkened. Histogram equalisation redistributes the HDR histogram into the contrast range of 8 bit or 16 bit image. This mode makes use of a custom tonal curve which spreads out histogram peaks so that histogram becomes flat. An image with several relatively narrow peaks is more suitable for this operation.

4. Local adaptation: This mode is more flexible and one of utmost utility to photographers. In contrast to above methods, this one modifies here the amount of brightness or darkness based on pixels surrounding it i.e. locality based enhancement. This creates an illusion that the image has more contrast, which is of maximum requirement in contrast-impoverished HDR images.

---

[3] http://www.csse.uwa.edu.au/~pk

[4] http://www.earthboundlight.com/phototips/photoshop-cs2-hdr-32bit.html

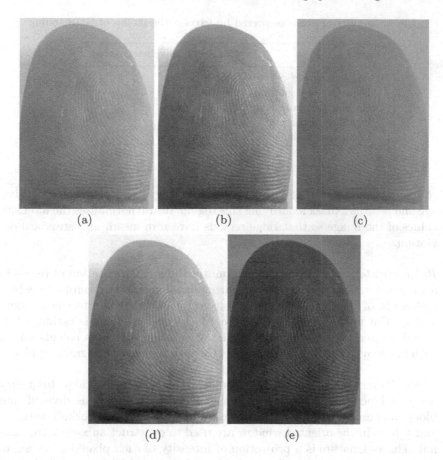

(a)   (b)   (c)

(d)   (e)

Fig. 2. (a) Image taken from a 5MP webcam with an LED torch (b) Image modified using Exposure and Gamma normalisation (c) Highlight compression (d) Histogram equalisation (e) Local adjustment

We examined image as shown in Fig. 2 using an LED torch and noted the ridge readings in various modes as mentioned above and depicted in Table 1.
These images showed that the best reading was observed when local adaption mode is used.

3   Algorithm

The algorithm is a step by step process to convert the fingerprint image into a binary image of ridges. The steps are laid down as follows:-

1. *Local adaptation*: This is a pre-processing step (as described in section 2.4,4) that improves the quality of image since it recovers maximum ridges.

Table 1. Number of pixels recovered by varying the modes of HDR toning

Modes	Number of pixels recovered
Original image	235601
Exposure and gamma	221009
Highlight Compression	257105
Equalize histogram	249169
Local adaptation	*275537*

2. *Ridge segmentation*: This module recognizes ridge areas of a fingerprint image and returns a mask identifying this region. It also normalises the intensity values of the image so that ridge regions have zero mean, unit standard deviation.

3. *Ridge orientation*: This function estimates the local orientation of ridges in a fingerprint. The widely used gradient-based method is employed which makes use of the fact that orientation vector is orthogonal to the gradient [5,7,9]. The image is segmented into blocks and gradient is estimated in x and y direction for every pixel. The orientation matrix is calculated for each block by taking the average of vectors orthogonal to the gradient pixels.

4. *Ridge Frequency*: This process calculates the fingerprint ridge frequency across a block of the fingerprint image. Firstly, the image is divided into blocks and an orientation window is calculated along each block. The ridges and valleys in the oriented window are used to construct an x-signature signal. The x-signature is a projection of intensity of each pixel orthogonal to the orientation window. The projection is a sinusoidal wave and the frequency of the wave gives the ridge frequency in that block.

5. *Ridge Filter*: This function enhances ridges in the fingerprint image via oriented filters. This function makes use of Gabor filters for enhancement which have found utility in fingerprint matching [6,8] and fingerprint classification [4]. Gabor filters are bandpass filters that are sensitive to frequency and orientation [1]. The fingerprints have a useful characteristic of well defined ridge orientation and ridge frequency. When the Gabor filter is applied on each pixel, it enhances the ridges oriented in the direction of local orientation and diminishes anything oriented otherwise. The filter thus enhance ridges and blurs the background, thus cancelling out noise as described by Thai [10].

All these steps have been shown in Fig. 3.

4   Experimental Details

The aim of this experiment is to find the variation in quality of image enhancement algorithm by varying the light intensity. For this experiment we have used

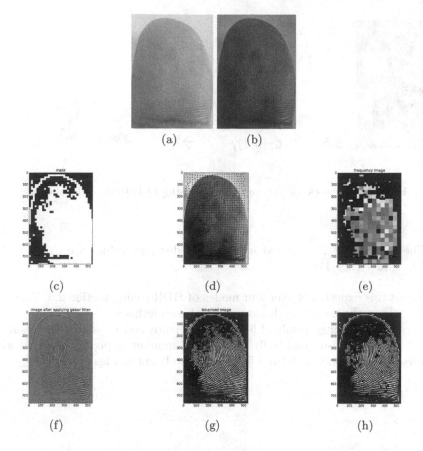

Fig. 3. (a) Original image (b) Preprocessed image with local adjustment (c) Mask after ridge segmentation (d) Ridge orientation (e) Ridge frequency (f) Ridge filter (g) Binary image (h) Final image

a 5MP webcam. The images have been taken in a dark room using a 6 LED high intensity torch.

4.1 Method Proposed

We have laid down the steps used to carry out these experiments.

1. We use a webcam W (having reasonably good resolution, say 1.2 MP) and fix it on table top.
2. Now we place the torch T parallel to the webcam and mark its distance d from the source S as shown in Fig. 4
3. Person X places his thumb on S, we record the image of thumb I_1.
4. Now we vary the position of T to a new value $d + y$ metres from S and take image I_2. The position of W is unchanged throughout the experiment.

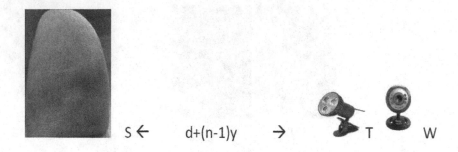

Fig. 4. Framework for varying intensity using LED torch and webcam

5. The position of T is varied n times. So distance values are $d, d + y, d + 2y, \ldots, d + (n - 1)y$.

We repeat this experiment over four modes of HDR toning section 2.4. Each cell of Table 2 records the pixels discovered by these methods.

We have collected fingerprints of 5 different persons and tabulated the result in Table 2. We have also graphically represented number of pixels recovered with distance for three persons from a 5 MP pixel webcam in Fig. 5.

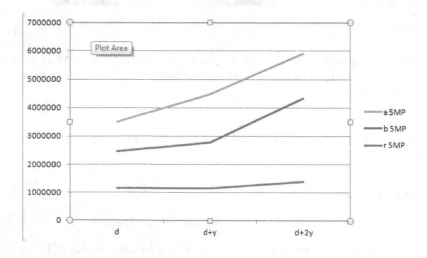

Fig. 5. 1. Number of pixels recovered by varying distance of source S from torch T on different person with 5MP camera

Table 2. Number of pixels recovered by varying distance of source S from torch T on different modes available with HDR toning for image I_1 and 5 MP camera

Image I_1, Webcam 5 MP	Distance of source S from torch T				
Methods	d	$d+y$	$d+2y$	$d+3y$	$d+4y$
No HDR	414464	570368	514816	515840	433664
Gamma Normalisation	627712	626432	674816	674816	706304
Highlight Compression	231936	462336	423936	423936	488448
Histogram Equalisation	1365760	1645824	586240	721408	1213440
Local Adaptation	4876544	4893184	4622592	4863744	4824320

5   Conclusion

Our experiments have shown that the quality of image is not lowered with variation of light as the number of pixels recovered have not varied a lot throughout our experiments. Thus our pre-processing technique makes the system robust to changes in amount of light intensity and can be employed in the fingerprint recognition system. We are presently working on implementing our system for real time identification systems, for the applications mentioned earlier.

Acknowledgements. The authors would like to thank IIT-Bombay MOOC (an online learning initiative sponsored by NMEICT [5]) for which this webcam based fingerprint system is being developed. It is also expected to be deployed in future versions of India's indigenous low-cost tablet 'Aakash'. Special thanks to Prof. D.B.Phatak (CSE Dept., IIT-Bombay), who is the principal investigator of this project, for his support.

References

1. Daugman, J.G.: Uncertainty relation for resolution in space, spatial frequency, and orientation optimized by two-dimensional visual cortical filters. JOSA A 2(7), 1160–1169 (1985)
2. Hong, L., Wan, Y., Jain, A.: Fingerprint image enhancement: Algorithm and performance evaluation. IEEE Transactions on Pattern Analysis and Machine Intelligence 20(8), 777–789 (1998)
3. Islam, M.R., Sayeed, M.S., Samraj, A., et al.: Fingerprint authentication system using a low-priced webcam. In: Proceedings of the International Conference on Data Management (ICDM 2008), IMT Ghaziabad, India, pp. 689–697 (2008)
4. Jain, A.K., Prabhakar, S., Hong, L.: A multichannel approach to fingerprint classification. IEEE Transactions on Pattern Analysis and Machine Intelligence 21(4), 348–359 (1999)
5. Kasaei, S., Deriche, M., Boashash, B.: Fingerprint feature extraction using block-direction on reconstructed images. In: IEEE Region 10 Annual Conference, Speech and Image Technologies for Computing and Telecommunications, Proceedings of the IEEE, TENCON 1997, vol. 1, pp. 303–306. IEEE (1997)

[5] http://www.it.iitb.ac.in/nmeict/home.do

6. Prabhakar, S., Jain, A.K., Wang, J., Pankanti, S., Bolle, R.: Minutia verification and classification for fingerprint matching. In: Proceedings of the 15th International Conference on Pattern Recognition, vol. 1, pp. 25–29. IEEE (2000)
7. Ratha, N.K., Chen, S., Jain, A.K.: Adaptive flow orientation-based feature extraction in fingerprint images. Pattern Recognition 28(11), 1657–1672 (1995)
8. Ross, A., Jain, A., Reisman, J.: A hybrid fingerprint matcher. Pattern Recognition 36(7), 1661–1673 (2003)
9. Simon-Zorita, D., Ortega-Garcia, J., Cruz-Llanas, S., Gonzalez-Rodriguez, J.: Minutiae extraction scheme for fingerprint recognition systems. In: Proceedings of the 2001 International Conference on Image Processing, vol. 3, pp. 254–257. IEEE (2001)
10. Thai, R.: Fingerprint image enhancement and minutiae extraction. The University of Western Australia (2003)

Supporting Annotation of Anatomical Landmarks Using Automatic Scale Selection

Sebastian Bernd Krah, Jürgen Brauer, Wolfgang Hübner, and Michael Arens

Fraunhofer Institute of Optronics, System Technologies and Image Exploitation
{sebastian.krah,juergen.brauer,wolfgang.huebner,
michael.arens}@iosb.fraunhofer.de

Abstract. The effectiveness of appearance based person models strongly relies on a sufficiently large number of high quality training samples. Generating training data in terms of bounding boxes is already a time consuming task. If more complex person models are used, like part-based models or models suitable for human pose estimation, the labeling process becomes infeasible. In the context of pose estimation, motion capturing is often used to generate ground truth data. A major problem with this approach is that motion capturing is usually done in artificial environments with only few persons. It is therefore difficult to generate classifiers which are able to localize anatomical landmarks on a moving person. In order to solve this problem we propose a solution to generate annotations of anatomical landmarks using a semi-automatic work flow, based on tracking and automatic scale selection.

The contribution of the paper is twofold. First, different tracking methods are evaluated in terms of their properties to follow anatomical structures on a moving person. Second, in order to determine the spatial extents of anatomical landmarks some simple but effective scale selection methods are proposed. The resulting person models are intended to generate a suitable basis for learning regression models for monocular pose estimation, as well as for training part-based models directly. Results of a comprehensive quantitative evaluation on the UMPM dataset are presented, while we also show examples of qualitative results on two challenging YouTube sequences.

Keywords: Semi-automatic annotation, Tracking of anatomical landmarks, Automatic scale selection.

1 Introduction

For training part-based person detectors or 2D human pose estimators, learning-based approaches often need training examples of the form (person image, 2D ground-truth landmark regions) (e.g., [4], [10], [5]). Unfortunately, such training data is currently only available for some few videos which were recorded with marker-based motion capture systems (e.g., UMPM [1], HumanEva [9]). For this, it is desirable to be able to annotate selected training videos that are similar to the image material during the envisaged application manually. But labeling a large amount of video frames only by means of manual annotation is time-consuming and laborious since the ground truth landmark regions have to be annotated in every video frame, e.g., by drawing a rectangle

F.J. Perales and J. Santos-Victor (Eds.): AMDO 2014, LNCS 8563, pp. 61–70, 2014.

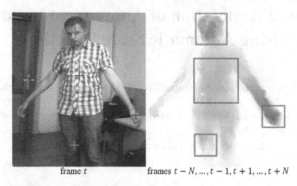

frame t frames $t - N, ..., t - 1, t + 1, ..., t + N$

Fig. 1. Semi-automatic landmark annotation. Left: manual annotation of 2D locations of anatomical landmarks for an anchor frame t. Right: using the manual annotation information we speed-up the ground-truth labeling process by first estimating the spatial extent of each landmark automatically and then track the landmarks to neighbored frames using variants of optical flow (visualized here: TV-L1 optical flow) and appearance based online tracking methods adapted to the task of landmark tracking.

around each of N landmarks. Here we want to generate such annotations automatically starting from so-called *weakly annotated anchor frames*, which are frames annotated by the user with the limitation that the user only labels the center location of each landmark, e.g., by a single point click. Determining the 2D region of each landmark and tracking the landmarks backwards and forwards in the video for some video frames will be done automatically and is the topic of this paper. There are two main contributions by this paper. First, we present a comparative evaluation of an appearance based visual tracker and different optical flow based tracking approaches in order to better assess which of both approaches is more appropriate for the task of landmark tracking. Second, we propose three methods that allow to estimate the scale of each landmark automatically, thereby lifting up the weak landmark annotation of the user by a 2D point to a full 2D rectangular region annotation. Together, this allows to annotate ground-truth data in a semi-automatic fashion, more than 18 times faster compared to a manual annotation, if automatic generated landmarks that do not deviate more than 3% of the object height from the true landmark locations are considered to be acceptable as training data.

Related Work. Tracking is a very active research area with many approaches presented in the last decades. [14] and [13] provide surveys of tracking approaches. Among the different appearance based tracking approaches, online tracking approaches, which update an appearance model of the object on-the-fly, have shown to be successful even in cases of strong appearance changes of the object. [12] provides an exhaustive evaluation of 25 current state-of-the-art online trackers, which renders the Compressive Tracking (CT) approach by Zhang et al. [16] as currently the best online tracking method. We therefore choose CT here as a representative for the class of appearance based trackers. Among optical flow based object tracking methods, dense (e.g.,[8]) and sparse optical flow (e.g., [7]) has been used. While dense optical flow methods are computational more demanding compared to sparse flow methods, they provide a higher accuracy. Since we do not focus on real-time ground-truth generation of training data, but allow for off-line annotation, we select the TV-L1 method [15] as a representative and basis for optical

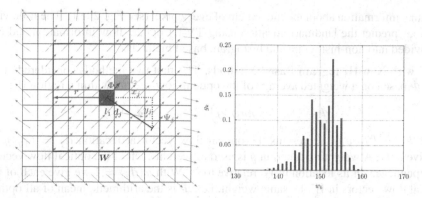

Fig. 2. Left: optical flow vector field. For the non-histogram based methods, the location of the landmark is predicted for the next frame using all optical flow vectors within a region W. Right: exemplary cutout of an angle-weight histogram.

flow based tracking. Ground truth training data is needed by many computer vision algorithms. Offline (e.g., ViPER [3]) and online labeling tools (e.g., LabelMe [6]) have been published, allowing to annotate, e.g., bounding boxes or polygons. Nevertheless, semi-automatic annotation is often restricted to linear interpolation which assumes constant velocity of the object. The VATIC annotation tool [11] is one of few tools that use object tracking in order to ease the annotation process. The tool uses a feature descriptor composed of a HOG descriptor and color features to model the appearance of manually annotated objects. For tracking a linear SVM is used. Nevertheless, a fixed appearance model of the object with a fixed spatial extent is not appropriate to track objects in cases of strong appearance changes, e.g., if the object size changes or in the case of in-depth-rotations. [2] addresses the task of dealing with partially labeled data as well. There the task is to learn a part-based model using images labeled only with bounding boxes around the objects. For this, part locations which are not labeled are treated as latent variables during the training procedure. In contrast to [2] here we consider the situation that parts are labeled, but only the 2D locations, while the 2D landmark regions are unknown.

In section 2 we present the details about the optical flow and appearance based tracking methods used to propagate the user annotation from the anchor frame backwards and forwards within a video. Section 3 introduces three methods to determine the size of a landmark automatically. The results of the comparative evaluation of optical flow and appearance based landmark tracking and the different landmark scale estimation methods are presented in section 4, while section 5 presents the conclusions.

2   Tracking of Landmarks

For tracking a landmark from a frame t_1 – where we already have an estimate of the location l_1 of the landmark – to a frame t_2 with unknown location l_2, we compute a prediction vector Φ, that describes the translation of the landmark, i.e., $l_2 = l_1 + \Phi$.

Optical Flow Based Tracking of Landmarks (OFT). For two consecutive video frames t_1 and t_2 we compute the TV-L1 optical flow, i.e., an optical flow field which contains information about the movement of every pixel (see Fig. 2 left). The following methods predict the landmark location using TV-L1 optical flow information and can be divided into non-histogram and histogram based methods.

OFT with Non-Histogram Based Methods. The first two methods considered compute Φ based on a weighted average of the optical flow vectors within a region W:

$$\Phi = \left(\Sigma_{d_j \in W} \, g(d_j) \cdot \Psi_j \right) \cdot \left(\Sigma_{d_j \in W} \, g(d_j) \right)^{-1}$$

Here $\Psi_j = (u_j, v_j)^\mathsf{T}$ represents the optical flow vector at location $d_j = (x_j, y_j)^\mathsf{T}$ relative to l_1. A weighting function g is used to weight each of the optical flow vectors in dependence on its location in W relative to l_1. With $g(d_j) = 1$ we give each of the optical flow vectors in W the same weight, i.e., Φ is the arithmetic mean of all optical flow vectors in W (method name: Φ). Since the spatial extent of a landmark is unknown it is more promising to weight optical flow vectors which are close to the considered landmark larger than those which are far away from l_1. This can be achieved by using a Gaussian kernel weighting function $g(d_j) = \mathcal{N}\left(\|d_j\|_2, r/3\right)$ (method name: Φ_G).

OFT with Histogram Based Methods. The non-histogram based methods do not take into account that (i) some of the optical flow vectors might be erroneous due to outliers or (ii) optical flow vectors can point into different directions if the region W contains image structures of other landmarks that move into other directions. The following histogram based approaches offer the possibility to tackle the problem of outliers (i) and contradictory optical flow information (ii). In the following, optical flow vectors are described by their length η^j and their angle ω^j, i.e., $\Psi_j = \left(\eta^j, \omega^j\right)^\mathsf{T}$ instead of their x- and y-translation components. Both following two methods first compute an angle-weight histogram that represents the information how often each angle ω^j occurs when considering all optical flow vectors in W, weighted by the lengths of the corresponding optical flow vectors. The angle-weight histogram is discretized into bins $\omega_k, (k = 1, ..., M)$ and for each angle bin a weight g_k is maintained. Each optical flow vector Ψ_j casts a vote into the next bin ω_k that corresponds to its angle ω^j, where the vote strength is set to η^j. Hence $g_k = \sum_{j=0, \omega_k = \omega^j}^{N-1} g(d_j) \cdot \eta^j$. Here $N \in \mathbb{N}$ represents the number of optical flow vectors in W. In Fig. 2 (right) we present an example of the computed weights g_k for some of the angle bins ω_k of such a angle-weight histogram computed for a region W of a real frame. The angle-weight histogram shows a clear peak which corresponds to a favored direction of the optical flow vectors within W. The idea to compute $\Phi = (\omega_\phi, l_\phi)^\mathsf{T}$ is to use only the optical flow vectors Ψ_j that belong to this favored direction. The favored direction corresponds to the bin ω_ϕ where the peak can be localized and the length of the landmark prediction vector is computed by:

$$l_\phi = \left(\Sigma_{j=0, \omega_\phi = \omega^j}^{N-1} \, g(d_j) \cdot \eta^j \right) \cdot \left(\Sigma_{j=0, \omega_\phi = \omega^j}^{N-1} \, g(d_j) \right)^{-1}$$

Here the length of each optical flow vector is weighted by a weighting function g again. We consider two variants in the following: (i) a weighted mean of the lengths η^j of all optical flow vectors that voted into bin ω_ϕ, i.e., $g(d_j) = 1$ (method name: Φ^H) and (ii) weighting each optical flow vector length by its distance to the landmark, i.e., $g(d_j) = \mathcal{N}\left(\|d_j\|_2, r/3\right)$ (method name: Φ_G^H).

Appearance Based Tracking of Landmarks (CT). As described in section 1 we use the Compressive Tracker (CT) [16] as a representative for the appearance based meth-

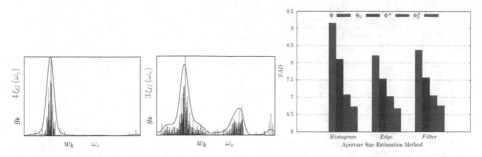

Fig. 3. Left+Mid: Angle-weight histograms for a landmark using a too small (left: one peak) and a too large landmark region (mid: two peaks). g_k: discrete histogram, ξ_G: continuous histogram using a Gaussian kernel density estimator. Right: Tracking errors for different combinations of optical flow and scale estimation methods.

ods. CT is an online tracker, i.e., starting from a selected image region, it generates an appearance model (AM) and updates the AM on-the-fly while tracking. In contrast to the optical flow based methods, we cannot recompute a new landmark region radius r for each new frame. Instead we compute the region size only once using the scale estimation methods described in the next section when we initialize a CT online tracker for each landmark in the anchor frames. The reason is that the AM that is established and updated for each landmark is not scale-invariant, i.e., the AM can only describe a fixed region size. For CT we use the reference implementation provided by the authors[1]. In the following we use ζ to denote CT related tracking results.

3   Automatic Scale Estimation

Due to the weak labeling scenario, the actual landmark region is not specified by the user, but only its 2D center location. In the following three methods are presented that can be used to estimate the spatial extent of a landmark automatically. The corresponding landmark region can then be used by the optical flow methods to estimate a landmark prediction vector or by the CT to update its AM.

Histogram Based (H). The motivation behind the first approach is that a too small or an appropriate landmark region radius will result in a angle-weight histogram with a single peak (Fig. 3 left), since only optical flow vectors of the corresponding landmark are included, i.e., image regions that consistently move into a single direction. If the region radius is too large, image structures of other landmarks will be included, i.e., some optical flow vectors in that region will point into a second direction – as long as these other image structures do not move into the same direction – and a second peak will emerge in the histogram (Fig. 3 middle). A rough estimate for the landmark can be computed therefore by starting with a small region radius r_0 and increase it incrementally by Δr until a second large peak occurs in the angle-weight histogram at radius r_1 and take $r = r_1 - \Delta r$ as a region radius estimate. Since the detection of local maxima in a discrete angle-weight histogram turns out to be not reliable enough, we use

---

[1] http://www4.comp.polyu.edu.hk/~cslzhang/CT/CT.htm

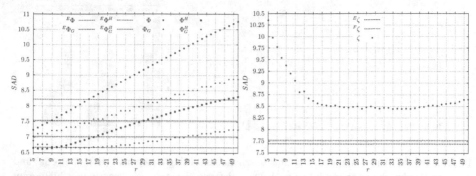

Fig. 4. Tracking errors for constant vs. estimated landmark scale. The plots show the landmark tracking errors for the different optical flow (left image, Φ) and CT (right image, ζ) based landmark tracking methods using constant scale (of 5-49 pixels) or dynamically estimated landmark scales based on the edge-based (E) or the filter-based (F) aperture size estimation. For easier comparison with the constant scale results the tracking errors using the dynamic scale estimation are shown as lines.

a Gaussian kernel density estimator $\kappa_G\left(\omega_k\right)$ to compute a continuous density estimate on basis of the discrete histogram.

Edge Based (E). The central idea of this method is that based on an edge image the region radius should be selected such that at least a minimum amount of edge pixels are contained in the region. Assuming the landmark region is more or less homogeneously, edge pixels will occur at the borders of the region. More precisely, we compute a Canny edge image, start with a region radius r_0 and increase it incrementally by Δr. For each region radius the number of edge pixels $E(r)$ in the corresponding region W is compared with a threshold Θ. The landmark region radius estimate is the first r, such that $E(r) > \Theta$.

Filter Based (F). The basic idea behind this third method is that the scale should be selected in such a way that the brightness of the region border differs significantly from its region center, similar to SIFT and SURF blob keypoint detection. Such a region radius can be computed by filtering image patches at the hypothesized landmark location $l_1 = (x, y)^\top$ with different blob filters, described each by a blob filter matrix:

$$B_r^{l_1} = \begin{cases} +1/N_+ \, , \sqrt{(x - r/2)^2 + (y - r/2)^2} < r/2 \\ -1/N_- \, , \text{else} \end{cases}$$

N_+ and N_- are normalization factors such that the positive and negative elements of the blob filter matrix sum up to 1 each. We convolve the image patch at the hypothesized landmark location with blob filter matrices of different radii r and take as estimate for the landmark region the radius r for which we get the strongest filter response.

4 Evaluation

Quantitative Analysis. For the quantitative evaluation we choose the UMPM benchmark [1] since it provides 3D motion capture data together with camera calibration data. This allows to project the 3D landmark coordinates into the image, thereby generating ground truth 2D landmark center locations which can be compared with the automatically generated landmark locations by the different tracking approaches proposed here. The manual annotation of *weakly annotated anchor frames* is simulated by using the provided ground truth information of landmarks every 99 frames of an UMPM video. Starting from an anchor frame the landmarks are tracked for 49 consecutive frames forwards and backwards. The tracking error is the average sum of absolute differences (SAD) between the UMPM ground truth landmark locations and the automatically generated landmark locations, where we average over all 15 landmarks considered and all evaluation frames. The distance between a ground truth and a tracked landmark location is measured in relative person (bounding box) height units and explicitly not in pixels in order to make the error measure independent of the displayed size of a person. Overall we used the 19 single person videos of the UMPM dataset, which corresponds to approx. 50 000 evaluation frames for each tracking method.

I. Dynamically Estimated vs. Constant Scale. Fig. 4 shows the tracking error when we use a constant scale (of 5 to 49 pixels) for each of the 49 frames left and right to the anchor frame or a dynamically estimated scale, using the edge-based (E) or the filter-based (F) method. The results allow to draw two main conclusions. First, the optical flow histogram-based methods yield better tracking results than the simple averaging methods (compare, e.g., Φ, Φ_G with Φ^H, Φ_G^H). Second, the methods that estimate the landmark scale dynamically (with preceding E and F) yield better average tracking errors than the constant scale methods (without preceding E and F), which is most clearly shown for the case of the CT (bottom plot).

II. Comparison of Scale Estimation Methods (H vs. E vs. F).
Fig. 3 right compares the average tracking errors for the different optical flow methods (Φ, Φ_G, Φ^H, Φ_G^H) combined with the three different scale estimation methods (H,E,F), where each combination is evaluated on approx. 50 000 frames and 15 landmark locations estimated for each frame. The plot allows to draw two further conclusions. First, we can see a clear ranking of the four different optical flow methods w.r.t. the tracking error, namely: $\Phi >$ $\Phi_G > \Phi^H > \Phi_G^H$. Second, there are no large significant differences in the errors depending on the scale estimation method, i.e., $H \approx E \approx F$.

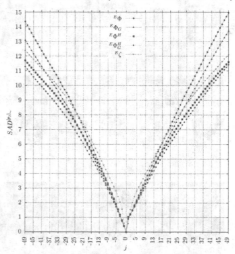

III. Tracking Error as a Function of the Distance to the Anchor Frame. In the figure at the right we show the average tracking error as a function of the distance to the anchor frame for the different optical flow based methods (Φ) and the CT ($^E\zeta$) using an edge-based scale estimation (E). The plot allows to answer the question how far we can track the landmarks to the left and right starting from an anchor frame (frame

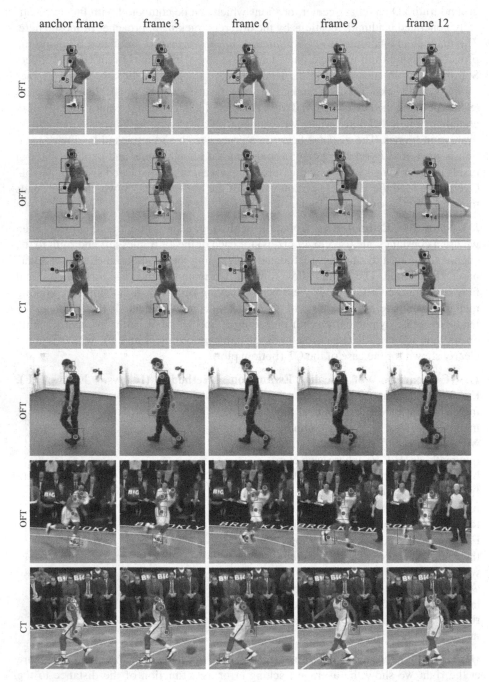

Fig. 5. Qualitative OFT and CT landmark tracking results. Results for three different YouTube badminton sequences (row 1-3), an UMPM sequence (row 4), and two different YouTube basketball sequences (row 6-7). Left column: manually annotated. All other columns: automatically annotated using landmark OFT and CT based tracking with automatic scale selection.

0) if we allow for an average tracking error of maximally Θ percent. When accepting an average landmark tracking error of $\Theta = 5\%$ of the person height, we can use the annotated frames up to 17 frames left and right from the anchor frame without the need of any further manual post-processing, i.e., for each weakly annotated anchor frame, we can generate 34 automatically annotated frames with estimated landmark centers and landmark regions.

IV. Optical Flow vs. Appearance Based Tracking. The best optical flow based landmark tracking method ($^{E}\Phi_G^H$) that exploits the edge-based approach to estimate the landmark scale yields a tracking error of 6.7% and the CT based tracker with edge-based scale estimation an error of 7.7% (of the person height) when tracking 49 frames to the left and right, i.e., automatically annotating 98 frames given one weakly annotated anchor frame. This seems to indicate that there is no large difference between the optical flow and appearance based landmark tracking approaches proposed here.

Qualitative Analysis. In Fig. 5 we show some qualitative examples of tracking results on a UMPM sequence and two challenging YouTube sport sequences showing fast movements with motion blur and some background clutter in the case of the basketball sequence. For some anchor frames we manually labeled four different landmarks (head, shoulder, hand, foot) and used the optical flow (Φ_G^H) and the CT (ζ) tracking methods to track the landmarks. The landmark region scales were estimated using the E method and are depicted by the rectangles, while the black dot denotes the estimated landmark center. Note the large differences in the estimated landmark scales when considering different landmarks. The estimated scales of the head and the left shoulder are very similar for different frames and correspond to the extents of the head and the shoulder, which is interesting, since we do not have specified which image structures belong to the head or the shoulder anywhere. Remember that the user only labels the landmark centers and does not provide segmentation information for the landmarks. The scale corresponds to the landmark extents here since edge pixels occur at the borders to other landmarks (for the head at the border to the torso, and for the shoulder at the border to the head and the end of the T-shirt sleeves). The estimated scale for the foot often ends at the edge of the sock to the lower leg. For the badminton sequence which shows a relative homogeneous background the hand region ends typically at the elbow, while for the basketball sequence the hand region is significantly smaller, since there is much background clutter present that belongs to other image structures than the hand.

5   Conclusions

The paper addressed the task of supporting the generation of ground-truth landmark annotations by tracking anatomical landmarks on highly articulated objects given a few manually annotated anchor frames. We explored four different optical flow based methods and a state-of-the-art appearance based method (CT) in combination with three different simple scale selection methods, which are used to obtain a region from which to use the optical flow vectors to compute a landmark prediction vector or to update the appearance model of the CT tracker. Each method was evaluated on approx. 50 000 frames of the UMPM benchmark and the quantitative results show that there is no large difference between the simple optical flow based methods and the CT tracking method. Since a simple histogram-based detection of the main flow direction with Gaussian weighting ($^E\Phi_G^H$) results in even slightly smaller tracking errors compared to the much more complex CT method, we propose to use this method for landmark tracking. Re-estimating the scale of each landmark for each new frame yields significantly better tracking results than using a fixed scale, while no large differences between the three scale estimation methods (H,E,F) concerning the tracking errors were observed. Even though the optical flow based approaches in combination with one of the three scale estimation methods renders as a simplistic approach for landmark tracking, we can automatically annotate approx. 34 frames for each weakly annotated frame if average landmark localizations errors of up to 5% of the person height are acceptable and thereby speed-up the manual annotation process by a corresponding factor of 34 as well.

References

1. van der Aa, N., Luo, X., Giezeman, G., Tan, R., Veltkamp, R.: Utrecht Multi-Person Motion (UMPM) benchmark: A multi-person dataset with synchronized video and motion capture data for evaluation of articulated human motion and interaction. In: Proc. of Human Interaction in Computer Vision (HICV) Workshop (2011)
2. Felzenszwalb, P.F., Girshick, R.B., McAllester, D., Ramanan, D.: Object Detection with Discriminatively Trained Part Based Models. IEEE Trans. on PAMI 32(9), 1627–1645 (2010)
3. Mihalcik, D., Doermann, D.: The Design and Implementation of ViPER. Tech. rep., University of Maryland (2003)
4. Mori, G., Malik, J.: Recovering 3D Human Body Configurations Using Shape Contexts. IEEE Trans. on PAMI 28(7), 1052–1062 (2006)
5. Müller, J., Arens, M.: Human Pose Estimation with Implicit Shape Models. In: Proc. of ACM ARTEMIS 2010, pp. 9–14. ACM, New York (2010)
6. Russell, B.C., Torralba, A., Murphy, K.P., Freeman, W.T.: LabelMe: A Database and Web-Based Tool for Image Annotation. Int. J. Comput. Vision 77(1-3), 157–173 (2008)
7. Salmane, H., Ruichek, Y., Khoudour, L.: Object Tracking Using Harris Corner Points Based Optical Flow Propagation and Kalman Filter. In: Proc. of 14th IEEE Intelligent Transportation Systems Conference (ITSC 2011), Washington D.C., USA, pp. 67–73 (2011)
8. Schikora, M., Koch, W., Cremers, D.: Multi-Object Tracking via High Accuracy Optical Flow and Finite Set Statistics. In: Int. Conf. on Acoustics, Speech and Signal Processing, ICASSP (2011)
9. Sigal, L., Balan, A., Black, M.: HumanEva: Synchronized Video and Motion Capture Dataset and Baseline Algorithm for Evaluation of Articulated Human Motion. Int. Journal of Computer Vision 87(1), 4–27 (2010)
10. Sigal, L., Black, M.J.: Predicting 3D People from 2D Pictures. In: Proc. of Int. Conf. on Articulated Motion and Deformable Objects (AMDO). pp. 185–195 (2006)
11. Vondrick, C., Patterson, D., Ramanan, D.: Efficiently Scaling up Crowdsourced Video Annotation. Int. Journal of Computer Vision, 1–21 (2012), doi:10.1007/s11263-012-0564-1
12. Wu, Y., Lim, J., Yang, M.H.: Online Object Tracking: A Benchmark. In: Proc. of CVPR 2013 (2013)
13. Yang, H., Shao, L., Zheng, F., Wang, L., Song, Z.: Recent advances and trends in visual tracking: A review. Neurocomputing 74(18), 3823–3831 (2011)
14. Yilmaz, A., Javed, O., Shah, M.: Object tracking: A survey. ACM Computing Surveys 38(4) (2006)
15. Zach, C., Pock, T., Bischof, H.: A duality based approach for realtime TV-L1 optical flow. In: Pattern Recognition, pp. 214–223. Springer (2007)
16. Zhang, K., Zhang, L., Yang, M.-H.: Real-time compressive tracking. In: Fitzgibbon, A., Lazebnik, S., Perona, P., Sato, Y., Schmid, C. (eds.) ECCV 2012, Part III. LNCS, vol. 7574, pp. 864–877. Springer, Heidelberg (2012)

Human Hand Motion Recognition Using an Extended Particle Filter

Chutisant Kerdvibulvech

Rangsit University, 52/347 Muang-Ake, Paholyothin Rd, Lak-Hok,
Patum Thani 12000, Thailand
chutisant.k@rsu.ac.th

Abstract. This paper presents a method to recognize hand motion using an extended particle filter in real-time. We integrate a deterministic clustering algorithm and particle filter together. The skin color of a human hand is firstly segmented by using a Bayesian classifier. Next, during online process, the adaptive algorithm is used to calculate skin color probabilities. By using the online adaptation, this method is able to cope extremely well with luminance changes. After that, we determine the probabilities of the fingertips by using semicircle models for fitting curves to fingertips. Following this, the deterministic clustering algorithm is utilized to search for regions of interest (ROIs), and then the standard particle filter is also performed for motion recognition robustly. Representative experimental results, even when occlusion exists, have been included.

Keywords: Human Hand, Motion Recognition, Extended Particle Filter, Finger Recognition, Online Adaptive, Real-time, Luminance.

1   Introduction

Researches about hand motion recognition are recently and interestingly a popular topic. Consequently, computer vision has been applied to many kinds of application to assist human motion tracking. In this paper, we aim to track the human hand motion and the fingertip positions. It is not easy to achieve for tracking the fingers because some fingers are not stretched out separately. Thus the existing fingertip tracking methods are indirectly applicable to the self-occlusion fingertip tracking as the fingers are usually bent. Moreover, the background is sometimes non-uniform which makes it more difficult for background segmentation. As a result it is more complicated to locate the fingertip positions correctly. Our method for tracking the fingertips solves these problems.

After obtaining the input images, we first segment the hand from the background using a color detection algorithm. To determine the color probabilities of being skin color, during the pre-processing we apply a Bayesian classifier during an offline interactive training phase [1]. Online adaptation of skin probability is then used to refine the classifier automatically using added training images [2]. Following this, we determine probabilities for fingertips by cropping the models of semicircle shape for a

F.J. Perales and J. Santos-Victor (Eds.): AMDO 2014, LNCS 8563, pp. 71–80, 2014.
© Springer International Publishing Switzerland 2014

fit to the fingertip [3]. After that, we superimpose the circular models, and then we normalize the results which will be used as the fingertip probability map for tracking. Next, we apply a deterministic clustering algorithm [4]. This clustering algorithm uses to search for regions of interest (ROIs). Then we use a standard particle filter for tracking by distributing the particles inside the corresponding ROIs. This system enables us to visually track the fingertips even when some fingers are not fully stretched out or when the luminance changes.

2   Related Works

In this section, previous works about gesture recognition will be discussed. Related works have been shown useful for various gesture applications. Cooper et al. [5] built a system for sign language to recognize motion using sub-units. They utilize Markov Models and Sequential Pattern Boosting to encode the temporal changes and discriminative feature selection, respectively. Matilainen et al. [6] presented a finger tracking system using template matching for gesture recognition, focusing on mobile devices. Krejov and Bowden [7] presented a system using a weighted graph and the depth information of the hand for determining the geodesic maxima of the surface. More interestingly, in [8], Kereliuk et. al detected the positions of fingertips. They used the circular Hough transform to detect fingertips by using the assumption from circular of the fingertips.

Nonetheless, these gesture recognition methods are indirectly applicable to the fingertip tracking when the self-occlusion occurs. Also in [7], the hand and wrist localisation works not so smoothly and robustly, while from our experiments, utilizing the Hough transform to detect the fingertips in [8] is not robust enough. This is because fingertip edges cannot be easily detected due to the noise around the fingertips. Also, they did not aim to deal with luminance changes in online process.

To tackle these problems, we try our best to segment the skin color of hand robustly. However, the control of the lighting is still very challenging for skin color detection. Changing the levels of light and limited contrasts prevent correct registration, especially when there is a cluttered background. A major decision has to be made when deriving a model of color. This step to select the color space to be employed is important. Once a suitable color space has been selected, one of the commonly used approaches for defining what constitutes color can be used on the coordinates of the space selected. Nevertheless, by using the simple threshold, it is very difficult to accurately classify the color when the luminance changes. Another method [9] is to use histogram models to detect skin-colored areas in each frame. Still, it cannot perform well for the luminance challenge.

Therefore, we use a Bayesian classifier by learning skin color probabilities from a small training image set and then adaptively learn the color probabilities from online input images. Applying this method, the first advantage is that it avoids the cumbersome process of manually generating a lot of training data. From small amount of training data, it adapts the probability according to the current luminance and converges to a proper value. For this reason, the major advantage of using this method is its ability to cope with changing luminance because it can adaptively describe the distribution of the skin color, and make the results more robust.

3   Method

The schematic of the implementation will be explained in this section. After capturing the images, we firstly apply a Bayesian classifier and an on-line adaptation of skin color probabilities for hand segmentation. As the next step, we apply a matching algorithm to determine the probabilities of the fingertips (i.e. fingertip probability map). Then, we extend the standard particle filter by utilizing the clustering algorithm to create ROIs for tracking. In this way, the positions of human hand and fingertips can be visually tracked.

3.1   Dynamic Background Subtraction

In this section, the method we used for background subtraction will be described. It is difficult because the background used can undecidedly be dynamic. At the first place, we calculate the color probabilities being skin color which will be then used to segment the hand region by applying [1]. The learning process is composed of two phases. In the first phase, the color probability is obtained from a small number of training images during an offline pre-process. In the second phase, we gradually update the probability automatically and adaptively from the additional training data images [2]. In our implementation, we set that the adapting process is disabled as soon as the training is deemed enough. Therefore, when we start to learn the online skin color adaptation, we assume that there is enough skin in the image. As soon as the online adapting process is enough as we prefer (i.e. the skin color probability converges to a proper value), we manually stop the adapting process. In this way, after finishing the online learning process, though the skin area disappears from the scene, it does not affect the skin color probability.

Therefore, this method allows us to get accurate color probability of the skin from only a small set of manually prepared training images. This is because the additional skin region does not need to be segmented manually. Also, because of the adaptive learning, it can be used robustly with changing luminance during the online operation.

After that, we determine the probabilities of the fingertips. We assume that the fingertip shape can be approximated with a semicircular shape while the rest of the hand is roughly straight. After segmenting the hand region, we use the semicircle models for a fit to the curved fingertip [3]. It is very difficult to obtain the accurate results if using only one model. This is because the fingers may have different orientations and sizes. Thus in our implementation, we use 6 models for fingertips. We match semicircle templates against the results of hand segmentation by using

$$R(x, y) = \frac{\sum_{x',y'}[T(x', y') - H(x+x', y+y')]^2}{\sqrt{[\sum_{x',y'}(T(x', y')^2)\sum_{x',y'}H(x+x', y+y')^2]}} \tag{1}$$

where $T(x, y)$ is a searched template at coordinates (x,y) and $H(x, y)$ is a hand segmentation result where the search is running. Following this, we summarize results of the fingertip models using $R_{sum}(x, y) = \sum_{i=1}^{N_0} R_i(x, y)$ where N_0 is a number of fingertip models. In our implementation, we use the sum of the matches of all fingertip models. We superimpose the models, and then we normalize results of each model. As a result, the probabilities to be fingertips of each pixel can be obtained.

3.2   Multi-tracking Recognition

Particle filter is a good framework to track objects in heavy clutter since it works well when the data models are not Gaussian. In many previous works, it has shown that it works robustly when the models are not linear. Its advantages include performing automatic track initialization and recovering from tracking failures. In this paper, we apply particle filter by taking the advantages of particle filter about automatic track initialization and recovering from lost tracks. For example, when the fingertips disappear from the scene and then appear back, we can still track the fingertips correctly due to the advantage of utilizing particle filter. However, standard particle filter works best for non-multiple object. To solve this problem, we extend the standard particle filter by applying a deterministic clustering approach as proposed in [4]. We create rectangular ROIs in each fingertip, and then we distribute the particles only inside the corresponding ROIs (while the standard particle filer will distribute particles all over the image).

The idea of clustering is to create rectangular ROIs by determining the consistency if contours found in the fingertip probability map i.e. $R_{normalized}(x, y)$ are consistent enough using a buffer. The intensity in the grayscale image illustrates the probabilities of the fingertips (higher brightness means higher probability). In this way, after we compute the grayscale image of the fingertip probability map, contours are extracted from the *FindContours* function implemented in the Intel OpenCV library. In other words, contours are meant the area of high probability of the fingertips. Ever contour found is put together in form of $Y_t = \{y_{1,t}^T, ..., y_{m_t,t}^T, ..., y_{M_t,t}^T\}^T$. We called this $Y_t = \{y_{1,t}^T, ..., y_{m_t,t}^T, ..., y_{M_t,t}^T\}^T$ a contour vector. At any particular time, there is a total of M_t contours found from the fingertip probability map image. The system receives a contour vector $Y_t = \{y_{1,t}^T, ..., y_{m_t,t}^T, ..., y_{M_t,t}^T\}^T$ from the fingertip probability map. Note that the number of M_t changes with time (because the received contours may be noise also).

Every $Z_t^{(j)}$, where $Z_t = \{Z_t^{(j)}, j = 1, ..., J_t\}$ and J_t is the number of ROIs found at t within Y_t, is created from a cluster of contours received in Y_t and is stored in terms of a set of time and contour indices, i.e. pairs of indices (t, m_t). We denote the mth contour of $y_{t'+1}$ and the lth contour of $y_{t'}$ by $y_{m,t'+1}$ and $y_{l,t'+1}$ respectively. The normalized distance $d_{m,l}(t'+1, t')$ between $y_{m,t'+1}$ and $y_{l,t'+1}$ can be calculated from intersection area between two contours. Our assumption is if the intersection area of two contours is high enough, these two contours should be put together (so the normalized distance $d_{m,l}(t'+1,t')$ will be set low). The minimum distance between two contours is also determined to calculate the normalized distance $d_{m,l}(t'+1,t')$. For every contour of $y_{t'+1}$, a set of normalized distances $\{d_{m,l}(t'+1,t'),t'\}_{m=1}^{M_{t'+1}}$ is calculated, where $m \in \{1,...,M_{t'+1}\}$. We assume that $d_{m*,l}(t'+1,t')$, $m* \in \{1,...,M_{t'+1}\}$ is the set minimum. The contours $\{y_{m*,t'+1}, y_{l,t'+1}\}$ in terms of the time and contour indices $(t'+1, m*_{t'+1})$ and $(t',l_{t'})$ will be stored together in $Z_t^{(j)}$ using

$$0 \le d_{m*,l}(t'+1,t') \le \eta_0 \tag{2}$$

where η_0 is a given threshold. If the contours of $y_{t'+1}$ cannot be stored together with $y_{l,t'}$, $y_{t'+1}$ will be skipped. Following this, the search procedure is done by using $y_{t'+p}, 1 < p \le \tau$ until the condition of Equation (2) is true.

Since the contours we observed may be produced from true targets or from noise, we also distinguish between the detected regions that are due to targets or noise by determining the consistency of contours. The minimum number of clustered contours, $\tau_{\min}$, in a region required is used to identify a target. For this reason, if $P_t^{(j)} \ge \tau_{\min}$, then the jth region is stored as originating from a target. If not, the jth region is discarded.

The deterministic clustering method mentioned above explains the ways for detecting and reducing the noise in Z_t. If a clutter region cannot be filtered out by the clustering method, it is not impossible to differentiate between this noise and other target areas. This is as the life span of the event represented by this noise area is obviously short when compared with that of a true target. After we detect the ROIs, we classify them into four cases: active regions, new regions, vanishing regions, and noise regions. We decide a *track-to-region* association vector using

$$\gamma_{k,t} = \begin{cases} j \ne 0, & \text{if track } k \text{ can be associated with } Z_t^{(j)} \\ 0, & \text{otherwise} \end{cases} \tag{3}$$

where $\gamma_t = [\gamma_{1,t},...,\gamma_{k,t},...,\gamma_{K,t}]^T$ and $j \in \{1,...,J_t\}$ and $\beta_t = [\beta_{1,t},...,\beta_{j,t},...,\beta_{J,t}]^T$ as a *region-to-track* association vector.

We use the probabilities to be fingertips of each pixel which were obtained before as the observation model. In fact, there are two possible ways to use skin color probability in the particle filter step. Firstly, we can use the skin color probability itself. Secondly, we do threshold before, and then use the binarized image. However, in our implementation, we use the second way in this paper. Denote a time-stamped sample-set, by $\{s_t^{(n)}, n = 1,..., N\}$, representing approximately the probability-density function $p(X_t)$ at time t: where N is the size of sample sets, $s_t^{(n)}$ is defined as the position of the nth particle at time t, $p(X_t)$ is the probability that a fingertip is at position $X = (x,y)^T$ at time t. Just as similar to the iterative process in the normal particle filter, three main stages are selection stage, predictive stage and measurement stage, respectively. In the selection stage, a sample $s'^{(n)}_t$ is chosen from the sample-set $s^{(n)}_{t-1}$ with probability weights $\pi^{(n)}_{t-1}$. $s'^{(n)}_t$ can be set as follows: $s'^{(n)}_t = s^{(n)}_{t-1}$. Each sample is propagated from the set s'_{t-1} by a propagation function, $g(s'^{(n)}_t)$, using

$$s^{(n)}_t = g(s'^{(n)}_t) + noise \tag{4}$$

where noise is given as a Gaussian distribution in the predictive step. In this way, we use only the noise information by defining $g(x) = x$ in Equation (4). In the measurement stage, we generate weights from the probability-density function $p(X_t)$ to obtain the sample-set representation $\{(s^{(n)}_t, \pi^{(n)}_t)\}$ of the state-density for time t using

$$\pi^{(n)}_t = p(X_t = s^{(n)}_t) = R_{normalized}(x, y) \tag{5}$$

where $p(X_t = s^{(n)}_t)$ is the probability that a fingertip is at position $s^{(n)}_t$. Following this, we normalize the total weights, using the condition $\sum_n \pi^{(n)}_t = 1$. Once the N samples have been constructed, we estimate moments of the tracked position at time-step t as using

$$\varepsilon[f(X_t)] = \sum_{n=1}^{N} \pi^{(n)}_t s^{(n)}_t \tag{6}$$

where $\varepsilon[f(X_t)]$ represents the centroid of fingertip. As a result, after performing the clustering algorithm and particle filter, each fingertip can be achievably recognized.

4   Results

Representative results from our experiments are shown in this section. Figure 1 presents an example of finger tracking using the extended particle filter. The reported experimental result was acquired and processed online using an Intel® Core™ i5-3317U CPU computer running MS Windows at 1.70 GHz. The top-left image depicts the input images which are captured from a single USB camera with resolution 320x240. This camera captures a scene where a user is showing his hand. The top-right images represent the hand segmentation adaptively. The bottom-left images show the fingertip probability map after normalizing. The intensity in these grayscale images illustrates the probabilities of the fingertips. In the results, higher brightness means higher probability. After performing the clustering algorithm and extended particle filter, the tracked results of fingertip are finally shown in the bottom-right images.

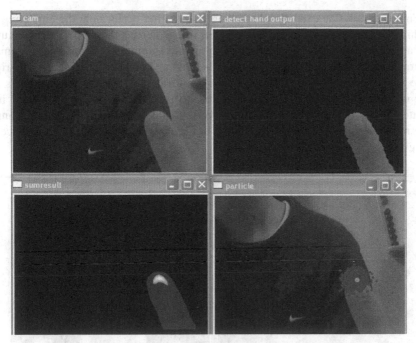

Fig. 1. During process of an extended particle filter to recognize

The accuracy of the particle filter depends on the propagation function. We have tried different propagation functions, including constant velocity motion model and acceleration motion model. However, our experimental results have revealed that using only noise information gives the best result. A possible reason is that the motions of fingertips we test are usually quite fast and constantly changing directions. Therefore the calculated velocities or accelerations in previous frame do not give accurate prediction of the next frame.

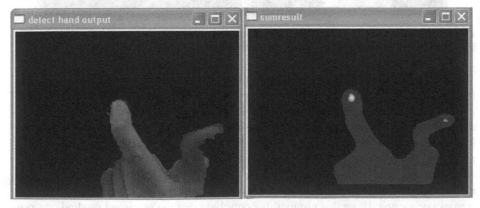

Fig. 2. During process of the clustering algorithm in the challenging positions, the tracking method can still perform well

Figure 2 shows an example of tracking results after performing the clustering algorithm in the challenging positions. The left image depicts the input image captured from a single camera after performing dynamic background subtraction. This camera captures a scene where a user is showing his hand and bending the fingers. The right image shows the results after clustering algorithm is done. Even though fingers are some occlusions, the tracking method is able to perform accurately. However, it is admittedly important to note that in some very challenging cases, the tracker cannot perform perfectly. For example, the thumb in Figure 2 is almost tracked well if comparing to the forefinger.

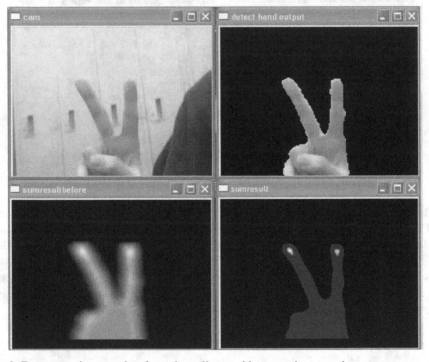

Fig. 3. Representative snapshot from the online tracking experiment at the commencement of the experiment while a user is showing his two fingers

Figure 3 shows some representative snapshot of the online experiment from the total 300 frames. Similarly, this camera captures a scene with a user. The top-right images represent the hand segmentation adaptively. The bottom-left images show the fingertip probability map. The intensity in these grayscale images illustrates the probabilities of the fingertips which will be used in the particle filter step. After performing the clustering algorithm and extended particle filter, the tracked results of fingertips are finally shown in the bottom-right images. The number of particles used in the system is 300 particles. The computation time for the sequence is about 12 frames per second. From this number, we conclude that the proposed method can run in real-time.

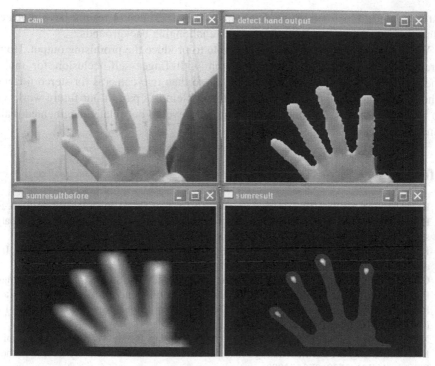

Fig. 4. The tracker can automatically determine the correct number of appeared fingertips.

At the commencement of the experiment, the hand of a user enters the field of camera's view. Then he starts to change his hand in different poses. In our method, the number of detected ROIs can be varied according to the number of fingertips appeared in the input images (the number of ROIs is automatically found by the algorithm described in the previous section). For example, there are two and four fingertips appearing in Figure 3 and Figure 4, respectively. However, it can be seen that the tracker can automatically determine the correct number of appeared fingertips. The experiments have revealed that the system can successfully track the fingertip positions even when the luminance markedly changes from the offline phase.

From our experiments, we believe the errors of tracking are low enough to make the proposed algorithm presented in this paper a suitable method for human hand motion recognition and fingertip tracking.

5   Conclusions

We have built a framework for tracking and recognizing the positions of the hand and the fingertips accurately. We segment the skin colored hand region of user by using a Bayesian classifier which can deal with considerable luminance changes. A matching algorithm is then used to determine the probabilities of the fingertips based on their primitives. Following this, we extend the particle filter by using a deterministic clustering algorithm for tracking fingertips. The experimental results have revealed that the proposed system is robust even with challenging backgrounds.

We believe that the current system is able to produce the promising output. However, the current system has the limitation with finger self-occlusion for multi-cameras. This usually happens when using more than two cameras for stereo images. In the future, we intend to further refine this problem. As part of our future work, we also intend to use this implementation to further develop our related-augmented reality and virtual reality applications [11].

References

1. Kerdvibulvech, C.: Real-Time Framework of Hand Tracking Based on Distance Transform. In: Proceedings of the Eleventh International Conference on Pattern Recognition and Image Analysis (PRIA-11-2013), Samara, Russian Federation (RAS and Springer), pp. 590–593 (2013)
2. Konstantinos, E.P., Antonis, A.A.: Integrating tracking with fine object segmentation. Image Vision Computing 31(10), 771–785 (2013)
3. Caglar, M.B., Lobo, N.: Open Hand Detection in a Cluttered Single Image using Finger Primitives. In: Proceedings of the IEEE International Conference on Computer Vision and Pattern Recognition Workshop (IEEE CVPR 2006 Workshop), New York, USA, p. 148 (2006) ISBN 0-7695-2646-2
4. Ng, W., Chan, T., So, H.C., Ho, K.C.: Particle Filtering Based Approach for Landmine Detection Using Ground Penetrating Radar. IEEE Transactions on Geoscience and Remote Sensing 46(11), 3739–3755 (2008)
5. Cooper, H., Ong, E., Pugeault, N., Bowden, R.: Sign Language Recognition using Sub-Units. Journal of Machine Learning Research 13, 2205–2231 (2012)
6. Matilainen, M., Hannuksela, J., Fan, L.: Finger tracking for gestural interaction in mobile devices. In: Proceedings of the Eighteen Scandinavian Conference on Image Analysis (SCIA 2013), Espoo, Finland (2013)
7. Krejov, P., Bowden, R.: Multitouchless: Real-Time Fingertip Detection and Tracking Using Geodesic Maxima. In: Proceedings of the Tenth IEEE International Conference on Automatic Face and Gesture Recognition (FG 2013), Shanghai, China (2013)
8. Kereliuk, C., Scherrer, B., Verfaille, V., Depalle, P., Wanderley, M.M.: Indirect Acquisition of Fingerings of Harmonic Notes on the Flute. In: Proceedings of the International Computer Music Conference (ICMC 2007), Copenhagen, Denmark, vol. I, pp. 263–266 (2007)
9. Asthana, A., Marks, T.K., Jones, M.J., Tieu, K.H., Rohith, M.V.: Fully automatic pose-invariant face recognition via 3D pose normalization. In: Proceedings of the International Conference on Computer Vision (ICCV 2011), pp. 937–944 (2011)
10. Wei, X., Phung, S.L., Bouzerdoum, A.: Object segmentation and classification using 3-D range camera. Journal Visual Communication and Image Representation 25(1), 74–85 (2014)
11. Kerdvibulvech, C.: Real-Time Adaptive Learning System Using Object Color Probability for Virtual Reality Applications. In: Proceedings of the ACM International Conference on Simulation and Modeling Methodologies, Technologies and Applications (ACM SIMULTECH 2011), Noordwijkerhout, Netherlands, pp. 200–204 (2011)

A Graph Based Segmentation Strategy
for Baggage Scanner Images

Yisleidy Linares Zaila[1], Marta L. Baguer Díaz-Romañach[1],
and Manuel González-Hidalgo[2]

[1] Universidad de La Habana, Cuba
ylz.yiyi@gmail.com,mbaguer@matcom.uh.cu
[2] University of the Balearic Islands, Computer Graphics,
Vision and Artificial Intelligence Group, Spain
manuel.gonzalez@uib.es

Abstract. Image processing and image analysis are often required in real life
scenarios. Segmentation is one of the key concepts used and for which has not
yet found a general solution that can be applied for every stage. In this paper a
graph based segmentation strategy is proposed aimed to images resulting from
baggage scanners used by the General Customs of the Republic of Cuba. This
strategy is a bottom up one that combines the Minimum Spanning Tree and the
mixing regions approaches. It defines a new standard for the two-component
merge that considers both global and local features of the image. The numerical
experiments show the effectiveness of the strategy for custom scanner images
and how it can be easily adapted to other image types such as natural images.

Keywords: Image segmentation, graph theory, minimal spanning tree.

1   Introduction

One of the first steps in any application of image processing is segmentation, so it is
of vital significance at this stage to obtain reliable results as a basis for further
processing. Currently, there is great diversity of segmentation based applications,
such as: indexing of images and videos, object detection, augmented reality applications, virtual reality, etc.

Identify and recognize an object in an image can be, at first glance, a simple task.
However, automating this so common share for the human eye, is a major challenge.
Proof of this is the wide range of alternatives with sometimes undesirable results.

Fig. 1. Baggage Scanner image

F.J. Perales and J. Santos-Victor (Eds.): AMDO 2014, LNCS 8563, pp. 81–93, 2014.

The motivation for this particular project responds to the need to facilitate the inspection of luggage. A good amount of X-ray equipment currently used for scanning of passenger baggage produces images like the one shown in Fig. 1. As you can see it is very difficult for a supervisor to identify individual objects contained in the baggage. The distinction of any dangerous or prohibited object turns out very difficult causing a large number of bags to be opened unnecessarily. This inspection process must also be done in real time so as not to interrupt the flow of people at airports. The solution to this problem may be subjected to a certain image preprocessing to reduce the number of false positives. We want to find a new representation of the image where the end user (customs officials) have a better understanding of it. One of the stages of this processing is precisely the segmentation. It is good to note this preprocessing should lay the foundation to address further in all its complexity, as these images have overlapping objects of different nature. In this stage of the processing we propose to "capture" as many objects as possible.

2   Segmentation: Some Concepts and Actually Alternatives

According to [1] the process of segmentation of an image can be defined as:

Definición 1. Let u_0 be an image on a 2-D, Ω domain. Segmentation is defined as the process of finding a visual meaning to u_0 partitioning the domain $\Omega = \Omega_0 \cup \Omega_1 \cup ... \cup \Omega_N$ Ω_i: object of the image, $i \geq 1$.

The term segmentation covers a wide range of processes through which the division of the image into different disjoint regions is obtained based on a certain homogeneity of these.

2.1   Basic Criteria

Generally the image segmentation algorithms are based on at least one of the following: low level features: refers to the intensity, color or texture of the pixels that make up the image. Virtually almost all segmentation techniques using these features.

Prior knowledge about the image: this is to take advantage of specific features of the images to be analyzed, for example when you want to find certain shapes. The design of such methods is not a trivial task and has been little work on the demonstration of its utility.

User interaction: these algorithms are called semi-automatic and allow the user, through their interactions, define which objects have to be segmented in an image.

2.2   Diverse Approaches

Given the variety of approaches and methods proposed targeting, the task of finding a suitable classification is almost as complicated as the problem of segmentation itself. In response to one of the general criteria, the algorithms can be classified into:

Methods based thresholds: Thresholds act as spacers for deciding which set of gray tones belong to a particular region. These techniques are based on the histogram of the image and are often combined with other so as to pre-process and post-process to get better results [2].

Edge-based methods: The basic idea is to find the edges in an image to determine the boundaries of each segment. These algorithms typically use gradient information of the image to locate the edges of the different areas [3].

Forms-based methods: These techniques are designed to find specific objects in the image and are divided into two main groups: i) models of shapes for specific purposes, which are designed by hand and carefully to solve a particular problem and ii) statistical models of shapes, those from semiautomatic techniques and are trained by examples of statistical analysis. These usually require solving an optimization problem to search for certain parameters and are used in the process of grouping regions [4], [5], [6], [7], [8].

Based region growing methods: The idea is to obtain a segmentation starting from the center of an object and growing toward the outside thereof to locate the edges that limit. The centers of the objects may be formed by one or more pixels and are called seeds. The main drawback of these algorithms is how to appropriately select these seeds. These methods are usually semiautomatic, the final user provides the information regarding the location of the seeds [9], [10], [11], [12].

Methods based on clustering techniques: These were the first approaches addressed in image segmentation. His appearance dates from 1938 with the theory of Werthei-mer. Usually these methods ignore the spatial information, focusing solely on characteristics such as color or texture. The method used in this category is the K-Means [13] and its equivalents [14], [15], [16] [17] .

Methods based on mathematical morphology: One of the most important methods of this category is the Watershed transform [18], which associates each region with a minimum gradient of the image.

Graph-based methods: Segmentation algorithms in this group began to develop from the 60s, it was not until the 90s that they became important to develop a range of techniques that feel their bases in these concepts. The method proposed in this paper belongs to this category, so then will delve a little deeper into this approach.

3   Graph Based Methods

After an analysis of the different variants and based on the nature of the problem to be solved, the use of graph theory as a basis for segmenting images mentioned class seems to be a good choice. It is desired to find a good solution in real time, that is, an algorithm is required to comply with user expectations in terms of both the quality of the results as to the speed of obtaining the data. In general, due to extensive study in recent decades on graph theory, it has a set of properties and mathematical tools that can be exploited for the development of methods with the characteristics described. One such a tool is the hierarchical structure that provides such methods which allows segmentation analysis at different levels, paying a post- image processing possible.

Moreover, this problem corresponds to a discrete space. The image consists of a finite set of pixels distributed in matrix form so their representation in a network does not require any discretization process to avoid making errors of this nature.

3.1   Representation of an Image on a Graph

Images are represented as weighted graphs, where nodes correspond to pixels or regions. The segmentation is obtained by dividing (cutting) the graph on the right level, so that the optimal choice will be an important point in the design of these methods.

Let $G = (V, E)$ be a graph where $V = \{v_1, v_2, \dots, v_n\}$ is the set of vertices which can represent pixels or regions corresponding to the image in the Euclidean space. Let E be the set of edges connecting vertices given pair of neighbors. Each $(v_i, v_j) \in E$ has an associated weight that measures the presence of some properties between the two vertices connected by that edge. One of the most widely used definition is assigned as the edge weight the absolute value of the difference of the intensities of the vertices (pixels) that form it.

A picture is partitioned into mutually exclusive components, so that each component A is a connected graph $G' = (V', E')$ where $V' \subseteq V, E' \subseteq E$ and E' contains only the edges that correspond to the nodes in V'. That is, non-empty sets $A_1, A_2, \dots, A_k$ form a partition of the graph G if $A_i \cap A_j = \emptyset$ $(i, j \in \{1, 2, \dots, k\}, i \neq j)$ and $A_1 \cup A_2 \cup \dots \cup A_k = G$. It is also required that in the segmentation obtained the elements of a component are similar in response to certain properties (color, texture, etc.) and elements in different components are different. To accomplish this in the original graph a set of cuts are applied, that means that edges with low similarity criteria joining different components are removed (see Fig. 2).

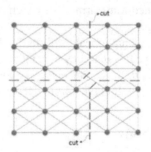

Fig. 2. Graph cut

A cut in a graph G means this is partitioned into two disjoint sets A, B and the value of this cut is generally defined as:

$$cut(A, B) = \sum_{u \in A, v \in B} w(u, v), \tag{1}$$

where u and v became vertices of two different partitions.

An important part of the graph-based methods that exists used the "Minimal Spanning Tree" known as MST. This is a very important concept in the graph theory. A spanning tree T of a graph G is a tree such that $T = (V, E')$ where $E' \subseteq E$. A graph can have several spanning trees. The MST is a spanning tree where the sum of the weights of the edges that comprise it is the minimum of all possible spanning trees. In [19], [20], [21] can be found algorithms to determine the MST. For example, the Prim algorithm [21], where the MST is built iteratively adding the lower boundary edge weight.

MST -based methods are essentially related to clustering techniques. Data are represented in an undirected graph with adjacency matrix. The edges correspond to neighboring vertices given a connection system (4 - neighbors, 8- neighbors). The different groups are obtained by removing edges of the graph forming sub- graphs mutually exclusive.

In [22] Morris used the MST for a hierarchical partitioning of the image. His method allows to obtain segmentations at different scales where similar pixels are located in the same group and the different pixels are separated. Cutting the MST by the heaviest edge, partitions of a graph are formed with the greatest difference between neighboring sub-graphs. In [22] some algorithms based on this idea are proposed. In each iteration a sub-graph is partitioned resulting in a final partition with the given number of sub- graphs. Apparently the algorithm in this way is inefficient, but the recursive variant proposed by Kwok [23] improves the speed of Morris's.

In [24] can be found an algorithm based on the advanced MST that uses both the internal differences of a sub - graph as well as the difference between two sub - graphs. This algorithm combines the MST and the mixing of regions obtaining results that satisfy some global properties. The key to this algorithm is the selection of the threshold. Two components are mixed if the link between them is less than the minimum between the edge of the higher cost of the MST of each component plus the threshold. The formal definition of this mix criterion would be as follows:

$$|e_t| < min\left(Int(C_1) + \frac{K}{|C_1|}, Int(C_2) + \frac{K}{|C_2|}\right) \tag{2}$$

where K is a constant, $|C_1|$ and $|C_2|$ are the cardinalities of C_1 and C_2 regions respectively. $Int(C_i)$ (internal difference of C_i) is the value of the heaviest edge in the MST of the component C_i, $|e_t|$ is the lower weight edge that connects with C_1 with C_2.

The MST -based methods work properly when the pixels in the same segment are very similar. Unfortunately this is not always the case, this is why many variants use this type of algorithm as an initial processing, using the results as input from other segmentation methods.

4   Implementation

In recent years there have been developed a number segmentation algorithms using graph theory. Some of these have the drawback of high computational cost, others are computationally efficient but do not provide acceptable results. Methods based on the

MST have a set of features that put it in an important place. Through these are obtained in a natural way different segmentation levels. They are easily adaptable to different problems, allowing to take into account global image features, which is taxed at a better result also can be obtained in real time.

In response to these advantages was decided to take as a starting point for our segmentation the algorithm based on MST mentioned in the previous section that uses features of dissimilarity in the edges. The main advantage of this strategy is that it is able to capture global properties of the image efficiently, at a cost of $O(m \log m)$, with m the total number of edges of the graph, which in practice consumes very little time. This feature puts it in a strong position for finding a segmentation that is neither too thick nor too thin because this problem could became NP -Hard [25], see [24]. Another important feature of the method is that in the mixing process, when analyzing the connecting edge o_q that connects two different components if these are not mixed, then one of them will be part of the final segmentation. The proof of this is quite simple. Two components C_i^{q-1}, C_j^{q-1} do not mix if $w(o_q) > Int(C_i^{q-1}) + \tau(C_i^{q-1})$ or $w(o_q) > Int(C_j^{q-1}) + \tau(C_j^{q-1})$. As the weights of the edges are sorted in no decreasing order, $w(o_q) \leq w(o_k)$, $\forall k \geq q + 1$. Therefore no other component is mixed with this and consequently $C_i^q = C_i^{q-1}$ or $C_j^q = C_j^{q-1}$. This feature means that the edge that facilitates the mixing of two components is exactly this with the lower weight. Thus the edges which cause the blend are exactly those obtained by the Kruskal algorithm [25] for the construction of the MST of each component.

As immediate disadvantage is the sensitivity to the parameter K. The size of the components that are obtained by the segmentation is directly proportional to the value of K, that is, for small values of K small components are obtained and for large values of K larger components are obtained. Thus, for images containing objects which occupy a large area high values of K value will provide a better outcome, whereas for objects with smaller area small values of K are recommended. Because of that fact the value of K depends on specific characteristics of the image. Moreover a small K results in over segmentation. In response to these problems we decided to perform a post- processing of the image. That is, taking the results obtained by this algorithm with not so big values of K, which generally constitutes an over segmentation, and define a new criterion for merging regions to provide a better result. With this new approach, inspired by [26], we give greater importance to the global features taking as initial approximation, the segmentation obtained in the above procedure. The first algorithm has a set of components under the criteria established mixing fulfill similar pixels correspond to the same region and different pixels belonging to different regions. This new algorithm has the same objective, just change the comparison test that determines if two components must be mixed or not.

Definition 2. Let C_1, C_2 be two adjacent components of the segmentation S obtained after applying the above algorithm, these components should be mixed if:

$$|M(C_1) - M(C_2)| \leq \sqrt{\tau(C_1) + \tau(C_2)} \, , \tag{3}$$

where $M(C_i)$ is the average of the intensities of the pixels that make up the component C_i and $\tau(C_i)$ is a C_i component dependent threshold function.

C_i is the ith component of a segmentation S, the threshold function $\tau(C_i)$ is defined as:

$$\tau(C_i) = g * \sqrt{\frac{1}{2Q|C_i|} \ln(|C_i| * |I|)} \,, \tag{4}$$

where $g = 255$ (maximum intensity), $|I|$ total image pixels and $|C_i|$ number of pixels of the C_i component.

The aim of this approach is that to small components are more prone to be merged and for that the term $\frac{1}{|C_i|}$ was used. However, as shown in the graph (Figure 3) this function decreases very rapidly, implying that the early decrease threshold, and the greater the degree of similarity is required between two components to be mixed resulting in over segmentation. As can also be seen in Figure 3 the term $\ln(|C_i| * |I|)$, smoothing function, increasing the acceptance range for larger components while maintaining the property of favoring the binding of small components. The parameter Q is used to facilitate finer or coarser segmentations. With a higher Q finer segmentations are achieved (greater number of regions) and for lower Q thicker segmentations (fewer regions).

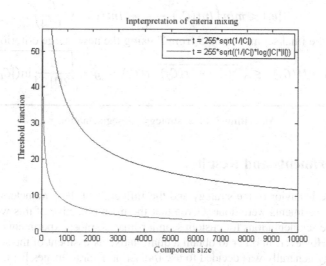

Fig. 3. Analysis of the threshold function

The results obtained so far are promising, however, in order to improve its performance we included the use of the color space CIELab and a base color Pantone catalog reference [27]. Using CIELab allows that slight variations of colors in nearby pixels are negligible and using the reference table of colors is achieved different shades of a color to be represented by a single reference color. Thus similar shades of colors are grouped into a single value and factors such as light, shadow and texture even in some cases, are almost negligible which allows for better segmentation avoiding over segmentation.

When we analyzes the images produced by the scanner of the custom that detected that each item is associated with a color, i.e. organic materials like clothes are colored orange, dark blue metal, plastic light green and dark brown wood. For this reason it was decided to create an own reference table for this type of image. Thus obtaining the best results.

The following algorithm (Algorithm 1) summarizes the proposed final strategy consists of three basic steps. The first phase of the algorithm makes an adjustment to the color image with reference to the basis of Pantone colors. This enables noise reduction and homogenization of similar hues. The second stage gets an initial segmentation of the image that presents problems while over segmentation provides a good initial guess for the next stage. The third step solves the over segmentation giving more importance to global features while taking into account local properties.

Input: Graph $G = (V, E)$, $8 - connected$, with n vertices and m edges
Output: A segmentation V into components $S = (C_1, C_2, ..., C_r)$
1. Readjust the original colors using the reference table Pantone
2. Obtain a segmentation T through the MST using as a merge criterion:
$$|e_t| < min\left(Int(C_1) + \frac{K}{|C_1|}, Int(C_2) + \frac{K}{|C_2|}\right)$$
3. Obtain the final segmentation S from T using the new merge criterion:
$$|M(C_1) - M(C_2)| \leq \sqrt{\tau(C_1) + \tau(C_2)}, \tau(C_i) = g * \sqrt{\frac{1}{2Q|C_i|}\ln(|C_i| * |I|)}$$

Algorithm 1. Final strategy for segmentation

5   Experiments and Results

To analyze the behavior of the strategy and the influence of the parameters that this requires three experiments were done. Given that the main objective of this work is to obtain acceptable segmentations for custom scanner images, most experiments are aimed at such images. However, in order to obtain a quantitative assessment of the segmentations and technology generally was decided to use the set of natural images from the database of Berkeley [28] and used as evaluation measures the Probabilistic Rand Index (PR Index) and the Normalized Probabilistic Rand Index (Index NPR) [29].

5.1   Experiment 1

Following the same order of the strategy, this first experiment aims to evaluate the performance of the algorithm varying the parameter K. For that we let run only the second stage of the strategy and the results were analyzed both visually, for images of custom scanners and quantitatively, using images from the Berkeley database.

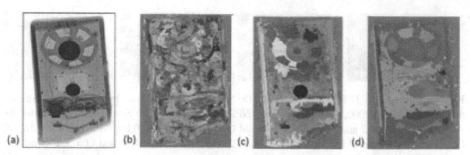

Fig. 4. (a) Custom image, (b) Algorithm (Step 2) with K = 300, (c) Algorithm (Step 2) with K = 3000, (d) Algorithm (Step 2) with K = 30000

Fig. 5. (a) Image 14037 Database Berkeley, (b) Algorithm (Step 2) with   K = 300, PR = 0.80, NPR = 0.39, (c) Algorithm (Step 2) with K = 3000 PR =0.81, NPR =0.42, (d) Algorithm (Step 2) with K = 30000, PR = 0.89, NPR = 0.6.

In the above figures it can be seen how as the value of K is increased larger regions are obtained. So if what you want is to extract an object that occupies a small area in the image you should choose a small K and vice versa. Moreover, the higher the value of K increased risk of various objects in the image belong to the same region, while a lower value of K increased risk of over segmentation.

5.2   Experiment 2

This second experiment is aimed at analyzing the behavior of the algorithm with the addition of the new merge criteria. This compares the segmentations obtained using the new condition with the results achieved in the first experiment.

Fig. 6. (a) Custom image, (b) Segmentation obtained by Algorithm 1 (Step 2) with K = 30000, (c) Segmentation obtained by Algorithm 1 (Steps 2 and 3) with K = 400 and Q = 1, (d) Segmentation obtained by Algorithm 1 (Steps 2 and 3) with K = 300 y Q = 6.

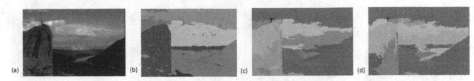

Fig. 7. (a) Image 14037 Berkeley Database, (b) Segmentation obtained by Algorithm 1 (Steps 2 and 3) with K = 30000, PR Index = 0.88, NPR Index = 0.57, (c) Segmentation obtained by Algorithm 1 (Steps 2 and 3) with K = 600 and Q = 4, PR Index = 0.89, NPR Index = 0.58, (d) Segmentation obtained by Algorithm 1 (Steps 2 and 3) with K = 800 and Q = 3, PR Index = 0.89, NPR Index = 0.58.

The above figures show the behavior of the new merge criterion. Note how was controlled largely over segmentation in this problem that was present in the second stage of the strategy. The most important result of this experiment is to be able to set both the K parameter as the Q. For $K = 400, Q = 2$ acceptable results are obtained for most of the test images.

5.3   Experiment 3

After falling values of K and Q for both custom images such as Berkeley, the next step is to analyze the behavior of the strategy as a whole, which means incorporating the use of colors and the Pantone reference colors created specifically for custom images. The algorithm is flexible to the degree of importance that is given to the representation of the pixels in the base of colors. The application has a parameter α taking values in [0,1] where 0 means the Pantone reference table is not used and 1 that this is used only. Any other value of α readjust the value of the pixel using either the original color as the reference. For this experiment we took $\alpha = \{0, 0.5, 1\}$. The parameters K and Q were taken equal to 400 and 2 respectively.

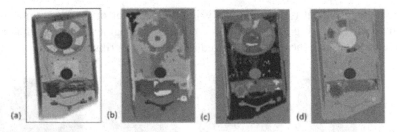

Fig. 8. (a) Custom image, (b) Segmentation without using reference colors with K = 400 and Q = 2, (c) Segmentation using Pantone reference colors with K = 400, Q = 2 and α = 1, (d) Segmentation using the reference colors for the custom images with K = 400, Q = 2and α = 1

In the figure above a marked improvement in results was achieved using reference colors being better those where we used the specific reference colors for the custom scanners. This shows the importance of using the particular characteristics of the problem to be solved. This behavior is similar for all custom images that were used in the experiment.

Concerning images from Berkeley results are not as absolutes. Considering experiments and consulted references [27], apparently this is because the basis of reference colors used is not the best fit for this type of images, so that the behavior is a little shaky providing better results in some images and worse in others.

6   Final Remarks

In this work a strategy for segmentation of images produced by a scanner passenger luggage is proposed. The first step in this research was to study the different alternatives to solve such problems. The proposed algorithm uses a technique based on graphs. This selection was made taking into account the fundamental objectives: i) a solution was needed on real time and of acceptable quality, ii) they had to find a 100 % automated solution, i.e., that did not require interaction with the user to be obtained. Graph theory provides a set of very useful tools for obtaining efficient solutions from the computational point of view. It also allows, naturally, to obtain segmentations at different levels and most graph-based techniques are readily adaptable to the characteristics of specific problems.

The first approach to the solution proposed a combination of the MST and a merge criterion for regions. This method presents two main problems, over segmentation and sensitivity to certain factors such as image noise, textures and lighting variations. The improvement of these results is achieved by applying the image preprocessing and post processing segmentation generated. The preprocessing is performed by using a color chart reference, known as Pantone, which aims to redefine the colors of the pixels concentrating the different shades of a color in a single color reference. While the post-processing is the definition of a new criterion for mixture having into account global image features without neglecting the local properties.

The results obtained for the context of the custom images can be said to meet the initial objectives of this work. It was possible to obtain an image segmentation within a reasonable time, which does not require interaction with the end user, as it managed to fix experimentally the values of the parameters required by the algorithm(K = 400, Q = 2). While these values are not optimal results are within an acceptable range in almost all test images. It is important to remember that regardless of the quality of segmentation, these images have the problem of overlapping objects, which prevents obtaining better segmentations in most scenarios.

As for natural images shown acceptable performance according to the PR and NPR index measurements used in the evaluation performed segmentations. If the target of labor would be oriented such images could think of several alternatives that could improve the solutions obtained, for example, the definition of a table of reference colors, similar to Pantone, which meets these images proceeded as with custom images.

As could be seen throughout the work, the world of image segmentation is varied. Determine the algorithm used for segmentation and the correctness thereof are tasks that have to take into account the particular characteristics of the type of images being analyzed , no segmentation algorithms are of general purpose, at least not with good results at any stage. Usually the algorithms proposed are aimed at a particular problem. In this sense the proposed algorithm is a first approach to the needs of the custom scenario and shows some flexibility through parameters that allow a good adaptability to other scenarios such as natural images. A final result in the form of two components, a class library .net with the implementation of the strategy designed and a visual application which allows you to check the behavior of the strategy depending on images and analyzed according to the variation of the parameters supported is provided.

Acknowledgements. This work was partially supported by the "Gobierno Balear, Grupos Competitivos, 2011, Num. 28/2011/44".

References

1. Chan, T., Shen, J.: Image Processing and Analysis. SIAM, Philadelphia (2005)
2. Saleh, S., Kalyankar, N.V., Khamitkar, S.D.: Image Segmentation by Using Threshold Techniques. Journal of Computing 2(5) (2010)
3. Bin, L., Yeganeh, M.S.: Comparison for Image Edge Detection Algorithms. Journal of Computer Engineering (IOSRJCE) 2(6), 1–4 (2012)
4. Koffka, K.: Principles of Gestalt Psycology, Lund Humphries (1935)
5. Zhang, D., Lu, G.: Evaluation of mpeg-7 shape descriptors against other shape descriptors. Multimedia Systems (2003)
6. Binford, T.: Visual Perception by computer, Conference on Systems and Control (1971)
7. Huttenlocher, D., Klanderman, D., Rucklige, A.: Comparing images using the hausdorff distance. IEEE Trans. on Pattern Analysis and Machine Intelligence (1993)
8. Ferrari, V., Tuytelaars, T., Van Gool, L.: Object detection by contour segment networks. In: Leonardis, A., Bischof, H., Pinz, A. (eds.) ECCV 2006. LNCS, vol. 3953, pp. 14–28. Springer, Heidelberg (2006)
9. Hojjatoleslami, S.A., Kittler, J.: Region Growing: A new approach. IEEE (1998)
10. Banerjee, B., Bhattacharjee, T., Chowdhury, N.: Color Image Segmentation Technique Using Natural Grouping of Pixels. University of Kolkata, India (2009)
11. Pan, Y., Douglas, J., Djouadi, S.M.: An Efficient Bottom-Up Image Segmentation Method Based on Region Growing, Region Competition and the Mumford Shah Functional. University of Tennessee, USA (2006)
12. Kamdi, S., Krishna, R.K.: Image Segmentation and Region Growing Algorithm. International Journal of Computer Technology ans Electronics Engineering (IJCTEE) 2(1) (2011)
13. Mcqueen, J.: Some Methods for Classification and Analysis on Multivariate Observations (1967)
14. Sag, T., Cunkas, M.: Development of Image Segmentation Techniques Using Swarm Intelligence. In: ICCIT, Konya, Turkey (2012)
15. Yerpude, A., Dubey, S.: Color Image Segmentations Using K-Medoids Clustering. International Journal Computer Technology & Applications 3(1), 152–154 (2012)
16. Cinque, L., Foresti, G., Lombardi, L.: A clustering fuzzy approach for image segmentation. The Journal of the Pattern Recognition Society 37, 1797–1807 (2004)
17. Dehariya, V., Shrivastava, S., Jain, R.: Clustering of Image Data Set Using K-Means and Fuzzy K-Means Algorithms. In: International Conference on CICN (2010)
18. Meyer, F.: The watershed concept and its use on segmentation: a brief history, Centre de Morphologie Mathématique, Paris (2012)

19. Kruskal, J.: On the Shortest Spanning Subtree of a Graph and the Traveling Salesman Problem. In: Proceedings of the American Mathematical Society (1956)
20. Dijkstra, E.: Some theorems on spanning subtrees of a graph (1960)
21. Prim, R.C.: Shortest connection networks and some generalizations (1957)
22. Morris, O.J., de Lee, M.J.: Graph theory for image analysis: An approach baesd on the shortest spanning tree (1986)
23. Kwok, S.H.: A Fast Recursive Shortest Spanning Tree for Image Segmentation and Edge Detection (1997)
24. Felzenswalb, P.F., Huttenlocher, D.P.: Efficient graph based image segmentation. International Journal of Computer Vision, 167–181 (2004)
25. Cormen, T.H., Leiserson, C.E., Rivest, R.L.: Introduction to Algorithm. MIT Laboratoy for Computer Science, Massachusetts (1990)
26. Nock, R., Nielsen, F.: Statistical Region Merging. IEEE Trans. on Pattern Analysis and Machine Intelligence 26(11) (2004)
27. Hernández, G., Sánchez, R.E.: Segmentación de imágenes naturales usando colores de referencia en el espacio CIELab. In: Perception, Cognition and Robotics Sinergy (2004)
28. Martin, D., Fowlkes, C., Tal, D., Malik, J.: Database of Human Segmented Natural Images ansd Its Application to Evaluating Segmentation Algorithms and Measuring Ecological Statistics. In: Conference on Computer Vision (2001)
29. Unnikrishnan, R., Pantofaru, C., Hebert, M.: Toward Objective Evaluation of Image Segmentation Algorithms. IEEE Trans. on Pattern Analysis and Machine Intelligence 29(6) (2007)
30. Cootes, T.F., Taylor, C.J., Cooper, D.H., Graham, J.: Active shape models: their training and application. Computing Vision and Image Undersatanding 61(1), 38–59 (1995)

Fast Upper Body Joint Tracking Using Kinect Pose Priors

Michael Burke* and Joan Lasenby

Department of Engineering, University of Cambridge, Cambridge, UK, CB2 1PZ
{mgb45,jl221}@cam.ac.uk

Abstract. Traditional approaches to upper body pose estimation using monocular vision rely on complex body models and a large variety of geometric constraints. We argue that this is not ideal and instead attempt to incorporate these constraints through priors obtained directly from training data, by fitting a Gaussian mixture model to a large dataset of recorded human body poses, tracked using a Kinect sensor. We combine this information with a random walk transition model to obtain an upper body model that can be viewed as a mixture of discrete Ornstein-Uhlenbeck processes, in that states behave as random walks, but drift towards a set of typically observed poses. The suggested model is designed with analytical tractability in mind and we show that the pose tracking can be Rao-Blackwellised using the mixture Kalman filter, allowing for computational efficiency while still incorporating bio-mechanical properties of the upper body.

Keywords: Human pose estimation, Mixture Kalman filter, Kinect, Monocular vision.

1 Background and Related Work

A vast amount of work has been conducted in the field of human pose estimation using monocular vision. Two approaches to pose estimation from static images have emerged, the first relying on tracking and generative models, and the second on morphological recognition. Morphological recognition techniques can be top-down, where entire bodies are recognised [8], or bottom-up [7][17], where bodies are recognised by locating various body parts or components. A number of top-down approaches rely on matching extracted silhouettes to a known database. This technique is applied in [9], where matched pose estimates are refined using a set of 3D body part constraints. This approach relies on multiple cameras though, and the extraction of silhouettes, which can be challenging. Further, the authors note that additional information is required to estimate poses where the

---

* This work was supported by funding from the Council for Scientific and Industrial Research (CSIR), South Africa and the Cambridge Commonwealth Trust under a CSIR-Cambridge Scholarship.

F.J. Perales and J. Santos-Victor (Eds.): AMDO 2014, LNCS 8563, pp. 94–105, 2014.

arms are close to the body, as silhouettes do not contain sufficient information to do so.

Many pose estimation techniques use segmentation to locate and extract human bodies. In work on pose estimation for sign-language videos, the authors of [2] leverage the layering of signers on video to extract bodies using co-segmentation, before estimating joint locations using a selection of random forests trained on a number of previously segmented bodies. Unfortunately, accurate segmentation is slow on general video sequences and not usually feasible for real time applications.

Bottom-up approaches to pose estimation are also used in tracking-based pose estimation approaches. The authors of [13] used a 21 degree-of-freedom generative model of human kinematics, shape and clothing in a data-driven Markov chain Monte Carlo (MCMC) search. Monte Carlo simulation or particle filtering is frequently used in pose estimation schemes. Particle filters represent the posterior belief in a state, conditioned on a set of measurements, by a set of random state samples drawn from this distribution.

The authors of [16] note that many particle filtering algorithms for 3D pose estimation often require the addition of extra noise to assist in the search for minima. They attempt to resolve this by using a complex body model and through careful design of the observation likelihood function, incorporating priors on the anthropometric data of internal proportions, parameter stabilisers, joint limits, and body part penetration avoidance.

Simulated annealing has been used to solve the high dimensional search problem associated with 3D pose estimation [5]. Here, a set of weighting functions are used to drive the particle filter search to possible solutions. The authors of [4] perform 3D tracking using multiple cameras and a simulated annealing search. In this case, generative body models are used to create edge and foreground templates, which are compared to those observed using a sum of squared distances metric.

Difficulties in 3D pose estimation from 2D images have led some researchers to focus on 2D pose estimation in images, a slightly better posed problem. MCMC estimation was used in [11] to fit a set of 2D quadrangles to humans in images, using an observation model combining colour measurements of the head and hands (learned after face detection), and line segments extracted from the torso.

Applying Monte Carlo search techniques to pose estimation has the benefit of allowing a number of constraints and priors to be incorporated. However, the large number of constraints and complex models required to direct the high dimensional search is hardly ideal, and somewhat inelegant, resulting in large processing burdens. The incorporation of these constraints through priors obtained directly from training data is proposed here, in an attempt to simplify the sampling stages.

The process of learning constraints from training data has been advocated in [18], who clustered 3D body positions according to various action categories, then used action recognition and 2D body parts detected using a deformable part model to predict 3D pose with a random forest. The use of action recognition restricts the possible pose search space, allowing for faster and more accurate pose estimation. The authors of [10] used 3D motion capture data to train a Gaussian mixture model prior, which when combined with a Gaussian error model of 2D tracked body parts allows a 3D pose estimate to be computed using Expectation maximisation. Our approach is similar to this as it also uses a Gaussian mixture prior to incorporate body constraints, but differs through the inclusion of temporal motion tracking using recursive Bayesian estimation. In addition, only a subset of body parts need to be detected for body tracking. A description of our pose estimation method follows.

2   Bayesian Filtering for Human Pose Estimation

Assuming the human body can be modelled as an unobserved Markov process with a set of joint states $\mathbf{x}_t$ at time t, recursive Bayesian estimation allows states to be updated as measurements $\mathbf{z}_t$ are made.

$$p\left(\mathbf{x}_t|\mathbf{z}_{1:t}\right) = \eta p\left(\mathbf{z}_t|\mathbf{x}_t\right) \int p\left(\mathbf{x}_t|\mathbf{x}_{t-1}\right) p\left(\mathbf{x}_{t-1}|\mathbf{z}_{1:t-1}\right) d\mathbf{x}_{t-1} \qquad (1)$$

Here, η is a normalising constant and the nomenclature $\mathbf{x}_{1:t}$ refers to the collection of states from time step 1 to t. This process allows for continual state estimation that includes temporal information, using a transition model to predict state changes and an observation model to introduce measurement information.

For human body tracking, the state vector $\mathbf{x}_t$ could comprise the 3D positions of all joints of interest, camera position and orientation, but this causes a number of estimation difficulties when only 2D image measurements obtained from a single camera's measurements are available. In this case, image measurements are a non-linear function of the camera position and orientation, which complicates the tracking problem significantly. This can be avoided by performing all filtering in the image plane and only returning to 3D coordinates when a state estimate is obtained. Let u/λ and v/λ be image coordinates of a body joint, $\mathbf{X} = [X, Y, Z, 1]^T$, observed by a camera with 6 degree-of-freedom pose and projection matrix $[\bar{\mathbf{p}}_1, \bar{\mathbf{p}}_2, \bar{\mathbf{p}}_3, \bar{\mathbf{p}}_4]$,

$$\lambda \begin{bmatrix} u/\lambda \\ v/\lambda \\ 1 \end{bmatrix} = \begin{bmatrix} \bar{\mathbf{p}}_1 & \bar{\mathbf{p}}_2 & \bar{\mathbf{p}}_3 & \bar{\mathbf{p}}_4 \end{bmatrix} \mathbf{X}. \qquad (2)$$

Selecting a state vector comprising the scale parameter λ, image plane coordinates u/λ, v/λ and camera pose allows us to make direct comparisons between state and measurements. Once a state estimate is made, returning to 3D coordinates is trivial, with

$$\begin{bmatrix} X \\ Y \\ Z \end{bmatrix} = \begin{bmatrix} \bar{\mathbf{p}}_1 & \bar{\mathbf{p}}_2 & \bar{\mathbf{p}}_3 \end{bmatrix}^{-1} \left(\begin{bmatrix} u \\ v \\ \lambda \end{bmatrix} - \bar{\mathbf{p}}_4 \right). \qquad (3)$$

2.1   Transition Model

Applying Bayes' rule, the transition model required for recursive Bayesian estimation can be computed as:

$$p\left(\mathbf{x}_t|\mathbf{x}_{t-1}\right) = \frac{p\left(\mathbf{x}_{t-1}|\mathbf{x}_t\right)p\left(\mathbf{x}_t\right)}{p\left(\mathbf{x}_{t-1}\right)}$$

$$= \frac{p\left(\mathbf{x}_{t-1}|\mathbf{x}_t\right)p\left(\mathbf{x}_t\right)}{\int p\left(\mathbf{x}_{t-1}|\mathbf{x}_t\right)p\left(\mathbf{x}_t\right)d\mathbf{x}_t}. \tag{4}$$

This decomposition is useful as it allows a prior distribution covering the probability of a human pose occurring to be used to incorporate likely human poses. This distribution is obtained offline, by fitting a Gaussian mixture model (GMM) to a large dataset of recorded human body poses. The positions of upper body joints of interest are tracked using a Kinect sensor [15]. Recorded 3D joint positions are then projected into 2D, assuming a pinhole camera with a known camera calibration matrix, $\mathbf{K}$, and a random set of camera viewpoints within a set of constraints. This provides a much larger set of recorded 2D joint positions. Figure 1a shows the original 3D recorded pose data, and the corresponding 2D pose data generated through the synthetic viewpoints is shown in Figure 1b to 1e.

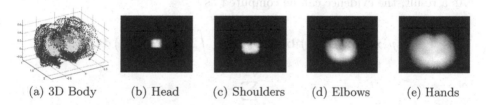

(a) 3D Body   (b) Head   (c) Shoulders   (d) Elbows   (e) Hands

Fig. 1. Upper body joint distributions are projected into 2D over a range of viewpoints to generate 2D joint position distributions (A limited range of viewpoints are used for illustration to allow for greater clarity). Lighter colours indicate more likely positions.

This large dataset is infeasible to work with, and so the Gaussian mixture model of this distribution is a useful form of dimension reduction. The Gaussian mixture model is denoted by $p\left(\mathbf{x}_t\right)$, the probability of an upper body pose $\mathbf{x}_t$ occurring,

$$p\left(\mathbf{x}_t\right) = \sum_{i=0}^{N-1} \pi_i \mathcal{N}\left(\mathbf{x}_t|\boldsymbol{\mu}_i, \boldsymbol{\Sigma}_i\right). \tag{5}$$

Learning the GMM can be computationally intensive and a large number of mixture components may be required. This is remedied by assuming independent left and right arms, and training two mixture models instead.

It is unlikely that states will vary much between time steps, and so we use a random walk to describe the motion between states: $\mathbf{x}_{t-1} = \mathbf{x}_t + \epsilon$, with $\epsilon \sim \mathcal{N}(\mathbf{0}, \mathbf{Q})$, or

$$p(\mathbf{x}_{t-1}|\mathbf{x}_t) = \mathcal{N}(\mathbf{x}_{t-1}|\mathbf{x}_t, \mathbf{Q}). \tag{6}$$

The covariance matrix $\mathbf{Q}$ in (6) is assumed to be a diagonal matrix with each diagonal term selected empirically with image dimensions in mind.

The prior learned from the training data inherently contains kinematic constraints, as well as information on more commonly observed poses. It is also extremely compact and simple. Using this prior, and the fact that the product of two multivariate normal densities over random variable $\mathbf{x}$ is another multivariate normal and scaling constant, we can write

$$p(\mathbf{x}_{t-1}|\mathbf{x}_t) p(\mathbf{x}_t) = \sum_{i=0}^{N-1} \pi_i c_i \mathcal{N}(\mathbf{x}_t|\boldsymbol{\mu}_c^i, \boldsymbol{\Sigma}_c^i) \tag{7}$$

with $c_i = \mathcal{N}(\mathbf{x}_{t-1}|\boldsymbol{\mu}_i, \mathbf{Q} + \boldsymbol{\Sigma}_i)$ and

$$\boldsymbol{\Sigma}_c^i = \left(\mathbf{Q}^{-1} + \boldsymbol{\Sigma}_\mathbf{i}^{-1}\right)^{-1}, \tag{8}$$

$$\boldsymbol{\mu}_c^i = \left(\mathbf{Q}^{-1} + \boldsymbol{\Sigma}_\mathbf{i}^{-1}\right)^{-1} \left(\mathbf{Q}^{-1}\mathbf{x}_{t-1} + \boldsymbol{\Sigma}_\mathbf{i}^{-1}\boldsymbol{\mu}_i\right). \tag{9}$$

Here, we have used the fact that (6) can be re-written as $\mathcal{N}(\mathbf{x}_t|\mathbf{x}_{t-1}, \mathbf{Q})$ because the Gaussian distribution is symmetric.

As a result, the evidence can be computed as

$$\int p(\mathbf{x}_{t-1}|\mathbf{x}_t) p(\mathbf{x}_t) \, d\mathbf{x}_t = \sum_{i=0}^{N-1} \pi_i c_i \int \mathcal{N}(\mathbf{x}_t|\boldsymbol{\mu}_c^i, \boldsymbol{\Sigma}_c^i) \, d\mathbf{x}_t$$

$$= \sum_{i=0}^{N-1} \pi_i c_i \tag{10}$$

This provides the final transition model

$$p(\mathbf{x}_t|\mathbf{x}_{t-1}) = \frac{\sum_{i=0}^{N-1} \pi_i c_i \mathcal{N}(\mathbf{x}_t|\boldsymbol{\mu}_c^i, \boldsymbol{\Sigma}_c^i)}{\sum_{i=0}^{N-1} \pi_i c_i}. \tag{11}$$

This model can be viewed as a mixture of discrete Ornstein-Uhlenbeck processes, in that states exhibit random walk behaviour, but drift towards a set of typically observed mean poses.

2.2   Observation Model

The observation model used here is assumed to be a Gaussian centred about the difference between a subset of states and measurements,

$$p(\mathbf{z}_t|\mathbf{x}_t) = \mathcal{N}(\mathbf{z}_t|\mathbf{H}\mathbf{x}_t, \mathbf{R}). \tag{12}$$

The pose state contains the image positions of the head, neck, shoulders, elbows and hands, but it is assumed that only the head, neck and hand states can be measured. These measurements correspond to the subset of states used in the measurement model of (12), selected using $\mathbf{H}$. The covariance matrix $\mathbf{R}$ is assumed to be a diagonal matrix with empirically selected diagonal terms, corresponding to a maximum measurement error in pixels, selected with image dimensions in mind.

2.3 Particle Filter Approximation

An analytical solution to the integral in (1) is not always easily computed and often an approximation is required. One way of performing this is to approximate the target distribution using a discrete set of N_s samples,

$$p\left(\mathbf{x}_t|\mathbf{z}_{1:t}\right) \approx \sum_{k=1}^{N_s} w_t^k \delta\left(\mathbf{x}_t - \mathbf{x}_t^k\right), \tag{13}$$

where the weights w_t^k are chosen using importance sampling,

$$w_t^k \propto w_{t-1}^k \frac{p\left(\mathbf{z}_t|\mathbf{x}_t^k\right) p\left(\mathbf{x}_t^k|\mathbf{x}_{t-1}^k\right)}{q\left(\mathbf{x}_t^k|\mathbf{x}_{t-1}^k, \mathbf{z}_t\right)}. \tag{14}$$

Unfortunately, sequential importance sampling often suffers from degeneracy problems [6], where the weights of most particles become negligible after a few iterations. This is remedied by resampling, which generates a new set of particles by sampling with replacement according to the importance weights. This typically eliminates particles that have small weights and adds emphasis to those with larger importance.

Care needs to be taken as to the selection of the proposal density $q\left(\mathbf{x}_t^k|\mathbf{x}_{t-1}^k, \mathbf{z}_t\right)$. Ideally this should be as close to the target density as possible. The sampling importance resampling (SIR) or bootstrap filter, discussed in detail in [14], is frequently used for recursive Bayesian filtering. Here, the proposal density is usually chosen to be equal to the transition density,

$$q\left(\mathbf{x}_t|\mathbf{x}_{t-1}, \mathbf{z}_t\right) = p\left(\mathbf{x}_t|\mathbf{x}_{t-1}\right). \tag{15}$$

This reduces the importance weight calculation to

$$w_t^k \propto w_{t-1}^k p\left(\mathbf{z}_t|\mathbf{x}_t^k\right). \tag{16}$$

Unfortunately, drawing samples from the Gaussian mixture model of (11) is rather computationally intensive. Sampling from this GMM requires N_s draws from a uniform distribution to select a mixture component according to the model's mixture weights, and a further N_s draws from different Gaussians (due to the dependence of (11) on previous states) to select particles. As an alternative solution, we propose that samples be drawn from the far simpler density

$p(\mathbf{x}_{t-1}|\mathbf{x}_t)$, which results in the weight update equation of

$$w_t^k \propto \frac{p(\mathbf{z}_t|\mathbf{x}_t^k)p(\mathbf{x}_t^k)}{\left[\int p(\mathbf{x}_{t-1}|\mathbf{x}_t)p(\mathbf{x}_t)\,\mathrm{d}\mathbf{x}_t\right]_{x_{t-1}^k}}. \qquad (17)$$

An even more efficient approximation could neglect the scaling term entirely, although this could potentially introduce evidence bias in the tails of the distribution.

Particle filter tracking in high dimensions typically relies on good initial particle estimates. In an attempt to remedy this, we start with much larger joint variance along the diagonals of $\mathbf{Q}$ in (6) and slowly reduce this over a burn-in period, to allow for an initial particle convergence phase. This can be considered a form of simulated annealing, which has been used previously for pose tracking in [5].

2.4   Mixture Kalman Filter

The particle filter is a useful approximation when dealing with complex probability distributions, which cannot be analytically integrated. However, the use of a Gaussian mixture model in the transition density and a conjugate Gaussian observation model allows us to Rao-Blackwellise the particle filter by performing integrations optimally using a number of Kalman filters to track mixture components, in a manner similar to that described by [1]. This approach, termed the mixture Kalman filter, has been applied to a number of conditionally linear dynamic models [3].

Our goal is to calculate the posterior distribution, $p(\mathbf{x}_t|\mathbf{z}_{1:t})$, given a sequence of measurements. We start by partitioning the prior model learned from Kinect training data using an indicator variable i_t, which refers to the i-th mixture component in the distribution,

$$p(\mathbf{x}_t) = \sum_{i=1}^{N} \pi_i \mathcal{N}(\mathbf{x}_t|\boldsymbol{\mu}_i, \boldsymbol{\Sigma}_i) = \sum_{i=1}^{N} p(i_t)p(\mathbf{x}_t|i_t). \qquad (18)$$

Applying the random walk transition density selected in (6) to each mixture component provides the transition density for the body pose conditioned on the indicator variable and previous state,

$$p(\mathbf{x}_t|\mathbf{x}_{t-1}, i_t) = \mathcal{N}(\mathbf{x}_t|\boldsymbol{\mu}_c^i, \boldsymbol{\Sigma}_c^i), \qquad (19)$$

with $\boldsymbol{\Sigma}_c^i$ and $\boldsymbol{\mu}_c^i$ calculated using (8) and (9) respectively.

Equations (19) and (12) are of the form required for optimal Bayesian filtering using the Kalman filter [12], which marginalises out historical states and provides the posterior distribution of a state conditioned on a history of measurements and mixture components,

$$p(\mathbf{x}_t|\mathbf{z}_{1:t}, i_{1:t}) = \mathcal{N}\left(\mathbf{x}_t|\mathbf{x}_{t|t}^i, \mathbf{P}_{t|t}^i\right), \qquad (20)$$

where $\mathbf{x}_{t|t}^i$ refers to the estimated mean state for a mixture component and $\mathbf{P}_{t|t}^i$ the covariance associated with this estimate.

Using this information, the probability of the indicator variable conditioned on the sequence of measurements, $p\left(i_{1:t}|\mathbf{z}_{1:t}\right)$, can be used to obtain the target distribution

$$p\left(\mathbf{x}_t|\mathbf{z}_{1:t}\right) = \sum_i^N p\left(\mathbf{x}_t|\mathbf{z}_{1:t}, i_{1:t}\right) p\left(i_{1:t}|\mathbf{z}_{1:t}\right). \tag{21}$$

Note that N should increase with each iteration, but we restrict it to a finite set of trajectories, one for each component in the mixture model. The discrete conditional indicator probability is obtained by marginalising the joint state indicator distribution,

$$\begin{aligned} p\left(i_{1:t}|\mathbf{z}_{1:t}\right) &= \int p\left(\mathbf{x}_t, i_{1:t}|\mathbf{z}_{1:t}\right) \mathrm{d}\mathbf{x}_t \\ &= \int \frac{p\left(\mathbf{z}_t|\mathbf{x}_t, i_t\right) p\left(\mathbf{x}_t|i_{1:t}, \mathbf{z}_{1:t-1}\right) p\left(i_{1:t}|\mathbf{z}_{1:t-1}\right)}{p\left(\mathbf{z}_t|\mathbf{z}_{1:t-1}\right)} \mathrm{d}\mathbf{x}_t \\ &\propto p\left(i_t\right) p\left(i_{1:t-1}|\mathbf{z}_{1:t-1}\right) \int p\left(\mathbf{z}_t|\mathbf{x}_t, i_t\right) p\left(\mathbf{x}_t|i_{1:t}, \mathbf{z}_{1:t-1}\right) \mathrm{d}\mathbf{x}_t. \end{aligned} \tag{22}$$

The contents of the integral in (22) are known, with $p\left(\mathbf{z}_t|\mathbf{x}_t, i_t\right)$ the normal measurement model of (12) and $p\left(\mathbf{x}_t|i_{1:t}, \mathbf{z}_{1:t-1}\right)$ the result of the Kalman filter prediction step, also Gaussian, which we shall denote as $\mathcal{N}\left(\mathbf{x}_t|\mathbf{x}_{t|t-1}^i, \mathbf{P}_{t|t-1}^i\right)$. Here $\mathbf{x}_{t|t-1}^i$ refers to the predicted mean state, and $\mathbf{P}_{t|t-1}^i$ the covariance of this prediction. As a result, (22) reduces to an iterative form

$$p\left(i_{1:t}|\mathbf{z}_{1:t}\right) = \eta \mathcal{N}\left(\mathbf{z}_t\middle|\mathbf{H}\mathbf{x}_{t|t-1}^i, \mathbf{H}\mathbf{P}_{t|t-1}^i\mathbf{H}^{\mathrm{T}} + \mathbf{R}\right) p\left(i_t\right) p\left(i_{1:t-1}|\mathbf{z}_{1:t-1}\right), \tag{23}$$

with η a normalising constant.

Using this density, a maximum a posteriori estimate for the upper body pose is then obtained through a weighted combination of updated mixture means,

$$\hat{\mathbf{x}}_t \approx \sum_{i=1}^N \mathbf{x}_{t|t}^i p\left(i_{1:t}|\mathbf{z}_{1:t}\right). \tag{24}$$

This pose estimate is easily calculated, requiring only a small number of parallel Kalman filters, so is far more efficient than a particle filter approximation. Finally, a 3D human body pose is obtained by evaluating (3) at the estimated state.

In practice, the discrete density $p\left(i_{1:t}|\mathbf{z}_{1:t}\right)$ can tend to zero for a given mixture component. This is not ideal, as it then becomes impossible for this mixture to contribute towards the pose estimate regardless of future measurements. This is undesirable as it effectively removes the mean-reverting properties of the process model. This is remedied by adding a small uniform prior, $\epsilon > 0$, to the density on each iteration. The size of ϵ controls the speed at which the process model is able to transition between reverting to the different mixture means in the pose prior.

3   Tracking Results

In the previous section, we introduced a motion model suitable for upper body tracking using recursive Bayesian estimation and discussed four tracking schemes that perform this. The first, a bootstrap particle filter, makes proposals from the GMM transition model in (11) and uses the weight update equation in (16). This sampling step is quite time consuming, and the second, faster scheme discussed draws samples from the simple reverse transition density in (6) for use with the weight update equation in (17). The third tracker neglects the scaling evidence term in the weight update equation of (17) to obtain an even faster approximation. Finally, the last tracking scheme introduced uses a slightly modified transition model, where noise is added to each mixture component independently, to allow for an iterative solution using a mixture Kalman filter.

Results obtained after applying the four tracking schemes discussed to manually annotated image sequences are provided here. Each of the schemes was applied to image sequences with a moving person, and the pose estimates compared to those obtained using the Kinect motion tracker. Independent datasets were used to learn the pose priors and test the pose estimates. Figure 2 shows the mean pixel error for each joint over the test sequence. No simulated annealing was used for the scheme sampling from the full Gaussian mixture model, as this required a larger level of noise in the transition model in order to avoid losing track of the joints completely. The figure shows that the best performance was obtained using the mixture Kalman filter (MKF). Of the particle filter approaches, the sampling scheme with no scaling converged and tracked the actual pose best, with rather poor tracking achieved when weighting was included. The theoretically preferred Gaussian mixture model sampling was unable to adequately track motion, presumably due to its slow convergence.

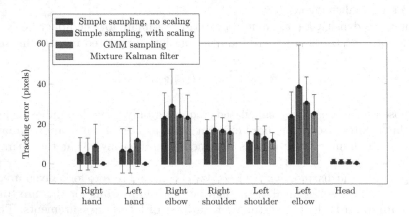

Fig. 2. Average joint error over an image sequence containing a moving person

A commonly used metric that assesses the performance of 2D pose estimation algorithms is the probability of correct pose (PCP) [17], which shows the percentage of correctly localised body parts, where a body part is deemed to be correctly localised if its end points fall within some fraction of the ground truth body part length. Figure 3 shows the PCP curves for each of the various tracking schemes (only forearm and upper arm localisation is considered). This metric highlights the performance of the Mixture Kalman filter. Good esti-

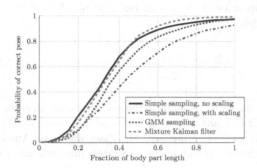

Fig. 3. Probability of correct pose (PCP) curves for the various tracking approaches show that the MKF and simple sampling (without scaling) strategies are generally the best estimators of pose

mates were obtained for elbow positions despite no measurements of these joints being made. Only the 2D positions of head, neck and hands were used as measurements, and elbow positions were inferred directly from the model. This is particularly encouraging, as elbows are often quite difficult to detect in images, due to their variable appearance.

Table 1 shows the average time taken for each filter iteration, when each of the suggested tracking schemes is used. It is clear that sampling from the full GMM is significantly more time consuming than the simple sampling, but that the mixture Kalman filter is far faster than all of the particle filter approximations.

Table 1. Average iteration times

Sampling strategy	Time
Simple sampling, with scaling (10000 particles)	0.046 s
Simple sampling, no scaling (10000 particles)	0.028 s
GMM sampling (10000 particles)	2.947 s
Mixture Kalman filter (30 mixture components)	0.015 s

4   Conclusions and Future Work

This paper has provided results on upper body pose tracking using Kinect joint priors and simple hand and head measurements, which are relatively easy to obtain in practice. Four tracking schemes have been considered and a mixture Kalman filter shown to provide fast and effective upper body pose estimation. The use of the proposed upper body model allows reliable pose estimates to be obtained indirectly for a number of joints that are often difficult to detect using traditional object recognition strategies. The suggested model is designed with computational efficiency and analytical tractability in mind, yet still incorporates bio-mechanical properties of the upper body, typically only included using more complex body models.

References

1. Alspach, D., Sorenson, H.: Nonlinear Bayesian estimation using Gaussian sum approximations. IEEE Transactions on Automatic Control 17(4), 439–448 (1972)
2. Charles, J., Pfister, T., Everingham, M., Zisserman, A.: Automatic and efficient human pose estimation for sign language videos. International Journal of Computer Vision (2013)
3. Chen, R., Liu, J.S.: Mixture Kalman filters. Journal of the Royal Statistical Society: Series B (Statistical Methodology) 62(3), 493–508 (2000)
4. Davison, A.J., Deutscher, J., Reid, I.D.: Markerless motion capture of complex full-body movement for character animation. In: Proceedings of the Eurographic Workshop on Computer Animation and Simulation, pp. 3–14. Springer-Verlag New York, Inc., New York (2001)
5. Deutscher, J., Blake, A., Reid, I.: Articulated body motion capture by annealed particle filtering. In: Proceedings of the IEEE Conference on Computer Vision and Pattern Recognition, vol. 2, pp. 126–133 (2000)
6. Doucet, A., Godsill, S., Andrieu, C.: On sequential Monte Carlo sampling methods for Bayesian filtering. Statistics and Computing 10(3), 197–208 (2000)
7. Eichner, M., Marin-Jimenez, M., Zisserman, A., Ferrari, V.: 2D articulated human pose estimation and retrieval in (almost) unconstrained still images. International Journal of Computer Vision 99, 190–214 (2012)
8. Gavrila, D.M., Davis, L.S.: Tracking of humans in action: A 3-D model-based approach. In: Proc. ARPA Image Understanding Workshop, pp. 737–746 (1996)
9. Germann, M., Popa, T., Ziegler, R., Keiser, R., Gross, M.H.: Space-time body pose estimation in uncontrolled environments. In: 3DIMPVT 2011, pp. 244–251 (2011)
10. Howe, N.R., Leventon, M.E., Freeman, W.T.: Bayesian reconstruction of 3D human motion from single-camera video. In: Advances in Neural Information Processing Systems. pp. 820–826. MIT Press (1999)
11. Hua, G., Yang, M., Wu, Y.: Learning to estimate human pose with data driven belief propagation. In: IEEE Computer Society Conference on Computer Vision and Pattern Recognition, CVPR 2005, vol. 2, pp. 747–754 (June 2005)
12. Kalman, R.E.: A new approach to linear filtering and prediction problems. Transactions of the ASME–Journal of Basic Engineering 82(Series D), 35–45 (1960)
13. Lee, M.W., Cohen, I.: Human upper body pose estimation in static images. In: Pajdla, T., Matas, J(G.) (eds.) ECCV 2004. LNCS, vol. 3022, pp. 126–138. Springer, Heidelberg (2004)
14. Ristic, B., Arulampalam, S., Gordon, N.: Beyond the Kalman Filter: Particle Filters for Tracking Applications. Artech House (2004)

15. Shotton, J., Fitzgibbon, A., Cook, M., Sharp, T., Finocchio, M., Moore, R., Kipman, A., Blake, A.: Real-time human pose recognition in parts from single depth images. In: Computer Vision and Pattern Recognition (June 2011)
16. Sminchisescu, C., Triggs, B.: Covariance-scaled sampling for monocular 3D body tracking. In: IEEE International Conference on Computer Vision and Pattern Recognition, Hawaii, vol. 1, pp. 447–454 (2001)
17. Yang, Y., Ramanan, D.: Articulated pose estimation with flexible mixtures-of-parts. In: Proceedings of the 2011 IEEE Conference on Computer Vision and Pattern Recognition, CVPR 2011, pp. 1385–1392. IEEE Computer Society, Washington, DC (2011)
18. Yu, T.H., Kim, T.K., Cipolla, R.: Unconstrained monocular 3D human pose estimation by action detection and cross-modality regression forest. In: Proceedings of the 2013 IEEE Conference on Computer Vision and Pattern Recognition, CVPR 2013, pp. 3642–3649. IEEE Computer Society, Washington, DC (2013)

From a Serious Training Simulator for Ship Maneuvering to an Entertainment Simulator

María José Abásolo[1,2], Cristian García Bauza[3,4], Marcos Lazo[3,4], Juan P. D´Amato[3,4],
Marcelo Vénere[3,5], Armando De Giusti[1], Cristina Manresa-Yee[6],
and Ramón Mas-Sansó[6]

[1] Universidad Nacional de La Plata, La Plata, 1900 Argentina
{mjabasolo,degiusti}@lidi.info.unlp.edu.ar
[2] Comisión de Investigaciones Científicas de la Provincia de Bs.As., Argentina
[3] PLADEMA, Universidad Nacional del Centro de la Pcia. de Bs.As., Tandil, 7000 Argentina
{crgarcia,venerem,mlazo,jpdamato}@exa.unicen.edu.ar
[4] CONICET, Argentina
[5] CNEA, Argentina
[6] Universitat de les Illes Balears, Palma, 07122 España
{cristina.manresa,ramon.mas}@uib.es

Abstract. This paper presents a ship-handling entertainment simulator that was developed to be used as a virtual reality experience in science exhibitions. It is a low-cost implementation that allows navigating a ship through a simple interface. Realistic 3D graphics area projected on a three panel screen implemented with computer monitors or HD LED TV. This simulator is an adaptation of a previous set of serious ship handling training simulators -called MELIPAL- that were developed for the Argentina Army. We describe how we adapted the original simulator to the new entertainment version, particularly the system architecture, the hardware, the 3D visualization and the user interface aspects.

Keywords: Ship handling, Entertainment simulator, Virtual Reality, Serious simulator, Training simulator, Computer graphics.

1 Introduction

The use of simulators to train operators is prior to the concept Virtual Reality (VR). In 1966 T. Furness built the first visual flight simulator for the USA Air Force. From this moment the attempts to get better flight simulators give a boost to the VR development due to the economical support of the Defense Department of the United States. Along this line, Pausch et al [1] presents a literature survey for military flight simulator visual systems. Ship simulators were also developed to avoid the high costs and difficulties of training military officers at sea in several countries. They requested the research of technologies that would enable the development of both realistic and inexpensive simulators for training ship-handling skills.

VR is widely used in education and training [2][3]. The use of virtual scenarios instead of real ones is basically due to three reasons: security, simplicity and economy.

F.J. Perales and J. Santos-Victor (Eds.): AMDO 2014, LNCS 8563, pp. 106–117, 2014.
© Springer International Publishing Switzerland 2014

Simulators are a category of applications that provide the user with a realistic experience in the management of vehicles or machinery by means of: control of the equipment through either identical real controls or a simplified interface, and the interaction of the vehicle with the environment using high realistic physical models. The challenges to be resolved in relation to the development of simulators are:

— Low-cost immersive environments
— Realistic real-time rendering of complex 3D models
— Accurate models of physical behavior

A realistic ship simulation model should include the simulation of ship movement and its interaction with marine environment, wind, current and waves [4][5][6][7][8].

In VR systems we can find different levels of immersion: from a low-cost non immersive systems based on conventional peripheral to fully immersive high-cost virtual reality systems. Daqaq [9] presents a fully immersive virtual simulation of ships and ship-mounted cranes that is carried out in a Cave Automated Virtual Environment. On the other hand, ship simulation computer games, such as Ship Simulator series [10], has been released in the last few years. They simulate maneuvering various ships in different environments under different weather conditions. It has been criticized for limitations in the replication of realistic controls and the lack of open architecture preventing users from creating their own vehicle.

This paper presents a ship handling simulator that was developed to be used as a social virtual reality experience in sciences exhibitions. This simulator is an adaptation of a previous developed set of ship-handling training simulators called MELIPAL-X. In the entertainment version we focused on the 3D realistic visualization of the environment, the physics behavior of the ship interacting with current and wind as well as the navigation through a friendly interface. It provides mechanisms to configure the simulated vehicle, the weather, time of day, geography, sea state and visibility. To increase the user immersion we increase the field of view by using three adjacent screens. It is a low-cost implementation that use either three computer monitors or Full HD LED TVs.

The rest of the paper is organized as follows: section 2 presents the MELIPAL-X series of ship-handling training simulators which formed the basis of the presented entertainment simulator, which is described in section 3; and finally section 4 presents the conclusions and future work.

2   Background: MELIPAL-x Ship-Handling Training Simulators

2.1   Chronology

The entertainment ship handling simulator presented in this paper was an adaptation of a series of serious ship training simulators -called MELIPAL-x- developed for the Argentina Army some years ago. In chronological order, the simulators were:

— MELIPAL-R (2001) Automatic Radar Plotting Aid (ARPA) Simulator;
— MELIPAL-P (2003) Fishing Boat Simulator ;
— MELIPAL-M (2008) Ship Maneuvers Simulator;

To support the above simulators, the following editor was also developed:

— MELIPAL-ED (2005) Virtual 3D scene editor.

All the above developments are described in the following subsections.

2.2   MELIPAL-R ARPA Simulator

MELIPAL-R simulator was developed in 2001 at the request of the Argentine National Nautical School and INVAP SE for training ship captain candidate students [11].

This ship-handling training simulator allows a student to control a ship in a realistic maritime environment - that includes seashore topography, buildings, other ships and buoys- in real time. One of the main requirements was the inclusion of an ARPA simulator.

Several students stations are monitored by an instructor, all of them distributed over a LAN. Each student's station shows the radar, the ship controls and the cartography. The ship controls are basically the helm and the power control. The system performs a simulation of boat displacement considering simplified models for boats ranging from supertankers, container conveyors and light boats. The cartography is presented with a standard commercial system which also allows a GPS signal entry that is also simulated by the system for automatic location of the ship on the map. Instructor's station has tools to select scenarios, to assign vessels, to create situations, to visualize student's movements and radars. It also has the ability to record an exercise for later playback and study.

A real radar is based on listening to the echoes generated by the emission of short electromagnetic pulse. This pulse must be collimated so that the echoes are from mainly address is being observed. A pulse has the appearance of a main lobe with some width in the desired direction and a number of side lobes.

In ship radars, this pulse is emitted horizontally in different directions, rotating the antenna at a rate of 14 to 20 revolutions per minute, with approximately 4000 emitting-listening process every 360 degrees.

The natural discretization of this problem can be done considering the lobe as a beam of rays. The emitting-listening process is done by finding the intersections of the rays with all polygons that represent the environment. The first intersection for each ray is then plotted on the screen. Otheguy et al. [12] detail the description of the optimization of the algorithm.

2.3   MELIPAL-P Fishing Boat Simulator

MELIPAL-P simulator was developed in 2003 at the request of the National School of Fishing for training fishing vessel operators [13].

It is based on the ARPA simulator MELIPAL-R including also the simulation of:

— A vertical echo sounder and sonar scanning, for determining the vertical distance between the bottom of the seabed and a certain part of the hull of a boat;
— A sextant, for measuring angles in celestial navigation;
— Fishing instrumental command interface
— Front and laterals views

2.4   MELIPAL-M Ship Maneuvers Simulator

MELIPAL-M simulator was developed in 2008 at the request of the Argentina Army to be used as a ship maneuvering simulator at the School of Navy Officers (fig.1). It is based on MELIPAL-R simulator, but it also adds the following characteristics:

— Realistic simulation climate effects, types of sea water, different sea states and different phases of the day. Our physics engine presented in [22], models adequate water surfaces and their interaction with objects using the Lattice Boltzmann method [14][15]. The surface is represented by a grid and its points are updated at every frame at an acceptable rate for an interactive application [23].
— Development of a simplified discrete mathematical model to predict the dynamics and kinematics of ship maneuver based on their characteristics, speed and instant acceleration [16]. Boat behavioral model combines a kinematic model of displacement, control equations for the tangential acceleration and rudder angle, and a model of lift and pitching.

Each training station is composed by:

— ARPA radar module, that simulates a real radar with all its functionality including target tracking commands;
— An Electronic Chart Display and Information System (ECDIS) module, that is a computer-based navigation information system that complies with International Maritime Organization (IMO) regulations and can be used as an alternative to paper nautical charts;
— Maneuver control interface, to control ship engines and helm. It also includes other instruments such as GPS navigation and echo-sounder for depth monitoring.

Fig. 1. Students at the School of Navy Officers controlling the MELIPAL-M simulator (left) and the displayed 3D view (right)

Figure 2 shows the command control (left), the radar (middle) and the cartography (right) visual interfaces. The helm and engine controls are operated by a joystick or a mouse.

The instructor station can organize and monitor an exercise creating a scene from a raster image of a navigation chart and, adding ships, buoys and, changing weather conditions - such as wind and localized rains and adding additional target vessels with predefined or interactive changing courses.

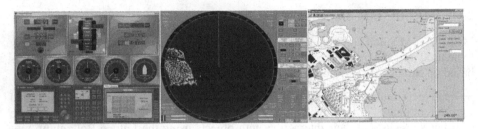

Fig. 2. MELIPAL-M command control (left), radar (middle) and cartography (right) visual interfaces

2.5   MELIPAL-ED Virtual 3D Scene Editor

MELIPAL-ED is an editor that allows the creation of 3D georeferenced scenes with customization of the weather and the addition of static and moving objects also with complex behavior (such as water, fire, smoke, etc.) [17].

The editor is connected to a database that contains a catalog of 3D models and a set of digital elevation models and satellite images of different training zones. The user creates the scene adding objects to the scene according to its global geographical position.

The created scenarios are then used in the visual modules of the existing simulators achieving realistic representations. To later achieve real time navigation a simplification algorithm of both topography and texture was used [18][19].

3   Entertainment Ship Simulator

3.1   System Requirements

To meet the goal of promoting science to the general public, we propose the adaptation of MELIPAL-M ship maneuvering simulator to obtain a prototype to be presented at exhibitions.

In this new entertainment version we focused on:

— Ship physics behavior considering conditions such as current and wind
— Realistic visualization of 3D environment
— Great immersion without sacrificing low-cost
— Simple navigation controls

— Personal settings about the vehicle type, the weather, time of the day, geography, sea state and visibility

Some of these requirements - such as the ship physics and the realistic visualization of the 3D environment- are met directly with the characteristics of the inherited module's implementation. The main difference between the original ship-training simulator and its new entertainment simulator version was the requirement of obtaining a low-cost implementation and at the same time to achieve the greatest immersion. Besides that we wanted to get a simply but attractive general aesthetic and also simplicity in navigation.

3.2   System Architecture

The developed system is formed by different components for every task such as:

— Launcher Module
— Command Interface Module
— 3D Visualization Module: physics engine + graphical engine

Instead of counting with the instructor module that we had in the original ship-handling simulator we have the launcher module, which basically provides a mechanism to set the scene parameters along with options to run the application.

The command interface module attends to the user's command inputs and communicates them to the visualization module.

The system is based on event-guided architecture over Impromptu Graphics Engine [20]. This graphical engine provides a complete support to visualize three-dimensional complex scenes with physics behaviour. To simulate the physical behavior of the virtual objects that compose the scene the Newton physics engine called Newton Game Dynamics [21] is used. The condition of every physic primitive is defined by its position and orientation in a certain time. The physical engine is the manager that calculates the new condition of the objects and updates it. The graphical engine requests this information for every object and applies the new values of position and orientation visualizing them on the screen.

3.3   Personal Settings

The launcher module allows the configuration of the following characteristics:

— Vehicle type: Meko 140 (Navy ship) or SpeedBoat (speed boat)
— Weather: clear, cloudy, rain, storm
— Time of the day: dawn, noon, afternoon, evening
— Maritime Scene: open sea, Mar Del Plata (Argentine coast)
— Sea State: quiet, moderate, enraged, wild
— Visibility: value between 0 to 100 which corresponds to the percentage of visibility

Figures 3 shows two different scene settings.

Fig. 3. Clear day and dawn mode (left). Rainy day and night mode with lights on buoys and ships (right).

3.4   Great immersion at Low-Cost

In VR systems we can consider different levels of immersion: from non-immersive systems based on conventional hardware peripheral to fully immersive high-cost virtual reality systems. The point is certainly to improve the degree of immersion in hybrid or intermediate systems. Current RV lenses allow seeing stereoscopic images but this is not enough for users to feel immersed. A much better solution is immersive rooms or caves but these require a lot of space and money. Besides its use is not trivial since it is necessary to synchronize multiple image projections.

In our case to increase the user immersion we increase the visual field using three adjacent screens for creating a vision wrap around the user. It is a low-cost implementation that uses a computer and three computer monitors or three High Definition LED TVs.

Historically, the rendering on multiple screens consisted in generating high resolution image for each screen and synchronized them via software. As the new generation video cards have real-time parallel processing they allow hardware synchronization up to three displays.

In 3D graphics applications, you have to set properly the perspective transformation parameters- which transform 3D scene to 2D images. To properly calculate the width and height of the final projected image it should be taken into account the number of monitors and its resolution. Also the sum of the screens increases the overall resolution requiring a higher fillrate[1].

Humans have eyes relatively close together and placed in the front of the face, so it allows a very accurate focused vision in size and distances with almost 180° in horizontal view - 60° central focused zone- and 100° in vertical view. Also to make a realistic visualization we have to set the Field Of View (FOV), ensuring that the objects

---

[1] Fillrate usually refers to the number of pixels a video card can render and write to video memory in a second.

have the same size as they would in real life. By default, the value of the graphics applications FOV is 90°. When greater than 90° FOV values are used, in order to cover a wide display, the final images begin to deform, stretching as it moves away from the center. Therefore, to generate a correct multi-display image is necessary to use another approach.

Whereas, if the FOV is less than 90° the image is not deformed, and the field overview can be divided to be displayed on 3 screens in 3 sub-fields of view, one for each screen. Figure 4 (left) outlines the arrangement of the three panel screen. A drawing canvas is associated to each screen in the rendering process using a FOV of 60°. The orientation of the lateral screens relative the central screen is then -60° and 60° respectively. The final result is getting a total FOV of approximately 180°. Considering the resolutions to be used on each display- in our case is 1980 x 1080 pixels- the distance of the camera (user) is determined. Then the scene is three times rendered with a fixed position but different orientation camera, each one corresponding to each screen.

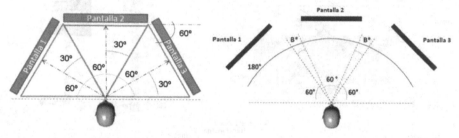

Fig. 4. Three screen spatial configuration, without taking into account the screen frames (left) and considering the screen frames (right)

Theoretically the three projected image compose the total image without discontinuity problems. However, when TVs or monitors are used , each screen has a frame or border -in the best case 1 cm wide- so that the effect of image continuity between screens is lost (see fig. 5, left). The hidden section behind the screen frame is called a bezel. To solve this problem we adjust an angle of overlap B* between the FOV of adjacent screens, so that the overlap is hidden behind the frame (see fig. 4, right). Figure 5 (right) shows how effect of continuity of the final image is achieved.

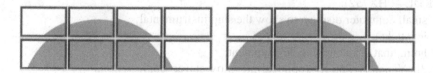

Fig. 5. Discontinuity between adjacent screens projected images (left) and the continuity achieved after considering the bezels (right)

3.5   Implementation

Figure 6 (left) outlines the ship simulator console. At the bottom, a panel box encloses the computer. It has wheels to allow easy transportation. Also it serves to allocate the peripherals over its top panel. The two main input peripheral are the helm for changing the ship heading, and the joystick for commanding the ship engines. A small display shows the main ship instrumental. Each of the screens that conforms the panoramic screen is arranged in a vertical support (see fig. 6, right).

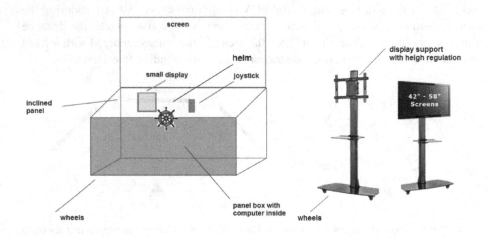

Fig. 6. An outline of the ship simulator console (left). Each screen is arranged in a vertical support (right)

The needed hardware is summarized as follows:

— 1 CPU Intel i7-3770K 8GB RAM;
— 1 Nvidia Geforce GTX690 video card;
— 1 Power supply (gold);
— 3 HD 3D LED TV with HDMI 1.4, particularly we tested 40" Sony 3D LED TV (KDL-40HX752);
— 1 small computer display, to show the ship instrumental;
— 1 joystick;
— 1 helm, that is an ongoing development;
— 1 3D Vision Nvidia Kit (optional), to allow stereoscopic vision.

Figure 7 shows a first prototype that is currently in a testing phase.

Fig. 7. Ship-handling entertainment simulator testing prototype

4 Conclusions and Future Work

This paper presents a ship-handling entertainment simulator that was developed to be used by the general public as a social virtual reality experience in sciences exhibitions. This simulator inherits its main characteristics from a previous developed set of ship-handling training simulators called MELIPAL-X. Particularly its use a simplified mathematical model that predicts the maneuver dynamics and the ship movements kinematics, based on the characteristics of the boat, the speed and the instantaneous accelerations. External forces influencing the ship - such as maritime currents and wind- are also taken into account. It provides mechanisms to configure the simulated vehicle, the weather, time of day, geography, sea state and visibility.

In contrast of using a commercial serious game - such as Ship Simulator series - it is possible to edit your own vessels and the particular environment. The 3D scene is based on real topographic models enriched with georeferenced 3D objects such as building, buoys, other ships, etc.

To increase the user immersion while maintaining the low-cost of the implementation, we increase the field of view by using three adjacent screens, either computer monitors or Full HD LED TVs.

We are testing the prototype while finishing the building the whole console. As a near future work we mention the development of the helm peripheral. We are working in the creation of different missions with different levels of complexity and also according to different ages. We are planning the first participation in a science fair aimed at students of different grade levels, in which we will conduct usability testing.

The accompanying videos of this paper are available at http://www.pladema.net/~cgarcia/FRIVIG.html

Acknowledgments. This research was partially supported by project A1/037910/11 FRIVIG. Formación de Recursos Humanos e Investigación en el Área de Visión por Computador e Informática Gráfica , granted by MAEC-AECID (Programa de Cooperación Interuniversitaria e Investigación Científica entre España e Iberoamérica) and by Ajudes grup competitiu UGIVIA granted by the Govern de les Illes Balears.

The adapted simulator presented here is based on previous developed set of ship-handling training simulators called MELIPAL, originally funded by the Argentine Armed Forces and INVAP SE.

References

1. Pausch, R., Crea, T., Conway, M.: A literature survey for virtual environments: military flight simulator visual systems and simulator sickness. Presence: Teleoperators and Virtual Environments 1(3), 344–363 (1992)
2. Lathan, C., Tracey, M., Sebrechts, M., Clawson, D., Higgins, G.: Using virtual environments as training simulators: Measuring transfer. In: Handbook of Virtual Environments: Design, Implementation and Applications, pp. 403–414. CRC Press (2002)
3. Pantelidis, V.: Reasons to Use Virtual Reality in Education and Training Courses and a Model to Determine When to Use Virtual Reality. In: Themes in Science and Technology Education. Special Issue, Klidarithmos Computer Books, pp. 59–70 (2010)
4. Magee, L.E.: Virtual Reality Simulator (VRS) for Training Ship Handling Skills. In: Virtual Reality, Training's Future? Defense Research Series, vol. 6, pp. 19–29 (1997)
5. Xiufeng, Z., Yicheng, J., Yong, Y., Zhihua, L.: Ship simulation using virtual reality technique. In: Proceeding of VRCAI 2004 Proceedings of the 2004 ACM SIGGRAPH International Conference on Virtual Reality Continuum and its Applications in Industry, pp. 282–285. ACM, New York (2004) ISBN:1-58113-884-9
6. Ueng, S., Lin, D., Liu, C.: A ship motion simulation system. Virtual Reality 12(1), 65–76 (2008)
7. Ning, Q.: The Study on Ship Navigation Method Based on Virtual Reality. In: Procedings of International Conference on Education Technology and Management Engineering. Lecture Notes in Information Technology, pp. 16–17 (2012)
8. Yeo, D., Cha, M., Mun, D.: Simulating ship and buoy motions arising from ocean waves in a ship handling simulator. In: Simulation, vol. 88(12), Society for Computer Simulation International, San Diego (2012)
9. Daqaq, M.: Virtual Reality Simulation of Ships and Ship-Mounted Cranes virtual simulation of ships and ship-mounted cranes. Masters of Science in Engineering Mechanics Thesis dissertation. Faculty of the Virginia Polytechnic Institute and State University (2003)
10. Ship Simulator Video Game, http://www.shipsim.com/
11. Boroni, G., Venere, M.: Un simulador distribuido para entrenamiento de operarios. Proceedings VIII Congreso Argentino de Ciencias de la Computación, 727–738 (2002) ISBN: 987-96-288-6-1
12. Otheguy, I., Soriano, M., Boroni, G., y Venere, M.: Simulation in real time of radar of horizontal scan. In: Proceedings of First South American Congress on Computational Mechanics, pp. 1203–1212 (2002) ISSN: 1666-6070
13. D' Amato, J., García Bauza, C., Vénere, M.: Simulación del Entorno de una Embarcación Pesquera. Actas de las 33 Jornadas Argentinas de Informática e Investigación Operativa (2004)
14. Chen, S., Doolen, G.D.: Lattice Boltzmann Method for Fluid Flows. Annual Review of Fluid Mechanics 30, 329–364 (1998)
15. Succi, S.: The Lattice Boltzmann Equation for Fluid Dynamics and Beyond. Oxford University Press (2001) ISBN 0-19-850398-9

16. Boroni, G., Vénere, M., Lotito, P., Clausse, A., Martinetti, O., Grasso, O.: Modelo predictivo de comportamiento de barcos. In: Proceedings of the X Workshop of Computer Science Research, Argentina (2008)
17. D' Amato, J., García Bauza, C., Vénere, M.: Editor de Escenarios para Aplicaciones de Realidad Virtual. Actas de las 34 Jornadas Argentinas de Informática e Investigación Operativa (2005)
18. Cifuentes, V., D' Amato, J., García Bauza, C., Lotito, P., Vénere, M., Clausse, A.: Análisis Multicriterio para la simplificación conjunta de geometría y textura de terrenos. CACIC 2006. Actas del XII Congreso Argentino de las Ciencias de la Computación (2006)
19. Cifuentes, V., D' Amato, J., García Bauza, C., Lotito, P., Vénere, M., Clausse, A.: Ray Casting para la Definición de Zonas de Interés en Simplificación Topográfica. Mecánica Computacional 25, 1177–1186 (2006) ISSN 1666-6070
20. García Bauza, C., Lazo, M., Vénere, M.: Incorporación de comportamiento físico en motores gráficos. Mecánica Computacional 27, 3023–3039 (2008)
21. Newton Game Dynamics - Physics Engine, http://newtondynamics.com
22. García Bauza, C., Boroni, G., Vénere, M., Clausse, A.: Real-time interactive animations of liquid surfaces with Lattice-Boltzmann engines. Aust. J. Basic & appl. Sci. 4(8), 3730–3740 (2010) ISSN 1991-8178
23. Lazo, M., García Bauza, C., Boroni, G., Vénere, M., Clausse, A.: Real-time physical engine for floating objects with two-way fluid-structure coupling. World Applied Sciences Journal 22(12), 1685–1694 (2013) ISSN 1818-4952

3D Human Motion Analysis for Reconstruction and Recognition

Chutisant Kerdvibulvech[1] and Koichiro Yamauchi[2]

[1]Rangsit University, 52/347 Muang-Ake, Paholyothin Rd, Lak-Hok,
Patum Thani 12000, Thailand
chutisant.k@rsu.ac.th
[2]Keio University, 3-14-1 Hiyoshi, Kohoku-ku 223-8522, Japan
yamauchi@hvrl.ics.keio.ac.jp

Abstract. In recent years, biometrics modalities with depth information are an interesting resource. As they can apply to many applications, range scanners have obviously become popular increasing the measurement accuracy and speed. In this paper, we propose a method for 3D human motion analysis for reconstruction and recognition. We use 3D gait signatures computed from 3D data that are obtained from a triangulation-based projector-camera system. The method consists of several steps: First, 3D human body data are acquired by using a projector-camera system. The body data are composed of representative poses that occur during the gait cycle of a walking human. Second, 3D human body model is fitted to the body data using a bottom-up approach to estimate its pose. Third, the entire gait sequence is recovered by interpolation of joint positions in the fitted body models. Representative results have been shown to ensure the robustness of the proposed method.

Keywords: 3D Human Body Data, Human Motion Analysis, Reconstruction, 3D Recognition, Human Body Model, 3D Model Fitting.

1 Introduction

Gait recognition aims for personal identification based on walking style. The use of recognition based on human gait has many advantages in various aspects as a contactless, exposed, and characteristic biometrics. If the habit of walking is changed consciously, the motion seems unnatural. In addition, gait involves not only surface shape, called static feature, but also continuous motion, called dynamic feature. Over the last few decades, recognition approaches using 3D biometrics have been proposed. This is because these reconstruction and recognition methods from 3D human motion analysis can apply to many recent applications in real life.

For example, Igual el al. [1] built a system that recognizes gait-based gender. They used depth cameras to capture and then extract the features in real-time. It was noted that this approach is robust to luminance changes since it discards the RGB information. Hu el al. [2] developed a probabilistic system with a measurement model to track

F.J. Perales and J. Santos-Victor (Eds.): AMDO 2014, LNCS 8563, pp. 118–127, 2014.
© Springer International Publishing Switzerland 2014

and understand human gait. The system used particle filtering to estimate the length between the generated leg model and the observed 3D points. Theoharis et al. [3] proposed a unified algorithm to fuse 3D facial and ear data. The mentioned methods reach high recognition rate when compared to a single modality approach. In [4], Ryu and Kamata proposed a frontal view gait recognition approach using 3D point clouds data of body of human. They called their method, "Spherical Space Model with Human Point Clouds" (SSM-HPC). Similarly, Gabel et al. [5] from Microsoft proposed a gait analysis system that focused on economical and non-intrusive issues based on the Kinect sensor. Moreover, in Sigal at al.'s work [6], it suggested that the 3D human pose tracker can be inferred by physical attributes, such as weight and gender, and mental aspects. As similar to [6], a sparse reconstruction based metric learning method was recently discussed in [7] to solve the problem of gender recognition and human identity from gait sequences. [8] used a hierarchical search to extract the lower body joint angles based on hybrid-dimensional features for human gait recognition. They used the hybrid-dimensional features to recognize the infrared gait.

In fact, there are many approaches for 2D and 3D biometrics. Here, Multi-Cam indicates a single or multi-camera system and Pro-Cam indicates a projector-camera system. While biometrics approaches using 3D face, finger, ear, and their multimodal data have been proposed, gait recognition methods still utilized video sequences. Therefore, we attempt to tackle human recognition using 3D gait biometrics where both the modeling and the test data are obtained in 3D. For this reason, their aforementioned works are different from ours.

Another possibility of recognition of a walking humans was discussed in [9] by Yamauchi et al. However, only the initial results were presented. This paper proposes a novel 3D human motion analysis for reconstruction and recognition. We use 3D gait biometrics from a projector-camera system. 3D human body data consisting of representative poses over one gait cycle are captured. 3D human body model is fitted to the body data using a bottom-up approach. Since the body data is dense and it is at a high resolution, we can interpolate the entire gait sequence to fill-in between gait acquisitions. Gait features are defined by both dynamic features and static features. The similarity measure based on gait features is used for recognition of a subject and his/her pose. Therefore, 3D human motion can successfully be recognized and reconstructed.

2   Human Motion Analysis

Figure 1 shows the gait cycle expressed by the swing phase and the stance phase from pose 1 to pose 4. Generally, gait consists of two distinct periods. First is a swing phase. This is a phase when the foot does not touch the ground moving the leg forward. Second is a stance phase. This phase is when the foot touches the ground. The gait cycle is expressed by the swing phase and the stance phase. The cycle begins with foot touch which marks the start of the swing phase. The body weight is transferred onto the other leg and the leg swings forward to meet the ground in front of the other foot. The cycle ends with the foot touch. The start of stance phase is when the heel strikes the ground. The ankle flexes to bring the foot flat on the ground and the body weight transferred onto it. The end of stance phase is when the heel leaves the ground. When pose 4 finishes, it goes to pose 1 again as cycle.

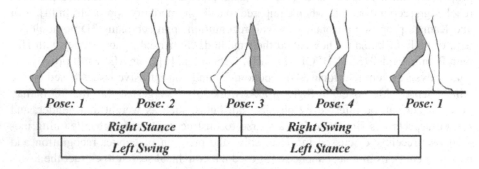

Fig. 1. Different phases of gait cycle

In this paper with 3D gait data, we assume that there are four measured poses as described in the above. The model of the human body we used comes from a kinematic tree. The tree consists of 12 segments. Figure 2 shows 3D human body model we used. The body segment is approximated by a 3D tapered cylinder which has one free parameter: the cylinder length. It has two degrees of freedom in rotational joints, in the local coordinate system. Upper torso is the root segment, i.e. the parent of lower torso, right upper leg, and left upper leg. Similarly, other segments are linked to parent segments by the rotational joints. The bounding angles of rotational joints are also important. The constraints are enforced in the form of bounding values of the joint angles. Within these constraints the model has enough range of movement to represent various poses. The whole body is rotated around three axes and the other segments are rotated around two axes. Here, neck is the fixed segment between head and upper torso, so the neck joint angles are not considered. The articulated structure of the human body has a total of 40 degrees of freedom (DOFs). The pose is described by a 6-D vector, p, representing global position and rotation, a 22-D vector, q, representing the joint angles, and a 12-D vector, r, representing the lengths of body part.

For easy to understand, we denote the combination of the representative four poses as s. Joint DOF values concatenated along the kinematic tree define the kinematic pose, k, as a tuple, [p, q, r, s], where $p \in R6$, $q \in R22$, $r \in R12$, $s = \{s1, s2, s3, s4\}$. In the previous works, segments are linked to parent segments by either 1-DOF (hinge), 2-DOF (saddle) or 3-DOF (ball and socket) rotational joints [10]. We use only 2-DOF rotational joints, because the 3D tapered cylinder has rotational symmetry along the direction orthogonal to the radial direction. As a result, we eliminate the twist of body parts as an unnecessary variable with only 2-DOF information.

The method for modeling a walking human use a body axes estimation. The intuition behind the principal component analysis (PCA) is to find a set of base vectors, so that they explain the maximum amount of variance of the data. An example of applying PCA for recognition can be found in [11]. PCA is applied to determine coronal axis (Xm-axis), vertical axis (Ym-axis), and sagittal axis (Zm-axis). The method to determining the three axes and the centroid incorporates two separate steps. First, we compute the eigenvectors and the mean vector using whole human body data. The first eigenvector, e1, and the mean vector, e0, define the vertical axis and the centroid. The range data of arms and legs do not affect the estimation of the vertical axis and the centroid adversely because they are at symmetric positions in a horizontal direction. Second, we compute the eigenvectors using the extracted range data of torso after torso detection. The second eigenvector, e'2, and the third eigenvector, e'3, define the coronal axis and the sagittal axis, respectively. The range data of torso is convex and has symmetrical shape even if a subject is walking, so that the two axes can be estimated correctly.

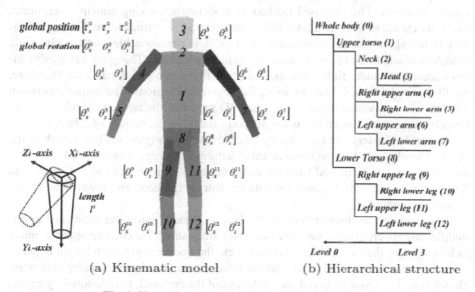

(a) Kinematic model   (b) Hierarchical structure

Fig. 2. Human body model we used in the experiments

By a triangulation-based projector-camera system, in this implementation, we measure 3D human body data with human in the walking postures. Following these data collection we separate the human body data into six regions, and then 3D human body model is fitted to the segmented body parts in a top-down hierarchy from head to legs. The body model is refined by the Iterative Closest Point (ICP) algorithm during the optimization process. The human body data are segmented into six regions: head/neck, torso, right arm, left arm, right leg, and left leg. It can be written as $x_0 = \{x_1, x_2, x_3, x_4, x_5, x_6\}$. The subscript, reg, indicates the region number. We use body axes, three segments, and six major regions which include a total of twelve body parts. Here, r. and l. indicate right and left, u. and l. indicate upper and lower (e.g. r. l. arm is right lower arm). In the following we present a fully automatic parts-based segmentation method. The description will be as follows.

To begin with, we measure 3D human body data by a triangulation-based projector-camera system with human in the walking postures. Following these data collection we separate the human body data into six regions, and then 3D human body model is fitted to the segmented body parts in a top-down hierarchy from head to legs. The body model is refined by the ICP algorithm during the optimization process. We first consider human body modeling. As discussed in [12], modeling methods usually fail when applied to real data. The real data captured by a projector-camera system have obviously some critical problems. For instance, the projector-camera system cannot cover well particular body parts. The groin region, axillary region, and the side of a human body are some examples. In this way, 3D points of the real data are dependently distributed as explained in [13]. Moreover, the body sways and deep color clothes have detrimental effects which appear as holes and gaps. To solve these mentioned problems, we present a modeling method for dealing with the problems occurring in real data. The proposed method to modeling a walking human incorporates two separate steps. First is model fitting, and second is optimization. The segmentation is useful for coarse registration, because it is unreasonable to fit a kinematic model to articulated objects without any prior knowledge. The prior knowledge allows automatic model fitting and the reduction in the computational cost. Therefore, we fit the model to body data by using the segmented regions. The distance between 3D data of a segmented region, $x_{reg \cdot j}$, and 3D model of the tapered cylinder, $y_{i \cdot j}$, is linearly minimized. Note that j is the 3D point index on the surface of a human body. The tapered cylinders can be fitted by determining two angles and one length in the order of levels 1, 2, 3 of the hierarchical structure. With regard to the head and neck, the parameters are estimated from the distribution of 3D points in the X-Y plane and Y-Z plane, respectively because the data for hair on the head and lower head region cannot be captured.

To decompose the human body, body data are divided into three segments: upper, middle, and lower. We use the cross-sectional areas along Y-axis. The upper segment in height larger than v includes head and heck, the middle segment in height between v and w includes torso and arms, and the lower segment in height smaller than w includes legs. The cross-sectional area in height of the centroid, g, is denoted by cg and the cross-sectional areas in height v, w are denoted by cv, cw are given by

$$cv = E1*cg \quad \text{and} \quad cw = E2*cg, \tag{1}$$

where E1 and E2 are height parameters. They are estimated by searching for the similar values in a vertical direction. Therefore, the body data is separated into the three segments.

The ICP algorithm provides fine registration by minimizing the distance between the body data and kinematic model [14]. The key steps of the algorithm are: (a) Uniform sampling of points on both shapes. (b) Matching each selected point to the closest sample in the other shape. (c) Uniform weighting of point pairs. (d) Rejecting pairs with distances lager than some multiple of the standard deviation. (e) Point-to-point error metric. (f) Standard select-match minimizes iteration.

The distance between 3D data of the entire body, defined as $x_{o \cdot j}$, and 3D model of the tapered cylinder, defined as $z_{i \cdot j}$, to be iteratively minimized is

$$d_f = (1/L) \text{ SUM } (\tilde{x}_{0,j} - R z_{i,j}) \tag{2}$$

where R is 3*3 rotation matrix including two angles of x and z, and L is the number of corresponding points. The tapered cylinders are adjusted by changing the two angles in the order of the levels 1, 2, 3 of the hierarchical structure.

Generally, gait features are divided into two types: (a) dynamic features and (b) static features. Both dynamic and static features are important for estimating the recognition. For example, the length of stride is one of the significant features of human gait. It can be computed by the leg length and its varying angles between poses. In addition, all the joint positions can be computed by using the same method. Therefore, both dynamic features and static features are used for recognition. We define the dynamic features as joint angles, $q_{m,n}$, and static features as lengths of the body parts, $r_{m,n}$. Here, m is the personal identification number, and n is the pose index. We will also discuss about the advantages of using both static and dynamic features in the following section.

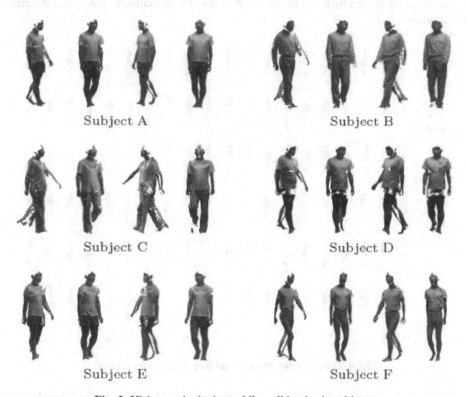

Subject A   Subject B

Subject C   Subject D

Subject E   Subject F

Fig. 3. 3D human body data while walking in six subjects

3   Results

In this section, representative results will be shown. The experiments were performed on the body data set collected by the human body measurement system. It contains twenty-four body data from the representative four poses of six subjects $X \in \{A, B, C, D, E, F\}$.

The body data of representative poses are captured by a human body measurement system, Cartesia 3D Body Scanner of SPACE-VISION [15]. The system consists of nine projector-camera pairs, which acquires nine range data in 2 seconds with 640 × 480 pixels, 3 mm depth resolution, and 3 mm measurement accuracy. We define that the one gait cycle is composed of twenty frames Y ∈ {1, 2, 3,…, 20}. The speed is given by dividing the stride length by the number of poses and the direction is given manually. Four of them are representative poses, indicated by the frame index 1, 6, 11, and 16, and the others are interpolated poses, indicated by the frame index 2-5, 7-10, 12-15, and 17-20.

After that, we measure the results. The measurement results of walking humans are depicted in Figure 3. Representative reconstruction and recognition results for 3D human motion data are depicted. The number of measuring points is about 1/2 to one million depending on the subject and the pose. For the training data, two gait sequences are recovered by using two combinations of representative poses and symmetrical poses.

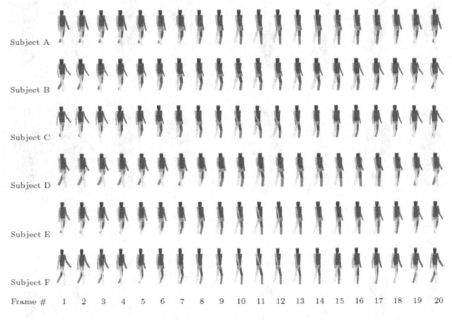

Fig. 4. Gait sequence from six subjects in different frames

Figure 4 depicts the full results of gait reconstruction also. It is defined that the one gait cycle is composed of twenty frames. The speed is given by dividing the stride length by the number of poses and the direction is not given automatically. The frame index 1, 6, 11, and 16 are representative poses, while the other frame indexes are calculated poses (from twenty).

Identification rate and average pose error are computed in order to estimate the quantitative accuracy of the proposed method. The identification rate is obtained by dividing the number of recognized subjects by the number of testing data. The pose error is the frame difference between the estimated pose and the ideal pose. From our experiment, we achieve 98.96 percent identification rate using dynamic features and 100 percent using both dynamic and static features. When only static features are tested, the method fails to recognize markedly. When only dynamic features are used, the method fails to recognize testing data for Subject D with pose 14 who is now incorrectly recognized as Subject B with pose 13. Although bodies for these two subjects are different, their joint angles, i.e. leg and arm swings, are quite similar. Additional explanation of 3D static features about this reason can be found in [16]. Overall, both dynamic and static features are clearly useful for gait recognition.

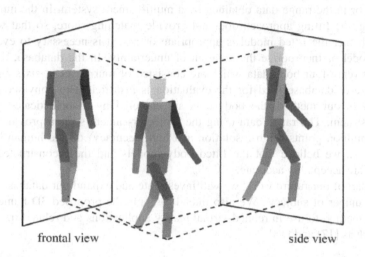

frontal view   side view

Fig. 5. Virtual front and side views for comparing 3D gait biometrics with a single view

Most of the previous gait recognition approaches often rely on only 2D gait biometrics. To compare 3D gait biometrics with a single view, frontal view and side view are synthesized from our data by orthographic projection as shown in Figure 5. After that, we use 2D gait biometrics for the quantitative experiment. From our experimental results, we achieve 95.83 percent using dynamic feature. Using both dynamic and static features, we reach 100 percent for the identification rate. Furthermore, we achieve 0.57 and 1.29, using dynamic feature and using both features for the average pose error, respectively. When we use only dynamic feature, the approach fails to recognize testing data Subject B with pose 4, Subject D with pose 7, Subject D with pose 8, and Subject D with pose 14 who should not be recognized as the training data for Subject C with pose 4, Subject A with pose 7, Subject A with pose 8, and Subject B with pose 13. We believe that these numbers are suitable enough to make this proposed method newly useful for 3D human motion analysis for reconstruction and recognition.

Nevertheless, it is important to note to readers that, in this proposed system, using either static feature or dynamic feature solely cannot achieve the sufficiently accurate results. Our experimental results have revealed that the system performs acceptably and well when dynamic feature is integrated with the using of static feature to obtain the identification rate.

4   Conclusions and Future Works

This paper proposed a new approach for 3D human motion analysis using reconstruction and recognition technology based on 3D gait biometrics. One of the significant weaknesses of current gait recognition methods has been the lack of enough pixels on the human body to fit the kinematic human body model accurately in the video sequences or in the range data obtained by a multi-camera system. In the human body modeling, the fitting approach does not provide matching score, so that we cannot judge whether the fitted model is appropriate or not. It is necessary to evaluate the fitted model or incorporate the notation of uncertainty. In the database, there are a total of twenty-four body data which are consisted of four poses of six subjects. The small size of database used for the evaluation is insufficient to convince about the efficacy. In our method, the body data are captured by a sophisticated projector-camera system. The range data using the projector-camera system provided approximately million points (high resolution and high accuracy) on the human body. For this reason, we believe that the fitted body models and the reconstructed gait sequences are acceptably accurate.

As part of our future work, we will investigate and expand our database to collect a huge number of subjects. We also intend to apply the proposed 3D human motion analysis method to use in related-virtual reality applications and related-tracking systems such as [17] and [18].

References

1. Igual, L., Lapedriza, A., Borras, R.: Robust gait-based gender classification using depth cameras. EURASIP Journal on Image and Video Processing (JIVP) 1, 11 p. (2013)
2. Hu, R.Z.-L., Cheriton, R.D., Hartfiel, A., Tung, J., Fakih, A.: 3D Pose tracking of walker users' lower limb with a structured-light camera on a moving platform. In: Proceedings of the IEEE Conference on Computer Vision and Pattern Recognition Workshops (CVPR Workshops), June 20-25, pp. 29–36 (2011)
3. Theoharis, T., Passalis, G., Toderici, G., Kakadiaris, I.A.: Unified 3D face and ear recognition using wavelets on geometry images. Pattern Recognition 41(3), 796–804 (2008)
4. Ryu, J., Kamata, S.: Front view gait recognition using Spherical Space Model with Human Point Clouds. In: Proceedings of the IEEE International Conference on Image Processing (ICIP), September 11-14, pp. 3209–3212 (2011)
5. Gabel, M., Gilad-Bachrach, R., Renshow, E., Schuster, A.: Full Body Gait Analysis with Kinect. In: Proceedings of the 34th Annual International Conference of the IEEE Engineering in Medicine and Biology Society (EMBS), August 28-September 1, pp. 1964–1967 (2012)
6. Sigal, L., Fleet, D.J., Troje, N.F., Livne, M.: Human Attributes from 3D Pose Tracking. In: Daniilidis, K., Maragos, P., Paragios, N. (eds.) ECCV 2010, Part III. LNCS, vol. 6313, pp. 243–257. Springer, Heidelberg (2010)

7. Lu, J., Wang, G., Moulin, P.: Human Identity and Gender Recognition from Gait Sequences With Arbitrary Walking Directions. IEEE Transactions on Information Forensics and Security 9(1), 51–61 (2014)
8. Wang, L., Zhang, L., Yang, Y., Qi, H., Wang, W., Abboud, R.: Human Gait Recognition based on Hybrid-Dimensional Features from Infrared Motion Image. In: Proceedings of the IEEE Conference on Computational Intelligence for Measurement Systems and Applications (CIMSA), July 2-4, pp. 69–72 (2012)
9. Yamauchi, K., Bhanu, B., Saito, H.: Recognition of walking humans in 3D: Initial results. In: Proceedings of the IEEE Conference on Computer Vision and Pattern Recognition Workshops (CVPR Workshops), June 20-25, pp. 45–52 (2009)
10. Vondrak, M., Signal, L., Jenkins, O.C.: Physical simulation for probabilistic motion tracking. In: Proceedings of the IEEE Conference on Computer Vision and Pattern Recognition (CVPR), pp. 1–8 (2008)
11. Kerdvibulvech, C., Saito, H.: Real-Time Guitar Chord Recognition System Using Stereo Cameras for Supporting Guitarists. Transactions on Electrical Engineering, Electronics, and Communications (ECTI) 5(2), 147–157 (2007)
12. Yu, H., Qin, S., Wight, D.K., Kang, J.: Generation of 3D human models with different levels of detail through point-based simplification. In: Proceedings of the International Conference on "Computer as a Tool", pp. 1982–1986 (2007)
13. Werghi, N., Rahayem, M., Kjellander, J.: An ordered topological representation of 3D triangular mesh facial surface: Concept and applications. EURASIP Journal on Advances in Signal Processing 1, 1–20 (2012)
14. Rusinkiewicz, S., Levoy, M.: Efficient variants of the ICP algorithm. In: Proceedings of the 3-D Digital Imaging and Modeling, pp. 145–152 (2001)
15. Yamauchi, K., Sato, Y.: 3D human body measurement by multiple range images. In: Proceedings of the IEEE International Conference on Pattern Recognition (ICPR), vol. 4, pp. 833–836 (2006)
16. Ariyanto, G., Nixon, M.S.: Model-based 3D gait biometrics. In: Proceedings of the IEEE International Joint Conference on Biometrics Compendium (IJCB), October 11-13, pp. 1–7 (2011)
17. Kerdvibulvech, C.: Real-Time Adaptive Learning System Using Object Color Probability for Virtual Reality Applications. In: Proceedings of the ACM International Conference on Simulation and Modeling Methodologies, Technologies and Applications (SIMULTECH), July 29-31, pp. 200–204 (2011)
18. Kerdvibulvech, C., Saito, H.: Model-Based Hand Tracking by Chamfer Distance and Adaptive Color Learning Using Particle Filter. EURASIP Journal on Image and Video Processing (JIVP), Article ID 724947, 10 p. (2009)

Interactive Multimodal Platform for Digital Signage

Helen V. Diez, Javier Barbadillo, Sara García,
Maria del Puy Carretero, Aitor Álvarez,
Jairo R. Sánchez, and David Oyarzun

Vicomteh-IK4, Paseo Mikeletegi 57, 20009 Donostia-San Sebastián, Spain
{hdiez,jbarbadillo,sgarcia,mcarretero,aalvarez,jrsanchez,doyarzun}
@vicomtech.org
http://www.vicomtech.org

Abstract. The main objective of the platform presented in this paper
is the integration of various modules into Web3D technology for Digital
Signage systems. The innovation of the platform consists on the development and integration of the following technologies; 1) autonomous virtual
character with natural behaviour, 2) text-to-speech synthesizer and voice
recognition 3) gesture recognition. The integration of these technologies
will enhance the user interface interaction and will improve the existing
Digital Signage solutions offering a new way of marketing to engage the
audience. The goal of this work is also to prove whether this new way of
e-commerce may improve sales and customer fidelity.

Keywords: Multimodal Platform, User-Interface-Interaction, Digital
Signage.

1 Introduction

In the latest years, technology and especially new media has empowered marketing and commerce areas with new tools that go towards ubiquity and more
and more faithful virtual representations of real products.

Nowadays, HTML5 and Web3D technologies are strongly pushing to web
standardization of new media. Good and serious examples of efforts that are
being done in this direction are the low level WebGL specification [1] and the
high-level X3DOM architecture [2].

These new approaches could provide the basic platform for creating innovative
marketing and e-commerce applications, which take advantage from potentiality
of all technological channels and devices in a standardized way.

With this premise, the work presented in this paper consists on the development and integration of a web-based 3D engine and software modules that
enable natural communication channels.

This technical work is built over three pillars:

- Coherent coexistence and communication among technologies coming from
  different disciplines and with different levels of maturity.

F.J. Perales and J. Santos-Victor (Eds.): AMDO 2014, LNCS 8563, pp. 128–137, 2014.

- Strong focus of usability, providing new interaction channels that make the human/computer communication more natural.
- Keep the message. That is, build technology that improves the way a message is transmitted to the user, not to condition the own message.

Therefore, these three pillars pretend to improve the channel related modules of the Shannon Weaver communication schema [3], as shown in Figure 1

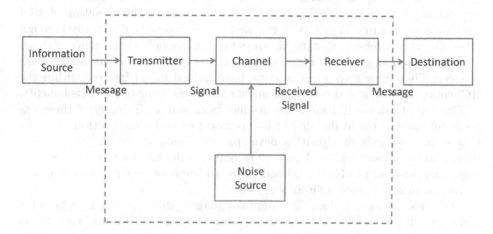

Fig. 1. Shannon Weaver communication schema on message transmission

A realistic marketing use case has been built over this integration. The use case is designed as an interactive marketing platform to be shown in digital screens in public spaces. The platform allows the end-user to interact through natural channels, such as gestures and voice.

Therefore, the platform developed acts as a testbed to experiment interaction practices that maximizes the way a digital message is sent to the end-user. The use case is considered ideal when the end-user is a potential customer in this case and so, the importance of properly transmiting the digital message is even more critical.

Moreover, the standardized feature of the technologies developed keeps the coherence of the information when it is shown in any additional device, from PCs to smartphones. A modular design allows the content creator to abstract the digital message from the interaction channels, providing a platform that easily adapts to and takes advantage from the interaction capabilities of each device where it is running.

The paper shows the technical work carried out to get a stable version of the whole platform. Beyond the potential technical capabilities of these new technologies, the marketing use case is being validated in a controlled but real environment to check the usability in the marketing area during these months.

The paper is organized as follows; Section 2 analyzes the related work regarding digital signage and user categorization, Section 3 explains the architecture followed to accomplish the goals of this work, describing in detail each of the modules involved. The final section is about conclusions and future work.

2   Related Work

Research on Human Computer Interaction (HCI) goes back to the 1980s [4], however the growig affordability of the devices using these interfaces and the accessibility to software development kits [5] have led to the evolution of HCI into Natural User Interfaces (NUI), this new way of interaction operates through intuitive actions related to natural, everyday human behaviour such as; touch screen interaction, gesture recognition, speech recognition or brain machine interfaces. These new ways of interaction have gained broad interest within the HCI community [6] and various experiments have been done to prove its benefits.

The use of Microsoft Kinect sensors has been crucial in many of these experiments due to the availability of its open-source and multi-platfom libraries that reduce the cost of algorithm development. Keane, S. et al. [7] present a survey on the Kinect sensor. A gesture recognition module based on the motion sensor included in the Kinect is used in [8] to improve user experience in the management of an office environment.

NUI is also being introduced into digital signage systems. Satho, I. [9] presents a framework for building and operating context-aware multimedia content on digital signage systems in public or private spaces and to demonstrate the utility of the framework, he presents a user-assistant that enables shopping with digital signage.

Chen, Q. et al. [10] describe a vision-based gesture recognition approach to interact with digital signage. Bauer, C. et al. [11] also introduce a conceptual framework for interactive digital signage which allows the development of various business strategies.

Adapting content according to the audience is one of the objectives pursued by the companies that offer digital signage. There are several studies that personalize content according to the audience. For example, Müller et al., [12] present a system that automatically learns the audience's preferences for certain content in different contexts and presents content accordingly.

Ravnic, R. and Solina, F. [13] developed a camera enhanced digital signage display that acquires audience measurement metrics with computer vision algorithms. The system also determines demographic metrics of gender and age groups. It was tested in a clothing boutique where the results showed that the average attention time is significantly higher when displaying the dynamic content as compared to the static content.

The introduction of autonomous characters into user interface platforms is also a matter of study. In 2006, Gribaudo, C. and Manfredi, G. [14] patented a modular digital assistant that detects user emotion and modifies its behaviour accordingly.

3   System Overview

During this work a 3D avatar able to interact with the user through different channels has been implemented. It has been designed using a modular schema that includes three main components: a web component, the speech component, and the gesture component.

The web component is responsible for displaying the virtual character along with the content of the signage application. It supports any browser that implements WebGL technology.

The speech component allows the user to interact with the virtual character using voice commands. It integrates speech recognition and synthesis technologies.

The gesture component integrates computer vision technologies for face and hands tracking. It allows the user to interact directly with the content using hand gestures, at the same time allowing the system to estimate the emotional state of the user through his face.

All the modules are integrated in a HTML5 compliant application that is used as the frontend of the signage system. However, part of the core of the speech and gesture components are native applications and must be executed in a desktop environment.

Following sections describe each module in detail.

3.1   Virtual Character

A main aspect of this work is the introduction of an autonomous virtual character into digital signage systems to act as a natural interface between the user and the content offered by the device. The role of the avatar will be to ease the communication between the audience and the digital information provided. Thus, users will experience a more natural and intuitive interaction emulating the one between real people. Likewise, the user can customize this interaction by accessing information according to his interests or preferences.

To achieve this virtual character with natural behaviour an animation engine based on WebGL technology as the one presented in this work [15] has been developed. This animation engine allows realistic simulation of both the avatar's face and body expressions. The engine is capable of real-time rendering of the lips when the avatar is speaking and it also interpolates the facial expressions depending on the avatar's mood.

As for the body language the avatar performs gestures and movements as humans do when communicating with others. A thorough study regarding natural hand, arm and body gestures has been done and animations emulating these movements have been designed.

Figure 2 represents the introduction of a virtual character with natural behaviour into a WebGL compatible browser. Nowadays most commonly used browsers support this technology (Firefox, Chrome, Opera, Safari).

Fig. 2. Integration of the virtual character into a WebGL compatible browser

3.2   Speech Synthesis and Recognition

The platform includes technologies for both automatic speech recognition and speech synthesis.

Regarding speech recognition, the Google Speech Recognizer for Spanish was integrated adapting the publicly available java API to the needs of the platform. During the recognition process, the audio is collected from the microphone. It is then encoded to FLAC and passed via an HTTPS POST to the Google speech web-service, which responds with a JSON object with the transcription. The Google Speech Recognizer is speaker-independent and provides two language models to be used, based on (1) web searches for short phrases and (2) a generic language model for dictation. Considering the needs of the project, the generic language model was used to allow continuous speech recognition.

The integration with the web platform has been done using a regular text file. The recognition software writes into the file the transcription which is consumed by a script using long pooling techniques. This integration forces the component to be deployed on the same machine as the virtual character, but in the future it could be done using the new HTML5 standards for audio input.

Two possible solutions were included in the platform for speech synthesis in Spanish. Like for speech recognition, the Google Speech Synthesis was integrated for text-to-speech conversion. In this case, the text is sent to the servers of Google via an HTTP REQUEST and a speech file in MP3 format is returned through an HTTP RESPONSE. Since the Google Synthesizer is limited to a maximum of 100 characters, the API was modified to enable the platform to synthesize longer texts. For this purpose, the input text is previously splitted on the full stops. Each sentence is then synthesized and all the returned audios are concatenated in a unique WAV file at the end.

As an alternative to Google, the Microsoft Speech Synthesizer was integrated in the platform. This technology is provided through the Microsoft.Speech. Synthesis namespace, which contains classes that allow user to easily integrate functionalities for speech synthesis. In order to extend the voicebank of the platform, a module for voice transformation was also included. This module transforms the synthesized voices modifying some prosodic features like the fundamental frequency, the speech rhythm and the energy. As a result, this module is able to modify the source speakers speech to make it sound like that of a different speaker.

3.3 Gesture Component

The platform implements a method for detecting and tracking the user's facial emotions and hand gestures. The system is composed by a Kinect device which captures video and a depth map, and it also includes a face detector for emotion recognition. The goal of the gesture component is to allow the interaction of the user with the avatar in both directions, resulting in a more natural experience. The avatar behaves according to the user's emotions and the user can perform gestures to communicate with the avatar.

The Kinect device captures video with an integrated camera and a depth map using infrared sensors. With the help of OpenNI and Nite APIs the system is able to detect and track human body parts and perform gesture recognition. Our system first detects the human body and then gets the head and the right and left hand positions. The 3D position is projected to 2D screen coordinates and the distance of the user with respect to the camera is obtained. This way the interaction is restricted to users that are facing the camera and close enough to it, avoiding interaction with people passing by.

In order to perform gesture recognition the user's hands are segmented from the rest of the body and tracked. The Nite API allows to track and detect the click gesture, the waving gesture and the rising hand gesture. The coordinates of the hand are also converted to screen coordinates so the user can use the hand as a mouse for selecting or clicking objects in a screen.

For the emotion detection process the face of the user is detected in combination with the head detection of the Kinect and a probabilistic face detector. First, the 2D position of the head is obtained from Kinect. If the distance to the camera is close enough the probabilistic detector is applied. Finally the face is detected and tracked and the system performs the emotion detection.

Our implementation of the emotion detection is based on the method proposed by [16]. When a face is detected in the screen a facial point mask is fitted to the face. This is achieved by first detecting facial features based on local image gradient analysis and then adjusting a deformable 3D face model to those features in the 2D plane. The mask represents the main facial features of a human face an it is able to track facial deformations computational efficiently and under challenging light conditions.

The emotion recognition method is based on the Facial Action Coding System developed in [17]. Every component of a facial movement is represented by an

Action Unit (AU) and therefore every facial expresion can be decomposed into AUs. An AU is independent of any interpretation as they are the result of the contraction or relaxation of one or more muscles. In our program an AU is represented by the movement of a point of the facial mask. For example, the hapiness expression is detected if the threshold of the AUs "cheek raiser" and "lip corner puller" is exceeded. Using the facial point mask makes it trivial to measure AUs and detect if a facial emotion is being performed. A threshold is set to skip low intensity muscle actions. Although there are up to 100 AUs our system just measures a few AUs related to the seven universal emotions: fear, surprise, sadness, anger, happiness, disgust and contempt.

Finallly the system filters the detected emotions to reduce them to three emotions of interest for our application: the user can be interested, neutral or not interested. The avatar will behave differently depending on the emotions recognized on the user.

To avoid sending massive information to the avatar controller, the gestures and emotions are filtered over the frames to generate statistics that are sent every certain number of frames.

The integration has been done in the same way as the speech component. In this case the component is deployed with an executable that writes the gesture and face information in a text file. The web component reads the file using long pooling techniques.

Fig. 3. Interactive Multimodal Platform for Digital Signage

4   Conclusions and Future Work

New multimedia sources are those that blend computer technology, with the audiovisual and telecommunications technology. They support a given language formed by image, sound, voice, written text, gestures and expressions and reach the user in a single marketer message.

Digitization is the universal tool that is profoundly transforming the international markets. This has eased the creation of new forms of marketing and industries dependent on these modes of information. The evolution of technology has changed the environment. The technological society of most developed countries live with new modes of experimental communication based on interactivity and the development of new forms of interdisciplinarity.

These digital technologies have completely changed the way information is transmitted. Due to its interactivity, the medium becomes the message itself. The multimedia models create a new, more powerful way to inform. New audiences are segmented and differentiated by gender, age and other components and the message focuses on this fact. These audiences are very selective with the message they receive because of their multiplicity.

New languages of human-machine communication are generated. Digital communication refers to the use of technology to achieve a certain purpose. The digital format of the medium indicates that the message content has something different and innovative. The format of the content is dependent on the medium, the distributor and the transmission system. The representation by digital screens in public spaces, allows private conversations and public environments simultaneously. It is a message created for the public, because the public participates by their expressions in the creation of the message. It is based on real-time interaction with an availability of 24 hours a day.

The transmitter, in this case the avatar, is in the same physical space as the receiver, so there is no distancing. A first approach takes place, it does not depend on the receiver who is surrounded by technology, but it depends on a transmitter / avatar searching for his receiver in their natural environment and a receiver that unintentionally becomes such.The figure of transmitter and receiver are constantly exchanged.

The message is not predetermined, it is dynamic, it is being created as the feedback happens. The receiver gives meaning to the message that has been sent massive / selectively. The audience tends to choose their messages, which improves the effectiveness of them. The range of possibilities the content displayed to the user is based on their characteristics and their willingness to receipt of the message, plus the response obtained along the communication between the avatar and the client.

Electronic technologies have a greater impact on the audience than more traditional media, since this support is also the means of reaching people and does not need more intermediaries. This way the message reaches out to the viewer, and the screen becomes the scenery for the reception.

The system has been tested in an academic atmosphere and it has proved to work recognizing and categorizing each user correctly. However, as future work we are planning to set the platform on a real scenario at a public space. This validation will serve the purpose of examining whether personalized marketing as the one proposed by our platform is better than traditional marketing systems.

To validate our system we will perform the following experiment; two groups of volunteers covering various age and gender ranges will be created. These volunteers will be invited to enter a mall in which the two trial systems have been set. Each group will try only one of the systems, once they have tried their corresponding system they will fill in a survey. In each corridor of the mall one of the marketing device systems will be set (Figure 3). Both systems will be monitored by Kinects in order to gather information regarding the amount of time people spend in front of the device. After the volunteers have walked through the corridors they will be invited to fill in a survey with questions such as:

1. did you stop in front of the device?
2. what struck your attention?
3. why did you leave?
4. did you find the experience amusing?
5. did you enjoy talking to the avatar?
6. did you find the communication with the avatar natural?
7. have you entered the store/s proposed by the system?
8. did you buy anything in any of the stores proposed by the system?
9. how would you improve the system?

The conclusions drawn from these surveys will direct further investigations in this field.

As mentioned in section 3.2 we also plan to standardize the voice capture from the microphone using WebRTC API [18], this communications standard developed by the W3C enables the embedding of audio and video in applications and websites. The WebRTC standard solves incompatibilities in real-time communications between browsers. This will also allow to integrate the Kinect device and video processing with HTML, which is currently handled by the Gesture Module plugin.

References

1. WebGL Specification, http://www.khronos.org/registry/webgl/specs/latest/1.0/ (retrieved on March 2014)
2. X3DOM Specification, http://www.x3dom.org/x3dom/doc/spec/ (retrieved on March 2014)
3. Weaver, W.: Recent contributions to the mathematical theory of communication. In: Shannon, C.E., Weaver, W. (eds.) The Mathematical Theory of Communication, pp. 1–28 (1949)
4. Myers, B.A.: A brief history of human-computer interaction technology. Interactions, 44–54 (1998)
5. Goth, G.: Brave nui world. Commun. ACM, 14–16 (2011)
6. Seow, S.C., Wixon, D., Morrison, A., Jacucci, G.: Natural user interfaces: the prospect and challenge of touch and gestural computing. In: Extended Abstracts on Human Factors in Computing Systems, CHI 2010, pp. 4453–4456. ACM (2010)

7. Keane, S., Hall, J., Perry, P.: Meet the Kinect: An Introduction to Programming Natural User Interfaces (2011)
8. Re, G.L., Morana, M., Ortolani, M.: Improving user experience via motion sensors in an ambient intelligence scenario (2013)
9. Satoh, I.: A framework for context-aware digital signage. In: Zhong, N., Callaghan, V., Ghorbani, A.A., Hu, B. (eds.) AMT 2011. LNCS, vol. 6890, pp. 251–262. Springer, Heidelberg (2011)
10. Chen, Q., Malric, F., Zhang, Y., Abid, M., Cordeiro, A., Petriu, E.M., Georganas, N.D.: Interacting with digital signage using hand gestures. In: Kamel, M., Campilho, A. (eds.) ICIAR 2009. LNCS, vol. 5627, pp. 347–358. Springer, Heidelberg (2009)
11. Bauer, C., Dohmen, P., Strausss, C.: Interactive Digital Signage-An Innovative Service and Its Future Strategies. In: 2011 International Conference on Emerging Intelligent Data and Web Technologies (EIDWT), pp. 137–142. IEEE (2011)
12. Müller, J., Exeler, J., Buzeck, M., Krüger, A.: Reflectivesigns: Digital signs that adapt to audience attention. In: Tokuda, H., Beigl, M., Friday, A., Brush, A.J.B., Tobe, Y. (eds.) Pervasive 2009. LNCS, vol. 5538, pp. 17–24. Springer, Heidelberg (2009)
13. Ravnik, R., Solina, F.: Audience measurement of digital signage: Quantitative study in real-world environment using computer vision. Interacting with Computers 25(3), 218–228 (2013)
14. Gribaudo, C., Manfredi, G.: Virtual Assistant With Real-Time Emotions. U.S. Patent Application 11/617,150, 28 Dic (2006)
15. Diez, H.V., Garcìa, S., Snchez, J.R., del Puy Carretero, M.: 3D animated agent for tutoring based on WebGL. In: Proceedings of the 18th International Conference on 3D Web Technology, pp. 129–134. ACM (2013)
16. Unzueta, L., Pimenta, W., Goenetxea, J., Santos, L.P., Dornaika, F.: Efficient generic face model fitting to images and videos. Image and Vision Computing 32(5), 321–334 (2014)
17. Ekman, P., Freisen, W.V., Ancoli, S.: Facial signs of emotional experience. Journal of Personality and Social Psychology 39(6), 1125–1134 (1980)
18. Web Real-Time Communications Working Group, et al. WebRTC 1.0: Real-time Communication Between Browsers (2012), http://dev.w3.org/2011/webrtc/editor/webrtc.html

Label Consistent Multiclass Discriminative Dictionary Learning for MRI Segmentation

Oualid M. Benkarim[1], Petia Radeva[1,2], and Laura Igual[1,2,*]

[1] Department of Applied Mathematics and Analysis, University of Barcelona, Spain
[2] Computer Vision Center of Barcelona, Spain
obenkabe7@alumnes.ub.edu, {petia.ivanova,ligual}@ub.edu

Abstract. The automatic segmentation of multiple subcortical structures in brain Magnetic Resonance Images (MRI) still remains a challenging task. In this paper, we address this problem using sparse representation and discriminative dictionary learning, which have shown promising results in compression, image denoising and recently in MRI segmentation. Particularly, we use multiclass dictionaries learned from a set of brain atlases to simultaneously segment multiple subcortical structures. We also impose dictionary atoms to be specialized in one given class using label consistent K-SVD, which can alleviate the bias produced by unbalanced libraries, present when dealing with small structures. The proposed method is compared with other state of the art approaches for the segmentation of the Basal Ganglia of 35 subjects of a public dataset. The promising results of the segmentation method show the efficiency of the multiclass discriminative dictionary learning algorithms in MRI segmentation problems.

Keywords: MRI segmentation, sparse representation, discriminative dictionary learning, multiclass classification.

1 Introduction

Many clinical applications rely on the segmentation of MRI brain structures, which allows to describe, for instance, how brain anatomy changes in relation with certain brain diseases. Since manual labeling by experts is subject to inter and intra rater variability and is also a highly laborious task, an automated technique is desirable to enable the routine analysis of brain MRIs in clinical use. Despite the large number of proposed techniques [1,6,7], MRI segmentation still remains a challenging task due to frequent image artifacts and poor contrast between the structures to segment.

Among these techniques, atlas-based methods [1] are the most commonly used. They use atlases, which consist of two image volumes: one intensity image and one labeled image, to segment target images without human assistance. The segmentation turns into a registration problem. To obtain a segmentation of the

* This work was partially founded by the projects TIN2012-38187-C03-01 and 2014 SGR 1219.

F.J. Perales and J. Santos-Victor (Eds.): AMDO 2014, LNCS 8563, pp. 138–147, 2014.

target image, the manual labeling of the atlas is transformed using the mapping determined during the registration; this process is called label propagation. The main drawback of this kind of techniques is that they implicitly assume that a single atlas endowed with a deformation model is a sufficiently rich representation of the whole population. Segmentation errors produced by atlas-based methods can be reduced by averaging techniques such as multi-atlas based segmentation; using several atlases to better capture the variability of target structures [2]. The keypoints of registration-based label propagation approaches concern the accuracy of the non-rigid registration and the fusion rules [5]. Recently, non-local patch-based segmentation techniques have been proposed [6], whose purpose is to relax the one-to-one constraint existing in non-rigid registration. This technique has two interesting properties: first, the natural redundancy of information contained in the image can be used to increase the numbers of samples considered during estimation; and second, the local intensity context (i.e., patch) can be used to produce a robust comparison of samples. The labeling of every voxel is performed by using similar image patches from coarsely aligned atlases, assigning weights to these patches according to their similarity. The final label is estimated by fusing the labels of the central voxels in the patch library.

Image similarities over small image patches may not be an optimal estimator [7]. In [8], segmentation is based on image patch reconstruction instead of similarity. A dictionary and a linear classifier are learned from the patch library of every voxel in the target image. Then, the target patch can be reconstructed by the corresponding dictionary and the label of the target voxel is estimated by the corresponding classifier. To the best of our knowledge, [8] is the only paper that has previously applied these techniques to subcortical structures segmentation (specifically, the Hippocampus). In this paper, we extend the MRI segmentation method in [8]. In particular, the proposed method is a multiclass dictionary leaning approach to simultaneously segment several subcortical brain structures. This method also incorporates a label consistent term [16] to impose dictionary atoms to be specialized in one given class. This can alleviate the bias produced by unbalanced patch libraries, which is the case in the boundaries of the brain structures.

The paper is organized as follows. Section 2 is devoted to review Sparse Representation and Dictionary Learning. In Section 3 we cope with the problem of MRI segmentation using these techniques and we introduce our method. Section 4 presents experimental results of our method compared with three state of the art methods. Section 5 finishes with conclusions and future work.

2 Related Work

2.1 Sparse Representation

Sparse representations have increasingly become recognized as providing extremely high performance for applications as diverse as image denoising [9] and image compression [10]. The aim of sparse coding is to reconstruct a signal as a linear combination of a small number of signal-atoms picked from a dictionary.

Using a dictionary $D \in \mathbb{R}^{n \times k}$, the representation of a given signal $y \in \mathbb{R}^n$ is $y = D\alpha$.

When the dictionary D is overcomplete, the linear system $y = D\alpha$ is under-determined since $k > n$, and an infinite number of solutions (if there are any) are available for the representation problem. Hence constraints on the solution must be set. In sparse representation we are interested in the sparsest of all such solutions. As a measure of sparsity, the ℓ^0 norm is used. In general, the sparse coding problem can be formulated as:

$$\min_{\alpha} \|\alpha\|_0 \quad \text{s. t.} \quad \|y - D\alpha\|_2^2 \leq \varepsilon, \tag{1}$$

where α is the vector of sparse coefficients of the signal y over D, $\varepsilon > 0$ is a given error tolerance, and $\|\cdot\|_0$ is the ℓ^0 norm.

Since the combinatorial ℓ^0 norm minimization is not convex, the ℓ^1 norm minimization, as the closest convex function to ℓ^0 norm minimization, is widely employed in sparse coding, and it has been shown that both norms are equivalent if the solution is sufficiently sparse. The solution to Eq. 1 is equivalent to the solution of the following problem:

$$\min_{\alpha} \|\alpha\|_1 \quad \text{s. t.} \quad \|y - D\alpha\|_2^2 \leq \varepsilon. \tag{2}$$

Using the Lagrangian method, this can be rewritten as:

$$\hat{y} = \min_{\alpha} \frac{1}{2} \|y - D\alpha\|_2^2 + \lambda \|\alpha\|_1, \tag{3}$$

where $\|y - D\alpha\|_2^2$ is the data fitting term, $\|\alpha\|_1$ is the sparsity-inducing regularization, and $\lambda > 0$ is a scalar regularization parameter that balances the trade-off between reconstruction error and sparsity.

Eq. 3 can be solved efficiently by several methods such as Lasso [11]. However, if there is a group of variables among which the pairwise correlations are very high, then the Lasso tends to select only one variable from the group and does not care which one is selected. Therefore, it is possible to strengthen further the prediction power of Lasso. The Elastic Net (EN) method, proposed in [12], often outperforms Lasso, while enjoying a similar sparsity of representation:

$$\hat{\alpha} = \arg\min_{\alpha} \|y - D\alpha\|_2^2 + \lambda_1 \|\alpha\|_1 + \frac{\lambda_2}{2} \|\alpha\|_2^2. \tag{4}$$

In addition, the EN method encourages a grouping effect where strongly correlated predictors tend to be in or out of the model together. The elastic net is particularly useful when the number of predictors n is much bigger than the number of observations m, which is our case dealing with neuroimages.

2.2 Dictionary Learning

An overcomplete dictionary that leads to sparse representations can either be predefined or designed by adapting its content to fit a given set of signal samples.

Recent publications have shown that learning dictionaries for image representation can significantly improve tasks such as image restoration [9]. Concretely, given a set of signals $Y = [y_1, \cdots, y_n]$, we assume that there exists a dictionary D that gave rise to the given signal samples via sparse combinations, i.e., there exists D, so that solving Eq. (1) for each y_i gives a sparse representation α_i. Learning a dictionary with k number of atoms and with a sparsity constraint T is addressed by solving the following problem:

$$\min_{\alpha,D} \|Y - D\alpha\|_2^2 \quad \text{s. t.} \quad \|\alpha\|_0 \leq T. \tag{5}$$

A number of practical algorithms have been developed for learning such dictionaries like *method of optimal directions* (MOD) proposed in [13] and the K-SVD algorithm [14]. Both K-SVD and MOD are iterative approaches designed to minimize Eq. (5) by first performing sparse coding and then updating the dictionary. Other method that scales to large datasets is the online optimization algorithm for dictionary leaning proposed in [17].

Nevertheless, K-SVD is not suitable for classification, where the dictionary should be not only representative, but also discriminative. Hence, some supervised dictionary learning approaches incorporate classification error into the objective function to construct a dictionary with discriminative power. Zhang and Li [15] developed the D-KSVD algorithm that uses the labels of training data to directly incorporate a linear classifier into the basic K-SVD algorithm and finally unifies the representation power and discriminate ability to train the dictionary and classifier simultaneously. D-KSVD algorithm solves the following problem:

$$\langle D, W, \alpha \rangle = \arg\min_{D,W,\alpha} \|Y - D\alpha\|_2 + \beta\|H - W\alpha\|_2 + \eta\|W\|_2 \tag{6}$$
$$\text{s. t. } \|\alpha\|_0 \leq T,$$

where W are the classifier parameters. Each column of H is a vector $h_i = [0, \cdots, 1, \cdots, 0]$, where the non-zero position indicates the class. So the term involving H is the classification error and $\|W\|_2$ is the regularization penalty.

Moreover, approaches such as D-KSVD consider only discriminativeness in the classifier construction, but do not guarantee the discriminativeness in the sparse representations of signals. Jiang et. al in [16], proposed the Label Consistent K-SVD (LC-KSVD) algorithm, which associates label information with each dictionary atom to enforce discriminability in sparse codes during the dictionary learning process. LC-KSVD solves the following problem:

$$\langle D, W, A, \alpha \rangle = \arg\min_{D,W,A,\alpha} \|Y - D\alpha\|_2 + \beta\|H - W\alpha\|_2 \tag{7}$$
$$+ \lambda\|Q - A\alpha\|_2 + \eta\|W\|_2 \quad \text{s. t. } \|\alpha\|_0 \leq T,$$

where $\|Q - A\alpha\|_2$ is the label consistent regularization term responsible for enforcing the creation of discriminative dictionaries, A is a linear transformation matrix and $Q = [q_1, \cdots, q_N] \in \mathbb{R}^{k \times N}$ are the discriminative sparse codes of elements in Y for classification. According to [16], for instance, $q_i = [q_i^1, \cdots, q_i^k]^t = [0, \cdots, 1, 1, \cdots, 0]^t \in \mathbb{R}^K$ is a discriminative sparse code corresponding to a given signal $y_i \in Y$, if the non-zero values of q_i occur at those indexes where the y_i and the dictionary atom d_k share the same label.

3   Multiclass Dictionary Learning for MRI Segmentation

In this section, we first review the MRI segmentation framework using Sparse Representation Classification (SRC) and Discriminative Dictionary Learning for Segmentation (DDLS) presented in [8]. Then, we introduce the Label Consistent Multiclass DDLS (LC-MDDLS) method for MRI segmentation, which is based on DDLS and also incorporates the *label consistency* (LC) property proposed in [16].

For a given target image I, we consider a training set of images previously registered to a normalized space. We select the N most similar training images based on the sum of squared intensity differences. For the segmentation of a set of subcortical structures in I, we extract a crop of the image, I_C defined by the dimensions of the union of the voxels belonging to these structures in the training images. The target voxels to segment are the ones in I_C. We define a *patch* as a bounding-box of a given size, S_p, around a target voxel. We create a patch library, P_L, from the set of N training images. As shown in figure 1, we extract a patch for each voxel in a search window, of a previously defined size, S_w, from all training images. Subsequently, we use P_L to classify the target voxel accordingly to one of the methods presented next.

3.1   Sparse Representation Based Classification

In SRC, the whole patch library is directly used as the dictionary in Eq. 4. The reconstruction error, r_j, using the coefficients α^j associated to class j is defined as

$$r_j(p_t) = \|p_t - P_L^j \hat{\alpha}^j\|. \tag{8}$$

Thereafter, the label value v_t for the target patch p_t is assigned as the class with the minimum reconstruction error over all classes:

$$v_t = \underset{j}{\operatorname{argmin}}(r_j(p_t)), \ \forall j = 1, \ldots, C, \tag{9}$$

where $C = 2$ is the number of classes (subcortical structure or background).

3.2   Discriminative Dictionary Learning for Segmentation

Using all training patches as the dictionary might incorporate noisy information and make the sparse coding process much more time-consuming. In contrast, DDLS learns a compact task-specific dictionary and a classifier for each target

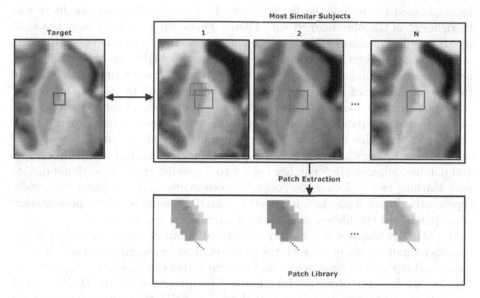

Fig. 1. Creation of the patch library for a given target patch. The red box represents the patch size and the green box corresponds to search window size.

voxel. In our case, the D-KSVD (Eq. 6) is used. In particular, the D-KSVD algorithm uses K-SVD to find the globally optimal solution for all the parameters simultaneously, rewriting Eq. 6 as follows

$$\langle D, W, \alpha \rangle = \arg \min_{D, W, \alpha} \| \begin{pmatrix} P_L \\ \sqrt{\beta} H \end{pmatrix} - \begin{pmatrix} D \\ \sqrt{\beta} W \end{pmatrix} \alpha \|_2 + \eta \| W \|_2 \qquad (10)$$
$$\text{s. t. } \| \alpha \|_0 \leq T.$$

For labeling, since the dictionary is small enough, the sparse representation $\hat{\alpha}_t$ of the target patch is computed using Lasso. The class label vector h_t for the target voxel is estimated by the learned classifier as follows

$$h_t = \hat{W}_t \hat{\alpha}_t. \qquad (11)$$

The index of the largest element in h_t is assigned as the label of the target voxel:

$$v_t = \arg\max_j h_t(j). \qquad (12)$$

3.3 Label Consistent Multiclass Discriminative Dictionary Learning for Segmentation (LC-MDDLS)

In LC-MDDLS, we use a multiclass approach to learn a classifier for all structures simultaneously. Consequently, H will have as many rows as structures to be segmented (including the background). In this way, learned classifiers will be richer than the ones learned with DDLS. Furthermore, DDLS lacks the ability to handle unbalanced libraries (i.e., more patches from one class than another). This problem is important in our case and highly recurrent in voxels near structure boundaries. Consider a target voxel in a structure boundary, due to inter-variability of atlases, extracted patches to create the library might not correspond to the target structure, therefore the patch library might have a higher number of patches belonging to other structures (or background) than the correct one. This imbalance will be transmitted to the learning process producing classifiers with poorer performance. Consider, for instance, a library of 100 patches, where only 5 patches belong to a specific class. Traditional dictionary learning can achieve a good overall reconstruction error without accurately representing these 5 patches; however, LC-MDDLS enforces the representation of all patches in the library as it uses discriminative sparse codes.

LC-MDDLS learns a single discriminative dictionary and a multiclass linear classifier simultaneously for each target voxel. Thence, learned dictionaries will have good representational power, and enforce better discrimination capabilities. Eq. 7 is used as the objective function and, as proposed in [16] D, W, and A are initialized before solving Eq. (7): We use K-SVD to learn an intermediate dictionary D_j for each group of patches in the patch library whose class is j. Then all intermediate dictionaries are combined to initialize D. We assign a label j to each atom in D based on the intermediate dictionary D_j it corresponds to and will remain fixed. On the other hand, W and A are initialized using multivariate ridge regression. The dictionary learning process here is similar to the one used in DDLS, although we need to add the label consistent term into the equation:

$$\langle D, W, \alpha \rangle = \arg\min_{D,W,\alpha} \| \begin{pmatrix} P_L \\ \sqrt{\beta} H \\ \sqrt{\lambda} Q \end{pmatrix} - \begin{pmatrix} D \\ \sqrt{\beta} W \\ \sqrt{\lambda} A \end{pmatrix} \alpha \|_2 \quad \text{s. t. } \|\alpha\|_0 \leq T. \quad (13)$$

After dictionary learning, the labeling procedure remains the same as the one used in DDLS (Eq. 11 and Eq. 12).

4   Experiments

This section is devoted to present the experiments whose objective is to segment the Basal Ganglia, composed of Accumbens, Caudate, Pallidum and Putamen structures.

Dataset. The dataset consists of 35 control subjects and their corresponding segmentations, made public by the MICCAI 2012 challenge[1]. They were all right handed and include 13 males and 22 females. Their ages ranged from 19 to 90

---

[1] https://masi.vuse.vanderbilt.edu/workshop2012

with an average of 32.4 years old. Dataset images consist of a de-faced T1-weighted structural MRI dataset and associated manually labeled volume with one label per voxel.

Evaluation Measure. All the experiments were evaluated by computing the Dice coefficient between a reference A and an automated segmentation B:

$$\kappa(A, B) = \frac{2|A \cap B|}{|A| + |B|} \tag{14}$$

Experimental Settings. For comparison, we consider as baseline methods: (1) the atlas-driven subcortical segmentation method included within the Freesurfer Software Suite[2], (2) SRC and (3) DDLS[3].

To speed up the dictionary learning phase, we have used the same sampling strategy proposed in [8]. Instead of creating a dictionary for each target voxel, dictionaries are created each $n = 3$ voxels. Segmentation of target voxels with no learned dictionary is performed using the dictionaries of the 6 nearest voxels for which we have computed the dictionaries.

Regarding the parameters, we have set $N = 10$, $K = 100$, $S_p = 5 \times 5 \times 5$ and $S_w = 3 \times 3 \times 3$. Using larger patch size or search window size for the whole Basal Ganglia is computationally expensive. Finally, a leave-one-out procedure was used in our validation strategy.

Computational Time. Experiments were carried out using a four core Intel Core i7-2630QM processor at 2.0 GHz with 4 GB of RAM. To segment the Basal Ganglia using SRC, DDLS and LC-MDDLS took around 18, 24, 17 minutes per subject, respectively (excluding the learning step in DDLS and LC-MDDLS).

Results. Table 1 contains the obtained average Dice overlaps for each of the Basal Ganglia structures and the whole Basal Ganglia (last column). As it can be seen, LC-MDDLS outperforms the rest of the methods in all the structures, specially in the Accumbens, being statistically significant with 10% significance level.

SRC and DDLS were used to separately segment each structure of the Basal Ganglia as proposed in [8]. For this reason, they present several important issues with respect to LC-MDDLS, as illustrated in figure 2:

1. SRC produces holes: voxels that lie sufficiently far from the boundary and, thus, clearly belong to the structure at hand are labeled as background. However, DDLS and LC-MDDLS are more robust against this problem because

---

[2] FreeSurfer Software Suite is an open source package for processing and analyzing (human) brain MRI images developed at the Martinos Center for Biomedical Imaging by the Laboratory for Computational Neuroimaging.

[3] SPAMS optimization toolbox (http://spams-devel.gforge.inria.fr) [17] was used in the learning step.

Table 1. Average Dice overlaps for Basal Ganglia structures

	Caudate	Accumbens	Pallidum	Putamen	Basal Ganglia
FS	0.82	0.552	0.741	0.786	0.725
SRC	0.869	0.758	0.828	0.876	0.833
DDLS	0.865	0.744	0.855	0.901	0.841
LC-MDDLS	0.873	0.764	0.866	0.906	0.852

of the intermediate dictionary learning process, where noisy information contained in the library is discarded.

2. Under-segmentations: SRC and DDLS segmentation results are, most of the time, smaller than they should be. This indicates that SRC and DDLS are not that accurate in boundaries, where intensities do change. This problem is also present in LC-MDDLS results, although segmentations are quite better.

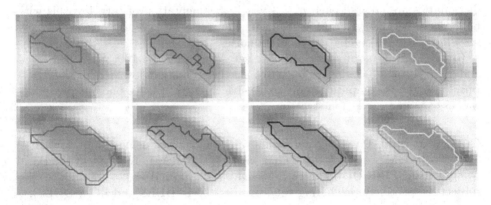

Fig. 2. Segmentation results of Accumbens (top) and Caudate (bottom) structures using (from left to right) FreeSurfer, SRC, DDLS and LC-MDDLS. Ground-truth segmentations are green.

5   Conclusions and Future Work

In this paper, we presented the LC-MDDLS method to perform segmentation of brain MRI subcortical structures. LC-MDDLS extends DDLS to segment multiple structures at the same time and also exploits discriminativeness in sparse codes in order to achieve dictionary atoms specialized in one given class, which can smooth the impact of unbalanced libraries. The evaluation on Basal Ganglia structures segmentation of a public dataset demonstrates the good accuracy and robustness of these methods. Particularly, LC-MDDLS provided the highest overlap compared with FreeSurfer, SRC and DDLS methods.

Although accurate segmentation results were achieved by LC-MDDLS, there are several aspects that may improve its performance. Future research might focus on adapting the dictionary learning procedure to use a weight matrix within the reconstruction loss term to balance the importance of the different classes. Another improvement can be the application of hierarchical dictionary learning techniques to model dependencies between dictionary elements.

References

1. Babalola, K., Patenaude, B., Aljabar, P., Schnabel, J., Kennedy, D., Crum, W., Smith, S., Cootes, T., Jenkinson, M., Rueckert, D.: An evaluation of four automatic methods of segmenting the subcortical structures in the brain. Neuroimage 47(4) (2009)
2. Aljabar, P., Heckemann, R., Hammers, A., Hajnal, J., Rueckert, D.: Multi-atlas based segmentation of brain images: Atlas selection and its effect on accuracy. Neuroimage 46(3), 726–738 (2009)
3. Scherrer, B., Forbes, F., Garbay, C., Dojat, M.: Fully bayesian joint model for MR brain scan tissue, structure segmentation. In: Metaxas, D., Axel, L., Fichtinger, G., Székely, G. (eds.) MICCAI 2008, Part II. LNCS, vol. 5242, pp. 1066–1074. Springer, Heidelberg (2008)
4. Wolz, R., Aljabar, P., Rueckert, D., Heckemann, R., Hammers, A.: Segmentation of subcortical structures and the hippocampus in brain mri using graph-cuts and subject-specific a-priori information. IEEE International Symposium on Biomedical Imaging: From Nano to Macro (ISBI), 470–473 (2009)
5. Rousseau, F., Habas, P., Studholme, C.: A supervised patch-based approach for human brain labeling. IEEE Trans. on MI 30(10) (2011)
6. Coupé, P., Manjón, J., Fonov, V., Pruessner, J., Robles, M., Collins, D.: Patch-based segmentation using expert priors: Application to hippocampus and ventricle segmentation. Neuroimage 54(2), 940–954 (2011)
7. Wang, H., Yushkevich, P.: Dependency prior for multi-atlas label fusion. In: ISBI: From Nano to Macro (ISBI), pp. 892–895 (2012)
8. Tong, T., Wolz, R., Coupé, P., Hajnal, J.V., Rueckert, D.: Segmentation of MR images via discriminative dictionary learning and sparse coding: Application to hippocampus labeling. Neuroimage 76, 11–23 (2013)
9. Elad, M., Aharon, M.: Image denoising via sparse and redundant representations over learned dictionaries. IEEE Trans. on IP 15(12) (2006)
10. Bryt, O., Elad, M.: Compression of facial images using the K-SVD algorithm. IEEE Trans. on IP 19(4) (2008)
11. Tibshirani, R.: Regression shrinkage and selection via the lasso. Journal of the Royal Statistical Society: Series B, 267–288 (1996)
12. Zou, H., Hastie, T.: Regularization and variable selection via the elastic net. Journal of the Royal Statistical Society: Series B 67(2), 301–320 (2005)
13. Engan, K., Aase, S.O., Husoy, J.H.: Frame based signal compression using method of optimal directions (MOD). IEEE Intern. Symp. Circ. Syst. (1999)
14. Aharon, M., Elad, M., Bruckstein, A.M.: The K-SVD: An algorithm for designing of overcomplete dictionaries for sparse representations. IEEE Trans. SP 54(11) (2006)
15. Zhang, Q., Li, B.: Discriminative K-SVD for dictionary learning in face recognition. In: CVPR, pp. 2691–2698 (2010)
16. Jiang, Z., Lin, Z., Davis, L.: Learning a discriminative dictionary for sparse coding via label consistent k-svd. In: CVPR, pp. 1697–1704 (2011)
17. Mairal, J., Bach, F., Ponce, J., Sapiro, G.: Online Dictionary Learning for Sparse Coding. In: International Conference on Machine Learning, Montreal, Canada (2009)

Real-Time Hand-Painted Graphics for Mobile Games

Fabian Di Fiore[1], Tom Schaessens[1], Robin Marx[2],
Frank Van Reeth[1], and Eddy Flerackers[1]

[1] Hasselt University - tUL - iMinds, Expertise Centre for Digital Media
Wetenschapspark 2 BE-3590 Diepenbeek, Belgium
{fabian.difiore,frank.vanreeth,eddy.flerackers}@uhasselt.be
http://www.edm.uhasselt.be
[2] LuGus Studios C-Mine (Crib) 12 BE-3600 Genk,
Belgium
robin@lugus-studios
http://www.lugus-studios.be

Abstract. In this paper we set out to find a digital painting technique which allows the recreation of scenes from childrens books or graphic novels for usage in mobile games. The idea is to give the impression that scenes are being hand-painted at the moment the player is moving through them.

To this end, we propose a technique for digital painting, *mesh-based strokes*, that combines the strengths of existing painting techniques while keeping the limitations of mobile devices in mind. In this new technique, instead of representing strokes as pixels in a raster, strokes are created as flat meshes following the contour of a brush stroke. Furthermore, in close cooperation with artists digital painting and animation tools are introduced to facilitate the creation of new digital brushes and scenes in order to capture the style from children's books. In this paper, the Bo childrens book series is used as a case study [1].

We believe our system is effective in terms of ease-of-use, performs better on mobile hardware than traditional techniques and offers a new fresh perspective on stylised animation in mobile games.

Keywords: Computer Animation, Painterly Animation, Mobile Games.

1 Introduction

Motivation. There are many picture books and graphic novels with very dynamic and interesting styles. When digitising these books, for animations or games, backgrounds and scenes are often represented as images that appear instantaneously or fade-in in some way. The entertainment industry, however, is always in demand for alternatives to the often used collage style of these games.

Scenes themselves, for instance, could be employed to support the progression of the story: as the player continues, more and more is revealed. Therefore, we will investigate the interesting possibilities that come to mind if scenes could be recreated in the same way the artist made them (e.g., line by line, stroke by

F.J. Perales and J. Santos-Victor (Eds.): AMDO 2014, LNCS 8563, pp. 148–159, 2014.
© Springer International Publishing Switzerland 2014

stroke). In addition, even though mobile devices are becoming faster and more powerful, there is still a big performance difference compared to PCs. This is mainly due to the fact that mobile devices often have to operate on battery power, which means that low power usage is a priority which in turn comes at the cost of performance. Hence, we will need to pinpoint the main differences between mobile and PC architectures, and use this knowledge to optimise our implementation.

It is also our objective to allow the user to interactively create visually pleasing animations while keeping him/her in full control of the animation process. This is typically the case for smaller-scale productions where animators have to find their way more independently.

Contribution. In this paper we present a system to simulate hand-painted graphics in real-time. Our method allows for animated recreation of scenes and provides sufficient performance to be run on mobile devices. Along with the method of simulation, tools are developed to allow artists to quickly and intuitively create and animate scenes.

These tools will be integrated in the Unity3D game engine [2] which will be used in the creation of the Bo game.

Primarily our system features following characteristics:

- allowing traditional hand-painted strokes to be generated digitally;
- capturing the way an artist creates his picture books;
- animated recreation of captured scenes;
- optimisation for mobile devices;
- integration in existing engine (Unity3D)

The pictures in the inset (Figure 1) show an actual scenes from the Bo books as well as snapshots from the game created using our technique.

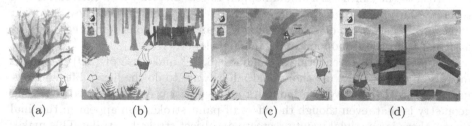

(a)   (b)   (c)   (d)

Fig. 1. a) Actual scene from the Bo books. b–d) Snapshots from our mobile game

Approach. As a case-study the visual style of Bo will be recreated [1]. Bo is a childrens book series featuring Bo, a transparent piglet, as the main character (see Figure 1(a)). The books are aimed at children between the ages of 4 and 6, and teach them how to deal with emotions, such as love, fear and anger. Throughout the books multiple traditional painting techniques are combined; Bo is drawn with a marker, backgrounds are painted abstractly with a paint roller, foreground elements are created using stencils and animals are often detailed watercolour paintings. This multitude of techniques makes Bo an ideal case-study.

In Section 2 existing techniques for digital painting will be analysed, and their feasibility within a mobile game determined. We will also look at common mobile hardware and its limitations. In Section 3 we propose a new digital painting technique, *mesh-based strokes*, based on the strengths and weaknesses of existing techniques. We will also elaborate on the digital copies of the brushes used in the Bo books and create the tools needed to let artists use these digital brushes. Next, we discuss how to animate the creation of strokes, and integrate this in a tool. In Section 4 we look at the results of our implementation. We compare the visual results, benchmark scenes created with the tool and analyse the usability of the tools themselves. Finally, Section 5 is our concluding section in which we also set the context for future work.

2   Related Work

In this section we discuss different methods for creating digital strokes. We will analyse the strengths and weaknesses in the light of real-time game performance and look at the software and hardware that will be used in the implementation of our proposed technique, to get a clearer image of pitfalls that might be faced.

Hand-Painted Look. A hand-painted look typically is achieved through *physical simulation, non-photorealistic rendering (NPR)* or *raster graphics.*

Regarding physically simulating the inner workings of paint, a great advantage of these techniques is that often the results are barely distinguishable from reality [3,4,5]. Also, since the techniques are simulating all the paint interactions from the brush to the canvas as it would happen in real life, they lend themselves well to create an animated recreation of a scene. This physical accuracy, however, comes at a cost. Most of these techniques can not be considered real-time, at least not from the standpoint of a game developer.

Non-photorealistic rendering techniques [6,7,8] make use of (3D) geometric models and, hence, can use the graphics hardware to do the heavy lifting allowing to run real-time, even on modern mobile devices. A downside to rendering geometry is that, even though the effect of paint strokes can appear in the final image, there is no trivial way to recreate an object stroke by stroke. This makes an animated recreation much more difficult.

Images can also be created and edited using raster-based image editors [9,10,11]. These rely heavily on writing and reading pixels and support multiple layers that can blend with one another using various blending modes. A clear benefit of raster graphics techniques is the real-time visualisation of what the artist is painting, in the same way as it will appear in the final image. However, they do lack the accuracy of physical simulation as there is no flow of medium, or movement of pigment particles.

Mobile GPU Performance. Since our system will be implemented on mobile devices, more specifically the iPad2, its crucial to get a clear understanding of the capabilities and limitations of the hardware. All of the iPad devices, as well as many other tablets and smartphones use the PowerVR graphics architecture [12].

The PowerVR architecture deviates from standard immediate mode rendering (IMR) graphics hardware in the way that it uses tile-based deferred rendering (TBDR) as a method of 3D rendering. The core design principle behind the TBDR architecture is to reduce the system memory bandwidth required by the GPU to a minimum, as transfer of data between system memory and GPU is one of the biggest causes of GPU power consumption. This makes TBDR-based architectures very interesting for mobile devices.

3   Approach

In this section we will focus mainly on recreating the visual style of Bo, as a case-study, even though the results of our technique can be used to simulate many different painting techniques.

The goal of recreating the visual style of Bo is not the physically accurate recreation of scenes rather than recreating the global appearance of the books, and doing so as if the scene was drawn live.

3.1   Mesh-Based Strokes

Following our discussion on achieving a hand-painted look (see Section 2), raster based graphics seems to be the best option as it allows for animated recreation of a scene, elements within a scene can change position — given that they are on a separate layer — and the artist is given a lot of freedom and control in the final result.

Benchmarking tests indicated that the combination of the ARM and PowerVR architectures is not very efficient at write-to-texture operations. Therefore, to combine the best of both worlds, we introduce *mesh-based strokes* which is a combination of NPR and raster graphics. In this new technique, instead of representing strokes as pixels in a raster, strokes are created as flat meshes following the contour of a brush stroke. This allows the same stroke-by-stroke creation as raster graphics or physical simulation. Creating the colour of the strokes is done through a GPU shader program, similar to the techniques used in NPR.

This allows us to exchange the slow write-to-texture operations with fast rendering of meshes on the GPU, while still allowing a stroke-by-stroke recreation. So we maintain the performance benefits of both NPR, and the stroke-by-stroke animatability of raster graphics.

3.2   Creating a Hand-Painted Look

Introduction to the Visual Style of Bo. The Bo childrens book series has a distinct graphical style. We identified several main characteristics to this style.

A *rubber paint roller* is used mainly for background elements such as the sky, the ground and foliage, setting the global atmosphere for each image (Figure 2(a)). To add more details to the scene, *paper cut stencils* are used, and brushed over using the paint roller (Figure 2(b)). All animals and insects in the Bo books are drawn realistically. They are painted separately, scanned and added into the final image using image processing software. Most other elements in the scenes are transparent (e.g., trees show through foliage and foreground objects blend with the background). In the final composition, the artist plays around with different layer blending modes, until the wanted result is achieved (see Figure 2(c)).

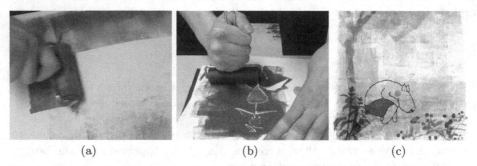

(a)   (b)   (c)

Fig. 2. Visual style of Bo. a) Rubber paint roller. b) Rolling the roller over a stencil. c) Final composition showing the blending of transparent elements.

Creating a Base Stroke. First, when drawing a stroke, a list of input points is sampled together with pressure sensitive (used to determine the width) and tilting data. The boundaries of these so-called brush footprints are then used to create the geometric mesh. Note that we do not use all the input samples directly as it would create a mesh with too many subdivisions. To prevent this, a minimum threshold distance is set between adjacent points.

One of the most clear characteristics of brushes is the fact that they contain a limited supply of paint. Hence, over time a brush stroke will fade out. Conceptually it seems easy to create a stroke that fades out over the length of a mesh by simply increasing the transparency gradually. However, as a shader has no context, it does not know if its drawing at the start or end of a stroke. Our solution lies in the usage of *uv*-coordinates: by adding a length-parameter as an additional *uv*-coordinate, fading out the stroke becomes possible.

The resulting mesh contains enough information to allow a shader to simulate common characteristics of brushes. The mesh itself allows to move back and forth, as one would with a brush or a paint roller, and the length-parameter gives the shader information about how far along a mesh it is painting allowing strokes to fade out.

Rubber Paint Roller. The fading of the roller strokes is implemented as a linear interpolation of the alpha value, according to the length-parameter set in the stroke mesh. In order to give the artist more freedom, two more parameters

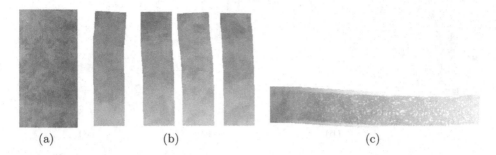

(a)   (b)   (c)

Fig. 3. Rubber Paint Roller. a) Image of a wide paint roller. b) Multiple differently coloured strokes using the same paint roller. c) Image showing the dried pattern within a brush stroke.

are introduced. *Fade offset* allows the stroke to be more transparent when beginning to draw whereas *fade multiplier* allows control over the speed at which a stroke fades out. Using these two parameters, a transparent, slowly fading stroke can be created that is very suitable for backgrounds, where individual strokes must not stand out. A thick, more opaque roller can be created for creating more prominent features of a scene.

As each stroke of the roller is unique, paint should never appear on the canvas in exactly the same way. Due to the way paint is applied to the physical roller, namely two or more dollops of paint next to each other through which the roller is rolled, there are three general blends of paint: (i) mostly one colour, with traces of the other, (ii) an even blend of both, or (iii) mostly the other colour with traces of the first. Figure 3 illustrates this by means of a very wide paint roller. When rolled through two dollops of paint, each side of the roller will have the colour of the paint that was most to its side, while the centre will have a patchy blend of both colours (Figure 3(a)). To create unique strokes each time using the same roller, for each stroke only a single narrow band is selected from the wide roller (Figure 3(b)).

Another feature is that when rolling back and forth in a fanning pattern, a pattern of white dots is created. This is due to the relief created by the paint itself as thin layers of dried paint on the surface of the roller prevent paint in between from touching the paper. To simulate this effect, we employ a black and white mask: white representing spots where the paint should adhere, black where it doesn't. This mask is added as a texture to the shader and multiplied with the transparency value (Figure 3(c)).

Other Brushes. Since the mesh which serves as a base for the brush strokes was created to be reusable, some other brushes were created as well. Here again, the brushes are based on brushes often found in the Bo books.

The *grass brush* creates the effect of individual blades of grass (Figure 4(a)). It is achieved by ripping of a corner of paper, dipping this in paint and quickly dragging it over the canvas. To simulate the effect of this brush, a mask was

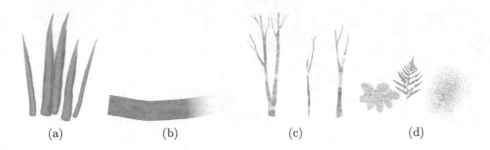

(a)   (b)   (c)   (d)

Fig. 4. Different kinds of brushes. a) Grass brush. b) Oily brush. c) Example of a stroke using the stencil roller brush with a birch tree stencil. d) Stamp brushes with various different masks.

applied and stretched over the entire length of a stroke based on the length-parameter from the mesh. This mask has a transparent inside and a defined outside similar to that of the real strokes. By stretching the mask over the length of the stroke, different sizes of grass can be created with the same shader.

The *oily brush* is a brush that was used in one of the Bo books to create the effect of thick grass. The brush clearly has visible brush fibres in the strokes and starts packed with thick paint. As pressure on the brush lessens, the brush becomes more transparent and grainy, until only the longest fibres are touching the paper. The stroke ends in only a few fibres still touching (Figure 4(b)). Two adjustable parameters were introduced: the (i) percentage to graininess to determine at which percentage of the stroke the thick paint ends and the graininess of the stroke becomes clear, and (ii) the percentage to fade to determine at which remaining percentage the stroke fades out to just a few brush fibres.

The *stencil roller* is a variation on the original paint roller to create the effect of rolling over a stencil (Figure 4(c)). The stencil is applied to the canvas and held in place while the paint roller is applied. The inside of the stencil has the same characteristics as the paint roller. The outside of the stencil has a double border: one as the hight of the stencils paper prevents the roller from reaching the canvas and another where the fibres on the edge of the stencil absorbed paint. To achieve this effect, a world-space mask was created, stating where paint from the roller could be seen, and where it couldn't. An extra texture in the paint roller shader serves as this mask. To achieve the same effect as a real stencil, the transparency value of the paint roller is changed according to the value of the stencil. Whenever the stencil is black, the alpha is kept as it is, whenever the stencil is white, the alpha is set to 0.

Stamps are the only types of brushes that do not use the same mesh as the paint roller, since stamps are not drawn as strokes but placed at once. Because of this, stamps are created by simply generating a quad mesh. To this mesh, a shader is added with a black and white mask; this masks shows the colour of the stamp where the colour is white, and is transparent where the colour is black. This allows any shape of stamp to be made, ranging form a sponge-like pattern to detailed leaves (Figure 4(d)).

3.3   Content Creation Pipeline Toolset

In order to allow the artist to create scenes, a toolset consisting of 2 separate tools was made: the brush editor and the animation tool.

Brush Editor. The brush editor allows artists to manage brushes. Brushes in this case are simply the collection of a shader and all of their parameters and textures.

For each scene the artist is restricted to one set of brushes. This is to ensure that the amount of different shaders used in a scene remains low, which optimises the amount of batched draw calls. A set of brushes can be used for multiple scenes. In the brush editor the artist can create new sets of brushes, as well as update previously created sets. A preview canvas is provided to test out new brushes, and to see how different brushes match together. There is also a simplified version of the painting controls from the animation tool, allowing the artist to set the length and width of strokes in order to preview those modifications accurately.

A simple editing screen is provided to change settings for the brush. These settings are a more user-friendly representation of the parameters used in the shaders. Here the artist can also select which textures to use. A screenshot of the Editor tool can be seen in Figure 5(a).

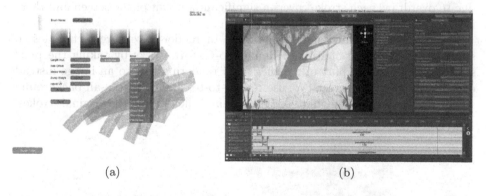

(a)   (b)

Fig. 5. a) Screenshot of the Bo brush editor tool. Here the settings for a roller brush are edited. b) Screenshot of the Bo animation tool.

Animation Tool. The animation tool allows the artist to draw scenes and animate the way in which they appear (Figure 5(b)).

The first step when beginning to create a scene is to load a set of brushes. Often brushes are themed to a certain setting, e.g., an autumn forest or a birch tree forest. Once brushes are loaded, the artist can select which brush to use, set the length and width for a stroke, and start painting. While painting, positions of points within the strokes are saved. This allows to recreate a stroke exactly as it was drawn. Besides this, the settings at the moment of drawing are saved. These settings include the selected brush, as well as the width and length for the stroke.

Another part of the tool is the animation timeline for which we used a free open-source timeline for Unity3D [13]. Strokes are given the ability to be added to the timeline. When added, a variable *percentageToDraw*, ranging from zero to one, can be modified through key frames. Each time the percentage to draw variable is altered, a new mesh, of which the length is that percentage of its total length, is generated. This allows the artist to make the stroke appear when and how he wants.

Recording functionality is also integrated in the tool. By default, each new stroke starts one frame after the previous one has ended. Afterwards the artist can fine-tune the effect by moving around key frames in the timeline.

4   Results

In this section we look at some of the scenes created using our mesh-based strokes technique. Figure 6 shows some actual scenes from the Bo books while in Figure 7 final snapshots of the Bo game can be seen.

On average, each scene contains 4500 vertices and 2400 triangles. Initially, running on an iPad2, the performance was quite low: the frame rate dropped quickly below 30 fps ending up at around 5 fps. This drop in frame rate is mainly due to overdraw: each stroke covers a significant amount of the screen and there is much overlap of strokes.

As a result, we examined the influence of render-to-texture techniques to speed up the drawing of strokes. Render-to-texture works by taking the pixel seen through the viewport of a camera and rendering this to an image instead of rendering it to the screen. We use render-to-texture to flatten all background strokes by rendering them all to one texture and then hiding the original strokes.

Fig. 6. Some actual scenes from the Bo books

Fig. 7. Snapshots from the game created using our technique

This ensures that instead of numerous overlapping transparent strokes, only one opaque background has to be rendered. This greatly improves performance yielding a consistent frame rate of 60 fps, even when animating.

Also, due to delegating most of the heavy lifting to the GPU, the CPU is still available to handle the game logic.

5   Conclusion and Future Work

In this paper we presented a digital painting technique which allows the recreation of scenes from childrens books or graphic novels for usage in mobile games.

Our technique allows a very flexible animation of strokes. This combined with our editing and animation tools gives the artist complete control over the animation of a scene. Through continuous optimisation of our techniques, we manage to stay well above the lowest acceptable frame rate of 30 fps making it run smoothly on mobile devices.

Comparing our results to the original images of the case study, we can conclude that our brushes and results resemble those of the original closely.

5.1   Discussion

One of the main issues with the tool at this time is the inability to use Unity3Ds undo functionality. At this point, it is not possible to detect an undo event consistently within Unity3D as the event is only sent to windows that have focus at the time of undoing. Since the drawing canvas is separate from the rest of the tool, no undo event is registered when drawing. This problem is partially omitted by providing custom undo and redo buttons with the required additional functionality.

Another disadvantage is that the artists have less creative freedom than when using off-the-shelf digital tools. Our tool, however, provides enough functionality to create scenes without any additional bells and whistles.

5.2   Future Work

A first possible improvement is broadening the amount of different brushes that can be simulated. There are many more styles to explore that can be recreated using the techniques from this paper including a multitude of other childrens books, as well as many graphic novels.

Improvements to the dynamic creation of the mesh can also be made. The current version works by generating a subdivision at certain distance intervals, this could be changed to a technique that bases subdivisions on the amount of curvature of a stroke. This would drastically lower the amount of geometry when drawing straight lines and create much smoother curves.

There is also still room for improvement in the brush creation and animation tools such as a movieclip system allowing the reuse of small animations.

Acknowledgements. We gratefully express our gratitude to the European Fund for Regional Development (ERDF) and the Flemish Government, which are kindly funding part of the research at the Expertise Centre for Digital Media.

References

1. Bo, V.: World Wide Web (2014), http://www.varkentjebo.net/
2. Unity3D. World Wide Web (2014), http://www.unity3d.com/
3. Curtis, C.J., Anderson, S.E., Seims, J.E., Fleischer, K.W., Salesin, D.H.: Computer-generated watercolor. In: Bo, V. (ed.) Proceedings of the 24th Annual Conference on Computer Graphics and Interactive Techniques, SIGGRAPH 1997, pp. 421–430. ACM Press/Addison-Wesley Publishing Co., New York, (1997)

4. Baxter, W.V., Wendt, J., Lin, M.C.: IMPaSTo: A realistic model for paint. In: Proc. of Symposium on Non-Photorealistic Animation and Rendering (NPAR), pp. 45–56 (June 2004)
5. Laerhoven, T.V., Reeth, F.V.: Real-time simulation of watery paint. Computer Animation and Virtual Worlds, 429–439 (2005)
6. Claes, J., Fiore, F.D., Vansichem, G., van Reeth, F.: Fast 3D cartoon rendering with improved quality by exploiting graphics hardware. In: Proceedings of Image and Vision Computing New Zealand (IVCNZ 2001), pp. 13–18. IVCNZ (November 2001)
7. Gooch, B., Gooch, A.A.: Non-Photorealistic Rendering. A. K. Peters Ltd., (2001) ISBN: 1568811330
8. Lei, S.I.E., Chang, C.-F.: Real-time rendering of watercolor effects for virtual environments. In: Aizawa, K., Nakamura, Y., Satoh, S. (eds.) PCM 2004. LNCS, vol. 3333, pp. 474–481. Springer, Heidelberg (2004)
9. GIMP. World Wide Web (2014), http://www.gimp.org/
10. Corel Painter. World Wide Web (2014), http://www.corel.com/corel/
11. Adobe Photoshop. World Wide Web (2014), http://www.photoshop.com/
12. Imagination Technologies. Powervr series5 graphics sgx architecture guide for developers (2011)
13. Adobe Photoshop. World Wide Web (2014), http://forum.unity3d.com/threads/135982-Animator-The-Ultimate-Timeline-Cutscene-Editor-for-Unity

Non-rigid Object Segmentation Using Robust Active Shape Models

Carlos Santiago*, Jacinto C. Nascimento, and Jorge S. Marques

ISR, Instituto Superior Técnico
Lisbon, Portugal
carlos.santiago@ist.utl.pt

Abstract. Statistical shape models have been extensively used in several image analysis problems, providing accurate estimates of object boundaries. However, their performance degrades if the object of interest is surrounded by a cluttered background, and the features extracted from the image contain outliers. Under these assumptions, most deformable models fail since they are attracted towards the outliers, leading to poor shape estimates. This paper proposes a *robust Active Shape Model*, based on a sensor model that takes into account both valid and invalid observations. A weight (*confidence degree*) is assigned to each observation. All the observations contribute to the estimation of the object boundary but with different weights. The estimation process is recursively performed by the Expectation-Maximization method and the weights are updated in each iteration. The algorithm was tested in ultrasound images of the left ventricle and compared with the output of classic Active Shape Models. The proposed algorithm performs significantly better.

1 Introduction

The segmentation of human organs in medical images is a challenging problem that has been addressed in several ways. Deformable models are amongst the most popular approaches since they separate geometric modeling of the contour from the visual features of the organ and background. Active Shape Models (ASMs) proposed in [1] are especially interesting since the shape model is trained from annotated data and the model learns not only the average shape of the object but also its deformation modes. This information is conveyed in a Gaussian prior that improves contour estimates and avoids unusual shapes.

Active Shape Models have been improved with respect to the way information is extracted from the image, trying to obtain more reliable features [2–7]. However, if the model is initialized far from the object contour and if the background is textured, a high number of outliers may be observed, attracting the elastic contour towards erroneous configurations. The performance of ASMs is therefore

---

* This work was supported in part by the FCT project [PEst-OE/EEI/LA0009/2013], by project "HEARTRACK"- PTDC/EEA-CRO/103462/2008 and under the FCT scholarship SFRH/BD/87347/2012.

F.J. Perales and J. Santos-Victor (Eds.): AMDO 2014, LNCS 8563, pp. 160–169, 2014.

hampered by invalid features since the model is not robust in the presence of outliers

Few works tried to address the robustness of ASMs. One notable exception is the work of Rogers et al. [8], which tries to overcome this problem by using a random sampling consensus method, RANSAC [9]. Another contribution to improve robustness was proposed by Nahed et al. [10] based on Robust Point Matching (RPM)[11] which tries to solve the matching problem between model points and observation points detected in the image. This algorithm is able to discard the observations considered as outliers in the matching process.

In this paper, we propose an alternative approach to estimate the ASM parameters in cluttered images. We explicitly assume that the feature points detected in the image contain outliers which do not belong to the object boundary. Each observation is associated to a binary label (valid/invalid) which is unknown; different sensor models are adopted to describe valid data and outliers. The estimation of the model parameters (global motion and shape deformation) in the presence of unobserved variables (binary labels) is carried out by the Expectation-Maximization method. The method developed in this paper is inspired in the work presented in [12] to improve the robustness of the snake algorithm. Experiments with ultrasound sequences of the heart show that the proposed method performs better that classic ASM in these experiments.

The remainder of this paper is organized as follows: Section 2 describes the problem and the proposed model; Section 3 describes parameter estimation by the Expectation-Maximization method; the application to ultrasound images of the heart is described in Section 4; and Section 5 concludes the paper.

2   Problem Formulation

Active Shape Models (ASM) [1] try to approximate the boundary of objects in images by sequences of 2D points (landmarks), $\mathbf{x} = (\mathbf{x}^1, \ldots, \mathbf{x}^N)$ with $\mathbf{x}^i \in \mathbb{R}^2$. Since the model is very flexible, a probabilistic model is adopted to constrain the set of admissible shapes. The 2D points are considered as a realization of random variables with joint Gaussian distribution, characterized by an average shape, $\bar{\mathbf{x}}$, and by a covariance matrix, $\mathbf{R}$. The covariance matrix defines the deformation modes that can be obtained by principal component analysis (PCA) $\mathbf{R} = \mathbf{W}\Lambda\mathbf{W}^T$ where $\mathbf{W}$ is a matrix of eigenvectors and Λ is a diagonal matrix of eigenvalues, λ_k. The average shape and the deformation modes are estimated in a two-stage training process involving [1]: (i) alignment of all training shapes and (ii) Principal Component Analysis (PCA).

This leads to a generative shape model in which the object contour is randomly generated by

$$\mathbf{x} \simeq \bar{\mathbf{x}} + \mathbf{D}\mathbf{b} , \tag{1}$$

where $\mathbf{D} \in \mathbb{R}^{2N \times K}$ is a matrix with K main deformation modes extracted from $\mathbf{W}$, and $\mathbf{b} \in \mathbb{R}^K$ is a Gaussian vector of coefficients (local deformation).

In addition, the contour undergoes a geometric transformation $\mathbf{T}_\theta$ (Euclidean similarity): each contour point is transformed by

$$\tilde{\mathbf{x}}^i = \mathbf{T}_\theta(\mathbf{x}^i) = \mathbf{A}(\bar{\mathbf{x}}^i + \mathbf{D}^i\mathbf{b}) + \mathbf{t} \ , \tag{2}$$

where $\mathbf{D}^i \in \mathbb{R}^{2 \times K}$ is the mode deformation matrix associated to the $i - th$ landmark and $\theta = (\mathbf{A}, \mathbf{t})$ are the transformation parameters (global motion).

When we wish to estimate the boundary of an object in a test image, an initial contour, $\tilde{\mathbf{x}} = (\tilde{\mathbf{x}}^1, \ldots, \tilde{\mathbf{x}}^N)$, is required to initiate the estimation process. Then, we search for edges (intensity transitions) along search lines orthogonal to the contour at each model point $\tilde{\mathbf{x}}^i$. Edge detection is performed along each line providing a set of edge points $\mathbf{Y}^i = \{\mathbf{y}^{ij}, j = 1, \ldots, M^i\}$. Multiple edges are detected in each line and many of them are outliers. Therefore, a binary label $k^{ij} \in \{0, 1\}$ is assigned to each edge point. We define $k^{ij} = 1$, if $\mathbf{y}^{ij}$ is a valid observation and $k^{ij} = 0$, otherwise. The probabilities of invalid and valid data $p_0 = P(k^{ij} = 0), p_1 = P(k^{ij} = 1)$ need to be estimated. Therefore, the model parameters comprise: global transformation parameters, local deformation parameters and the sensor probabilities $\psi = (\theta, \mathbf{b}, \mathbf{p})$, with $\mathbf{p} = (p_0, p_1)$.

Two sensor models will be considered. If an observation $\mathbf{y}^{ij}$ is valid ($k^{ij} = 1$), we assume that

$$\mathbf{y}^{ij} = \tilde{\mathbf{x}}^i + \mathbf{v}^i = \mathbf{A}(\bar{\mathbf{x}}^i + \mathbf{D}^i\mathbf{b}) + \mathbf{t} + \mathbf{v}^i \tag{3}$$

where $\mathbf{v}^i \sim \mathcal{N}(\mathbf{0}, \sigma^{i^2}\mathbf{I})$ is a Gaussian random variable with zero mean and variance $(\sigma^i)^2\mathbf{I}$, estimated from the training set. Therefore,

$$p\left(\mathbf{y}^{ij}\big|k^{ij}{=}1\right) = \mathcal{N}\left(\mathbf{y}^{ij}; \mathbf{A}(\bar{\mathbf{x}}^i + \mathbf{D}^i\mathbf{b}) + \mathbf{t}, (\sigma^i)^2\mathbf{I}\right). \tag{4}$$

If the observation $\mathbf{y}^{ij}$ is invalid ($k^{ij} = 0$), we assume it follows a uniform distribution $\mathcal{U}(V_{\tilde{\mathbf{x}}^i})$ within a validation gate $V_{\tilde{\mathbf{x}}^i}$ in the vicinity of $\tilde{\mathbf{x}}^i$, i.e. $p\left(\mathbf{y}^{ij}\big|k^{ij}{=}0\right) = \mathcal{U}(V_{\mathbf{x}^i})$.

These sensor models allow us to write a generative model for the observed data. Let $\mathbf{Y} = \{\mathbf{y}^{ij}\}$ be the set of all observations and $\mathbf{K} = \{k^{ij}\}$ the hidden labels. Assuming conditional independence, the complete likelihood function is given by

$$p(\mathbf{Y}, \mathbf{K}|\psi) = \prod_{i=1}^{N} \prod_{j=1}^{M^i} p(\mathbf{y}^{ij}|k^{ij}\psi)p(k^{ij}) \ . \tag{5}$$

The likelihood function $p(\mathbf{Y}|\psi)$ is obtained by marginalizing $p(\mathbf{Y}, \mathbf{K}|\psi)$ with respect to the hidden variables $\mathbf{K}$, leading to

$$p(\mathbf{Y}|\psi) = \sum_{\mathbf{K}} p(\mathbf{Y}, \mathbf{K}|\psi) \ . \tag{6}$$

This marginalization step is unfeasible in practice since the number of configurations of the variables $\mathbf{K}$ grows exponentially with the number of unknown labels. A direct estimation of the model parameters ψ by the Maximum Likelihood Method is unfeasible. Fortunately, this difficulty can be solved by using the Expectation-Maximization method.

3   Expectation Maximization Framework

Instead of maximizing the likelihood function (6), we use the Expectation-Maximization (EM) method [13]. The EM method computes an auxiliary function $Q(.,.)$ (E-step) and updates the parameter estimates $\widehat{\psi}$ by maximizing the auxiliary function (M-step). These two steps are repeated until convergence is achieved.

3.1   E-step

The auxiliary function $Q(.,.)$ is defined as the expected value of the complete log-likelihood function, given the observations $\mathbf{Y}$ and the most recent estimates of the parameters $\widehat{\psi}$

$$Q\left(\psi,\widehat{\psi}\right) = \mathbb{E}_{\mathbf{K}}\left[\log p\left(\mathbf{Y},\mathbf{K}|\psi\right)\middle|\mathbf{Y},\widehat{\psi}\right] \ . \tag{7}$$

The log-likelihood function is given by (see (5))

$$\log p\left(\mathbf{Y},\mathbf{K}|\psi\right) = \sum_{i=1}^{N}\sum_{j=1}^{M_i}\log p\left(\mathbf{y}^{ij}|k^{ij},\psi\right) + \log p\left(k^{ij}\right) .$$

Therefore,

$$Q\left(\psi,\widehat{\psi}\right) = \sum_{i=1}^{N}\sum_{j=1}^{M_i} w_0^{ij}\left[\log p\left(\mathbf{y}^{ij}|k^{ij}{=}0,\psi\right) + \log p_0\right]$$
$$+ w_1^{ij}\left[\log p\left(\mathbf{y}^{ij}|k^{ij}{=}1,\psi\right) + \log p_1\right], \tag{8}$$

with

$$w_1^{ij} = p\left(k^{ij}{=}1\middle|\mathbf{y}^{ij},\widehat{\psi}\right) \propto \widehat{p}_1\ \mathcal{N}\left(\mathbf{y}^{ij};\mathbf{T}_{\widehat{\theta}}(\bar{\mathbf{x}}^i + \mathbf{D}^i\widehat{\mathbf{b}}),\sigma^{i^2}\mathbf{I}\right) \tag{9}$$

and $w_0^{ij} = p\left(k^{ij}{=}0|\mathbf{y}^{ij}\right) = \widehat{p}_0\ \mathcal{U}\left(V_{\mathbf{x}^i}\right)$ such that $w_0^{ij} + w_1^{ij} = 1$. These weights correspond to the probability of the observation being a valid observation or an outlier.

3.2   M-step

Let us assume that the most recent estimates of the unknown parameters in iteration $t-1$ are given by $\widehat{\psi}(t-1)$. Parameter update is achieved by solving the following optimization problem

$$\widehat{\psi}(t) = \arg\max_{\psi}\ Q(\psi,\widehat{\psi}(t-1)) \tag{10}$$

The maximization with respect to $\psi = (\boldsymbol{\theta}, \mathbf{b}, \mathbf{p})$ is performed in three steps that will be described in the sequel.

Estimation of $\boldsymbol{\theta}$: First we optimize the auxiliary function $Q(.,.)$ with respect to $\mathbf{A} = \begin{bmatrix} a_1 & -a_2 \\ a_2 & a_1 \end{bmatrix}, \mathbf{t} = \begin{bmatrix} t_1 \\ t_2 \end{bmatrix}$. The optimization can be analytically done and leads to a linear system of equations

$$\begin{pmatrix} X_1 & -X_2 & W & 0 \\ X_2 & X_1 & 0 & W \\ Z & 0 & X_1 & X_2 \\ 0 & Z & -X_2 & X_1 \end{pmatrix} \begin{pmatrix} \widehat{a}_1(t) \\ \widehat{a}_2(t) \\ \widehat{t}_1(t) \\ \widehat{t}_2(t) \end{pmatrix} = \begin{pmatrix} Y_1 \\ Y_2 \\ C_1 \\ C_2 \end{pmatrix}, \tag{11}$$

where

$$X_1 = \sum_{i=1}^{N} \sum_{j=1}^{M_i} \frac{w_1^{ij}}{\sigma^{i2}} x_1^i \qquad Z = \sum_{i=1}^{N} \sum_{j=1}^{M_i} \frac{w_1^{ij}}{\sigma^{i2}} (x_1^{i\,2} + x_2^{i\,2})$$

$$X_2 = \sum_{i=1}^{N} \sum_{j=1}^{M_i} \frac{w_1^{ij}}{\sigma^{i2}} x_2^i \qquad W = \sum_{i=1}^{N} \sum_{j=1}^{M_i} \frac{w_1^{ij}}{\sigma^{i2}}$$

$$Y_1 = \sum_{i=1}^{N} \sum_{j=1}^{M_i} \frac{w_1^{ij}}{\sigma^{i2}} y_1^{ij} \qquad C_1 = \sum_{i=1}^{N} \sum_{j=1}^{M_i} \frac{w_1^{ij}}{\sigma^{i2}} (x_1^i y_1^{ij} + x_2^i y_2^{ij})$$

$$Y_2 = \sum_{i=1}^{N} \sum_{j=1}^{M_i} \frac{w_1^{ij}}{\sigma^{i2}} y_2^{ij} \qquad C_2 = \sum_{i=1}^{N} \sum_{j=1}^{M_i} \frac{w_1^{ij}}{\sigma^{i2}} (x_1^i y_2^{ij} - x_2^i y_1^{ij}) \ .$$

Estimation of $\mathbf{b}$: To update the deformation parameters, we maximize $Q(.,.)$ with respect to $\mathbf{b}$. This leads again to a linear system of equations

$$\left(\sum_{i=1}^{N} \sum_{j=1}^{M_i} \frac{w_1^{ij}}{\sigma^{i2}} \mathbf{D}^{i\top} \widehat{\mathbf{A}}^\top \widehat{\mathbf{A}} \mathbf{D}^i \right) \widehat{\mathbf{b}}(t) = \left(\sum_{i=1}^{N} \sum_{j=1}^{M_i} \frac{w_1^{ij}}{\sigma^{i2}} \mathbf{D}^{i\top} \widehat{\mathbf{A}}^\top \left[\mathbf{y}^{ij} - \widehat{\mathbf{A}} \bar{\mathbf{x}}^i - \widehat{\mathbf{t}} \right] \right) . \tag{12}$$

The deformation parameters obtained from (12) may correspond to an unexpected shape. Therefore, we use the protection mechanism proposed in [1]. First we compute the Mahalanobis distance, d, and compare it to threshold, $d_{\max}$,

$$d^2 = \sum_{l=1}^{K} \frac{\widehat{b}_l^2}{\lambda_l} \le d_{\max}^2. \tag{13}$$

where $\widehat{b}_l$ denotes the l-th component of $\widehat{\mathbf{b}}$, and λ_l is the eigenvalue associated to the l-th deformation mode. The threshold is chosen so that most of the shapes in the training set satisfy (13) (a typical value is $d_{\max} = 3$ [1]). If $\widehat{\mathbf{b}}$ does not satisfy (13), we rescale it as follows

$$\widehat{\mathbf{b}}(t) \leftarrow \widehat{\mathbf{b}}(t)\frac{d_{\max}}{d} \; , \qquad \text{if } d > d_{\max}. \tag{14}$$

Estimation of p: Finally, we update the probabilities of valid and invalid data by maximizing $Q(.,.)$ with respect to p_0, p_1. This yields

$$\widehat{p}_1(t) = \frac{\sum\limits_{i=1}^{N}\sum\limits_{j=1}^{M_i} w_1^{ij}}{\sum\limits_{i=1}^{N}\sum\limits_{j=1}^{M_i} w_1^{ij} + w_0^{ij}} \; , \qquad \widehat{p}_0(t) = 1 - \widehat{p}_1(t) \; . \tag{15}$$

The shape estimation algorithm described in this section will be denoted as **EM Robust Active Shape Model (EM-RASM)**.

4 Experimental Evaluation

This section shows examples and statistical results of the EM-RASM method applied to the segmentation of the endocardium of the left ventricle in ultrasound images.

In all the tests, the model was initialized with the average shape $\bar{\mathbf{x}}$ (i.e., $\mathbf{b} = \mathbf{0}$). The initial guess for the transformation parameters was obtained by aligning the average shape $\bar{\mathbf{x}}$ with a contour obtained by human input using the standard least squares method. The initial guess for the models probabilities was $p_0 = p_1 = 0.5$. We found no evidence suggesting that the initial values for these probabilities significantly changed the output of the algorithm.

In this work, the observation points were obtained by searching for edge points along lines orthogonal to the contour at each model point. The feature detection algorithm used was a matched filter designed for edge detection (see [14], Section 5.2). This detector convolves the intensity profile along each search line with an edge operator. Edge points correspond to the maxima of the filtered signal that can be detected by applying thresholding followed by non-maximum suppression. The threshold allows us to modify the sensitivity of the edge detector, which may depend on the application. The length of the search line is also application-dependent since it depends on the uncertainty associated to the contour.

The standard ASM [1] performs a similar search method, but the observation points correspond to the strongest edge along each search line, without guaranteeing that they belong to the object boundary. Consequently, the total number of detected observation points is typically greater in the EM-RASM approach.

4.1 Performance Measures

The segmentations were evaluated by comparing the obtained contours with the true object boundary (ground truth). The accuracy of the segmentations were quantitatively determined by using the Dice coefficient [15], and the average distance of each model point to the ground truth. The former metric measures the agreement between two contours as follows. Let R_1 be the region delimited by the first contour and R_2 the region delimited by the second contour. The Dice coefficient is computed as follows

$$D(R_1, R_2) = 2 \frac{A(R_1 \cap R_2)}{A(R_1) + A(R_2)}, \qquad (16)$$

where $A(\cdot)$ denotes the area of the region and $\cap$ denotes the intersection. A Dice coefficient of 1 means there is a perfect match between the two contours and a value of 0 means the corresponding regions do not even overlap.

4.2   Left Ventricle Segmentation

We applied the EM-RASM method in the segmentation of the left ventricle in 2D ultrasound image sequences. The dataset is composed of five 2D sequences (five different patients), each with 16-20 frames. The shape model was trained using medical annotations of the left ventricle contours (ground truth). Each training example was obtained by resampling, in arc-length, the medical contours with a fixed number of points from the bottom left to the apex (top) and from the bottom right to the apex. We tested the proposed algorithm and the standard ASM using a leave-one-sequence-out scheme, i.e., learning the shape model with four sequences and testing in a fifth, and repeating this for each test sequence.

As previously mentioned, the initial guess for the transformation parameters was obtained by aligning the average contour $\bar{x}$ with a contour obtained by human input using the standard least squares method. A different human input contour was used for each test sequence, and the resulting initial guess was used in all the frames of the sequence (i.e., we did not propagate the contours from one frame to the next).

Table 1. Performance statistics for the segmentation of the LV: average value and standard deviation

	ASM	EM-RASM
Dice coefficient	0.78 (0.06)	**0.88** (0.04)
Average distance	20.4 (4.6)	**10.3** (3.0)

Figure 1 (top) shows four examples of the segmentation obtained with EM-RASM and with the standard ASM. In all the examples, a large number of the detected observations (red dots) were outliers. The figure shows that the EM-RASM performed better than the standard ASM and was able to fit the

Ground Truth   **Standard ASM**   **EM-RASM**

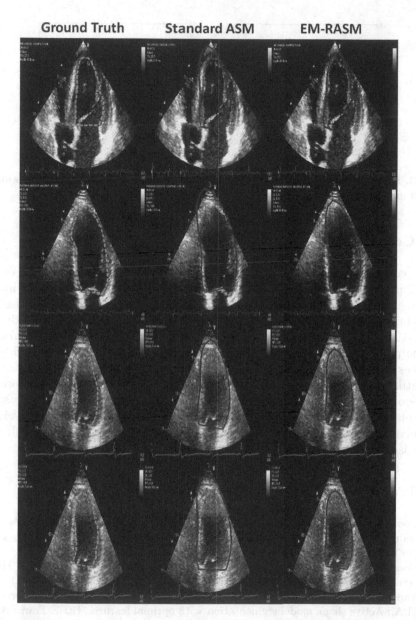

Fig. 1. Segmentation of the left ventricle in ultrasound images. The green dashed line shows the ground truth and the blue lines correspond to the estimated contour. The red dots represent the detected observations in the last iteration.

LV boundary, whereas the contour obtained using the standard ASM was hampered by the outliers. Statistical results are presented in Table 1 and in the boxplots of Figure 2, showing that the EM-RASM method, leads to a significant improvement in the segmentation accuracy.

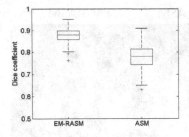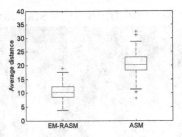

Fig. 2. Boxplots of the error metrics for the segmentation of the left ventricle in ultrasound images (the average distance is measured in pixels)

5   Conclusion

This paper combines active shape models (ASM) with robust estimation of the model pose and deformation using an outlier model. The estimation of the model parameters is achieved using the EM method, that assigns confidence degrees (weights) to each observation and take confidence degrees into account during the estimation of the model parameters. We show that this approach is robust in the presence of outliers since outlier observations tend to receive confidence degrees close to zero and have a small influence on the model estimates.

Future work should focus on extending the proposed framework to more reliable observations, such as edge strokes [12]. Since edge points along the same edge often belong to the same object in the image, the computation of the weights associated to observations can be improved. The use of application-specific features is another direction to be explored.

References

1. Cootes, T.F., Taylor, C.J., Cooper, D.H., Graham, J.: Active shape models-their training and application. Computer Vision and Image Understanding 61(1), 38–59 (1995)
2. Cootes, T.F., Edwards, G.J., Taylor, C.J.: Active appearance models. IEEE Transactions on Pattern Analysis and Machine Intelligence 23(6), 681–685 (2001)
3. Van Ginneken, B., Frangi, A.F., Staal, J.J., ter Haar Romeny, B.M., Viergever, M.A.: Active shape model segmentation with optimal features. IEEE Transactions on Medical Imaging 21(8), 924–933 (2002)
4. Wimmer, M., Stulp, K., Pietzsch, S., Radig, B.: Learning local objective functions for robust face model fitting. IEEE Transactions on Pattern Analysis and Machine Intelligence 30(8), 1357–1370 (2008)
5. Cristinacce, D., Cootes, T.F.: Automatic feature localisation with constrained local models. Pattern Recognition 41(10), 3054–3067 (2008)
6. Arbeláez, P., Maire, M., Fowlkes, C., Malik, J.: Contour detection and hierarchical image segmentation. IEEE Transactions on Pattern Analysis and Machine Intelligence 33(5), 898–916 (2011)

7. Cootes, T.F., Ionita, M.C., Lindner, C., Sauer, P.: Robust and accurate shape model fitting using random forest regression voting. In: Fitzgibbon, A., Lazebnik, S., Perona, P., Sato, Y., Schmid, C. (eds.) ECCV 2012, Part VII. LNCS, vol. 7578, pp. 278–291. Springer, Heidelberg (2012)
8. Rogers, M., Graham, J.: Robust active shape model search. In: Heyden, A., Sparr, G., Nielsen, M., Johansen, P. (eds.) ECCV 2002, Part IV. LNCS, vol. 2353, pp. 517–530. Springer, Heidelberg (2002)
9. Fischler, M.A., Bolles, R.C.: Random sample consensus: A paradigm for model fitting with applications to image analysis and automated cartography. Communications of the ACM 24(6), 381–395 (1981)
10. Abi-Nahed, J., Jolly, M.-P., Yang, G.Z.: Robust active shape models: A robust, generic and simple automatic segmentation tool. In: Larsen, R., Nielsen, M., Sporring, J. (eds.) MICCAI 2006. LNCS, vol. 4191, pp. 1–8. Springer, Heidelberg (2006)
11. Chui, H., Rangarajan, A.: A new point matching algorithm for non-rigid registration. Computer Vision and Image Understanding 89(2), 114–141 (2003)
12. Nascimento, J.C., Marques, J.S.: Adaptive snakes using the EM algorithm. IEEE Transactions on Image Processing 14(11), 1678–1686 (2005)
13. Dempster, A.P., Laird, N.M., Rubin, D.B.: Maximum likelihood from incomplete data via the em algorithm. Journal of the Royal Statistical Society. Series B (Methodological), 1–38 (1977)
14. Blake, A., Isard, M.: Active shape models. Springer (1998)
15. Dice, L.R.: Measures of the amount of ecologic association between species. Ecology 26(3), 297–302 (1945)

Rigging and Data Capture for the Facial Animation of Virtual Actors

Miquel Mascaró[1], Francisco J. Serón[2],
Francisco J. Perales[1], and Javier Varona[1]

[1] Universitat de les Illes Balears
[2] Universidad de Zaragoza
{miquel.mascaro,paco.perales,xavi.varona}@uib.es,
seron@unizar.es

Abstract. This paper presents a method of animating the facial expressions of virtual characters based on data capture processes. A presentation is given of a facial rigging system capable of simulating facial muscle activity in a realistic way. A distance-based methodology is outlined in which curves are calculated that define animation by the rig controllers, using data from Saragih's Face Tracker. The method's performance is tested by reproducing expressions from various different public databases of facial expressions.

Keywords: Facial animation. Facial rigging. Virtual avatars. Facial motion capture. Databases of facial expressions.

1 Introduction

Facial animation is still an unresolved issue in the field of interaction between man and the machine and more specifically in computer graphics. Facial animation poses many difficulties due to the time, cost and complexity that it involves. Traditionally many facial animation production processes were done by hand, individually for each character. Even in automated processes, like motion capture animation, it is common for some associated processes to be done manually, such as the cleansing and adjusting of captured data. Consequently, systems that automate part of this work and, at the same time, can be generalized to encompass different characters are of great interest.

There are two aspects involved in how to realistically portray certain facial expressions by virtual characters, and both form part of the objectives of this paper. On the one hand, a system is needed to simulate muscle activity in an accurate way, deforming the geometrical mesh of the character's face. On the other, a system is also required to set the animation keys, making sure that they are properly temporally distributed so that muscle activity takes place in a coherent way along the timeline, making the action credible for any spectator.

2 Related Work

Orvalho [1] recently presented a state-of-the-art report on facial animation, covering the entire rigging process. This study is of particular interest since, as well as including

F.J. Perales and J. Santos-Victor (Eds.): AMDO 2014, LNCS 8563, pp. 170–179, 2014.

definitions and specifications of the concept of rigging, it focuses on the problem of facial animation from a technical and artistic point of view, with particular emphasis on the production process. The main difficulties are the absence of a standard definition of what a facial rig is and the numerous possible configurations that animators use in facial animation. Orvalho defines facial rigging as the process of creating and then activating a series of controllers used to operate a 3D model. A rigging system is a structure capable of transforming a controller's motion data into facial geometry deformation data.

Some of the main contributions to facial rigging since 1996 include Maraffi [2], Gorden [3], Ritchie [4], Miller [5], McKinley [6], Bredow [7], Chang [8], Pardew [9], O'Neill [10], Vilagrassa [11], Alexander [12], Osipa [13] and Arghineti [14].

Even though a rigging system is capable of simulating facial muscle activity in a precise detailed way, in order to ensure valid animation, the animator must have a certain level of expertise in setting the animation keys properly along the timeline.

Since the early days through to the present, a hand mirror has been used by artists to reproduce facial expressions [15].

The problem of detecting faces and facial characteristics is a widely studied aspect of computer vision. In particular, Viola and Jones [16] and variations of the method like Varona, Manresa-Yee and Perales[17] and Castrillón[18] compare different methods based on this algorithm. Cerezo et al. [19] apply their results to the animation of a virtual character called Maxine.

Facial animation based on motion capture has been a key subject of research in recent years. An article by Phigin and Lewis [20] contains an extensive review of these systems.

Different approaches can be found that use simple cameras to collect facial data. Patras and Pantic [21] [22] detect the AUs that appear in video sequences. Saragih et al. [23] propose a solution based on the mean-shift algorithm, with regularization due to previous knowledge of the model.

Weise et al. [24] come up with a low-cost facial animation system that works with Kinect SDK. They present a new facial tracking algorithm, based on a series of existing facial animations that adapt a general mesh using data captured by a camera.

3 A Facial Rig to Describe Different Expressions

We have developed a rigging system that takes into account the following aspects:

A Diversity of Faces: The different shapes that our geometric models adopt must coincide with deformations caused by real muscle action.

The characters must have a structure that is essentially anthropomorphic, without it necessarily being realistic. That is why we chose to create two characters - a realistic and unrealistic one -, which would serve to test the reliability of the expressions we depict.

Inconsistent Facial Movements: To guarantee precise realistic movements, the rig must make it possible to simulate all the different muscle action outlined in the FACS [25]. Indeed, as Figure 1 shows, the rig that we have created is capable of

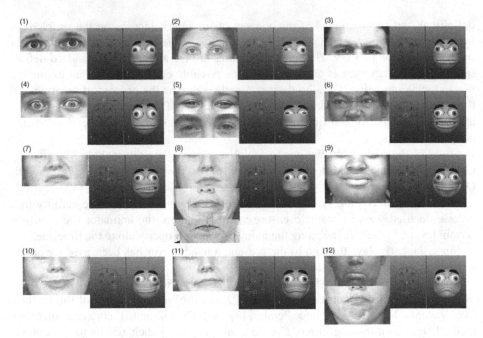

Fig. 1. Reproduction of some of the AUs of the FACS: (1) AU 1: Inner brow raiser, (2) AU 2: Outer brow raiser, (3) AU 4: Brow lowerer, (4) AU 5: Upper lid raiser, (5) AU 6: Cheek raiser, AU 7: Lid tightener, (6) AU 9: Nose wrinkler, (7) AU 10: Upper lid raiser, (8) AU 11: Naso-labial deepener, AU 20: Lip strechner, AU 24: Lip pressor, (9) AU 12: Lip corner puller, (10) AU 13: Cheek puffer, (11) AU 14: Dimpler, (12) AU 15: Lip corner depressor, AU 17: Chin raiser

reproducing the AUs described by Ekman and Friesen. In the image, the original photos describing the AUs are shown on the left while, on the right, a 3D window shows the interface of the rig and the primitive (unrealistic) character doing the same AU.

The Lack of a Standard Rule: There is no standard rule for defining the rigging system, although some widely used conventions exist, as is the case of geometric modelling with edge loop techniques [26]. These guarantee the topological coherence of the geometry and optimize the facial deformation process.

Animation. The classic keyframe animation technique, with keys defined by the rig manipulators, is the one that defines the character's movements. In general terms, the data generated by a motion capture device can be seen as a sequence of values or keys that evolve over time.

User Interface. The chosen system is an interface based on a 3D window with 2D manipulators, similar to solutions proposed by Alexander et al. [27] or Digital tutors [28]. This interface ensures tight control of the deformation of the geometric mesh in order to simulate facial muscles. At the same time, it is also an intuitive tool that easily facilitates all the actions described in the FACS. Table 1 shows the AU facial actions that the controllers of our system activate. In the table, the left and right symmetries caused by the AUs have been left out.

Tabla 1. Rig controllers and the AU they activate

Rig controller	AU
upsetSad	AU 1: Inner Brow Raiser, AU 4: Brow Lowerer, AU 9: Nose Wrinkler, AU 11: Nasolabial Deepener
shocked	AU 2: Outer Brow Raiser, AU 5: Upper Lid Raiser
twich	AU 6: Cheek Raiser, AU 7: Lid Tightener
sneer	AU 10: Upper Lip Raiser, AU 11: Nasolabial Deepener
smileFrown	AU 6: Cheek Raiser, AU 12: Lip Corner Puller, AU 13: Cheek Puffer AU 14: Dimpler, AU 15: Lip Corner Depressor, AU 17: Chin Raiser
jaw	AU 24: Lip Pressor, AU 25: Lips part, AU 26: Jaw Drop, AU 27: Mouth Stretch
blink	AU 41: Lid droop, AU 42: Slit, AU 42: Slit, AU 43: Eyes Closed, AU 44: Squint, AU 45: Blink, AU 46: Wink
neck	AU 55: Head Tilt Left, AU 56: Head Tilt Right

Deformers. To define the deformations of the characters' meshes, our rig uses a combination of skin and bone techniques based on *blendshape* [28] geometric interpolation. Jaw movements are controlled with the former (JawControl) while all the changes in the mesh used to represent all remaining facial muscle action are controlled with the latter. Once this deformation has been defined, its link with the linear transformation of its corresponding controller will be established.

4   Data Collection for the Simulation of Expressions

When it came to deciding on the right automatic facial tracking system to use, Face Tracker by Saragih[23] was chosen. This is because it is open source software and it does not require any kind of special hardware to collect the data. Also, it ensures versatility because it can be used with data captured by a camera, from video sequences that have been specifically recorded or are from existing databases, and from video sequences taken from any film.

The software gives us the position of the 66 points of a 2D face mesh on the flat image needed for each frame (See Figure 2). With these XY values for each point, 66 animation files for a 3D environment can be generated that show us the temporal evolution of each point collected by the tracking software.

Fig. 2. 2D Face Tracker mesh

5   The Calculation of the Facial Expression Controllers' Animation Values

To calculate the animation values of the rig controllers, we propose a method based on temporal rules similar to that of Pantic and Patras [22] for the automatic extraction of facial actions in image sequences. Our idea differs from theirs in that we are not interested in recognizing what facial action has occurred but, based on the detected movement, in converting the distances between points into suitable values for the rig controllers. For this purpose, Table 2 is taken into account, where the FP facial parameters and the tracker points that define them are linked to the rig controller that simulates the facial action.

The transformations applied to the manipulators will depend on a scaling factor ε of the video sequence data. This data will vary, depending on the image resolution and type of shot. As a result, the distance between the eyes - $FP1$ - is taken to approximate this scaling factor. Nonetheless, it is important to take into account the fact that, in the case of a primitive or cartoon character, it might be interesting to exaggerate the movements. Consequently, this scaling factor can be manually adjusted to suit the animator's interests.

The facial parameters from $FP2$ to $FP7$ are the ones used to deduce how to animate the eyebrows and eyes. This includes the shockedControl, upsetSadControl, brownRaiseControl (right and left), blinkControl (right and left) and twitchControl (right and left) controllers, while the parameters from $FP8$ to $FP15$ animate the mouth and cheeks, controlled through the rigging interface by the SmileFrownControl (right and left), sneerControl (right and left) and jawControl. Lastly, $FP16$ is used by the neckControl to portray twisting movements by the head. With the exception of $FP2$ and $FP4$, the other facial parameters are defined as distances between two points detailed in the third column of Table 2. $FP2$ and $FP4$ are calculated as mean distances.

To assign the time-related values that the different controllers will take, a frame from the sequence must be taken into consideration that depicts a neutral facial

Tabla 2. Facial parameters from the tracker points and the corresponding rig manipulators

FP1	Distance between eyes	39 - 42	Scaling factor
FP2	Half opening of lower lid (right)	46 - 47	rightTwich
FP3	Internal distance between eyebrow and eyelid (right)	22 - 27	upsetSad, shocked, rightBrownRaise
FP4	Half opening of lower lid (left)	40 - 41	leftTwich
FP5	Internal distance between eyebrow and lid (left)	21 - 27	upsetSad, shocked, leftBrownRaise
FP6	Distance of eye opening (right)	22 - 42	leftBlink
FP7	Distance of eye opening (left)	21 - 39	rightBlink
FP8	Width of mouth	48 - 54	smileFrown
FP9	Distance corner of mouth to nose (right)	33 - 54	rightSmileFrown
FP10	Distance corner of mouth to nose (left)	33 - 48	leftSmileFrown
FP11	Height of mouth	51 - 57	jaw
FP12	Vertical between mouth and nose	51 - 33	sneer
FP13	Distance between corner of mouth and nose-wing (right)	35 - 54	rightSneer
FP14	Distance between corner of mouth and nose-wing (left)	31 - 48	leftSneer
FP15	Vertical between chin and nose	8 - 33	jaw
FP16	Distance between oval of face	0 – 16	neck

expression, so that for a certain frame i, the value of controller C will be represented by the expression:

$$C_i = (FPx_i - FPx_0) * \varepsilon \qquad (1)$$

Where subindex 0 refers to the frame that represents the neutral expression, ε is the adjustment factor to the scale of the manipulator and FPx is the specific facial parameter of each controller in Table 2. In the final instance, value ε will depend on the animator, who is responsible for how exaggerated or gentle the expression is. In empirical terms, the visually correct values for ε can range from 0.1 to 0.3 for an image with a resolution of 640x490, corresponding to a frontal close-up of an individual.

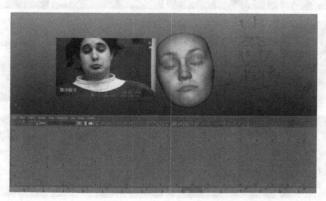

Fig. 3. Assignment of animation curves to the rigging system of Emily by *Face Ware Technologies*

Figure 3 shows an animation curve for the Jaw controller, generated with an ε value of 0.28, which is visually valid for a natural-looking or primitive character.

Depending on the range of values that the controller takes and the anthropometric properties of the expression to be simulated, formula (1) will be adjusted with values that are a multiple of ε.

The same animation curves generated for the controllers of our rigging system can be imported to other rigging configurations with visually correct results, for instance, to the rigging system created for the Emily [27] project by *FaceWare Technologies,* which can be downloaded free from the latter's website, or to those of *Creative Crash* [29].

6   Validation of the Method

In order to validate the results of the expression synthesis, public databases that include these types of expressions were used.

Databases of facial expressions like CK+ [30] or MMI [31] contain annotated facial expressions of all kinds. Studies have recently emerged that investigate the detection and classification of types of laughter, more specifically, the database of the BBC Smile Dataset [32]. The Uva-Nemo [34] database was generated to study the dynamics of spontaneous smiles in comparison with voluntary ones, while the MAHNOB Laughter database [35] has been used to differentiate between laughter and speech utterances and to detect laughter during speech.

Our facial animation method was applied to some randomly chosen sequences from the Cohn-Kanade, Uva-Nemo and MAHNOB databases. Satisfactory results were obtained when expressions were reproduced for both our natural-looking and primitive character. Figure 5 shows some of the results. The left side corresponds to sequences from BD Uva-Nemo and the right to MAHNOB.

Fig. 4. Examples of animation based on sequences from the Uva-Nemo and MAHNOB databases

7   Conclusions and Future Work

In this paper, we have presented a system of facial animation that allows an inexpert animator to reproduce an actor's facial expressions, previously recorded with a simple camera or from an existing video.

With this system, the animation can be exported to a facial animation rig using a simple 2D interface.

This approach is different from those used by other authors, since no kind of hardware device is needed, it does not depend on any specific 3D software and no specific cleansing process is required other than the standard system of smoothing animation curves featured in most 3D software.

A future study of specific expressions is planned in order to check how the system responds to subtle variations that give rise to changes in expression, like different expressions of joy, sadness etc.

The creation of a plug-in is also contemplated to integrate the system into a 3D software system like Blender or Maya.

Acknowledgements. This work was partially supported by the "Gobierno Balear, Grupos Competitivos, 2011, Num. 28/2011/44".

References

1. Orvalho, V., Bastos, P., Parke, F., Oliveira, B., Alvarez, X.: A Facial Rigging Survey, pp. 183–204 (2012)
2. Maraffi, C.: Maya Character Creation: Modeling and Animation Controls. New Riders (2004)
3. Gorden, J.: LightWave 3D 8 Cartoon Character Creation: Modeling & Texturing. Wordware Publishing, Inc., (2004)
4. Ritchie, K., Callery, J., Biri, K.: The Art of Rigging. CG Toolkit (2005)
5. Miller, E., Thuriot, P., Unay, J.: Maya Techniques: Hyper-Real Creature Creation, 2006th edn. Sybex (2006)
6. McKinley, M.: The Game Animator's Guide to Maya, Pap/Cdr. John Wiley & Sons (2006)
7. Bredow, R., Schaub, D., Kramer, D., Hausman, M., Dimian, D., Duguid, R.S.: Surf's up: The making of an animated documentary. In: ACM SIGGRAPH 2007 Courses, New York, NY, USA, pp. 1–123 (2007)
8. Chang, E., Jenkins, O.: Sketching Articulation and Pose for Facial Animation. In: Deng, Z., Neumann, U. (eds.) Data-Driven 3D Facial Animation, pp. 145–161. Springer, London (2007)
9. Pardew, L.: Character Emotion in 2D and 3D Animation, 1st edn. Course Technology Press, Boston (2007)
10. O'Neill, R.: Digital Character Development: Theory and Practice. Morgan Kaufmann Publishers Inc., San Francisco (2008)
11. Villagrassa, S., Susín, A.: FACe! 3D facial Animation System based on FACS. In: Rodríguez, F.S.O. (ed.) IV Iberoamerican Symposium in Computer Graphics – SIACG 2009, p. 209 (2009)
12. Alexander, O., Rogers, M., Lambeth, W., Chiang, M., Debevec, P.: Creating a Photoreal Digital Actor: The Digital Emily Project. In: Conference for Visual Media Production, CVMP 2009, pp. 176–187 (2009)

13. Osipa, J.: Stop Staring: Facial Modeling and Animation Done Right. John Wiley & Sons (2010)
14. Arghinenti, A.: Animation workflow in KILLZONE3™: A fast facial retargeting system for game characters. In: ACM SIGGRAPH 2011 Talks, New York, NY, USA, pp. 37:1–37:1 (2011)
15. Innes, L.: The Secret To Drawing Characters Consistently & Expressively, http://www.paperwingspodcast.com/2011/06/the-secret-to-drawin-expressive-consistent-characters/ (accessed: September 18, 2012)
16. Viola, P., Jones, M.: Rapid object detection using a boosted cascade of simple features. In: Proceedings of the 2001 IEEE Computer Society Conference on Computer Vision and Pattern Recognition, CVPR 2001, vol. 1, pp. I-511–I-518 (2001)
17. Varona, J., Manresa-Yee, C., Perales, F.J.: Hands-free vision-based interface for computer accessibility. Journal of Network and Computer Applications 31(4), 357–374 (2008)
18. Castrillón, M., Déniz, O., Hernández, D., Lorenzo, J.: A comparison of face and facial feature detectors based on the Viola–Jones general object detection framework. Machine Vision and Applications 22(3), 481–494 (2011)
19. Cerezo, E., Hupont, I., Manresa-Yee, C., Varona, J., Baldassarri, S., Perales, F.J., Seron, F.J.: Real-Time Facial Expression Recognition for Natural Interaction. In: Martí, J., Benedí, J.M., Mendonça, A.M., Serrat, J. (eds.) IbPRIA 2007. LNCS, vol. 4478, pp. 40–47. Springer, Heidelberg (2007)
20. Pighin, F., Lewis, J.P.: Facial motion retargeting. In: ACM SIGGRAPH 2006 Courses, New York, NY, USA (2006)
21. Patras, I., Pantic, M.: Particle filtering with factorized likelihoods for tracking facial features. In: Proceedings of the Sixth IEEE International Conference on Automatic Face and Gesture Recognition, 2004, pp. 97–102 (2004)
22. Pantic, M., Patras, I.: Detecting facial actions and their temporal segments in nearly frontal-view face image sequences. In: 2005 IEEE International Conference on Systems, Man and Cybernetics, vol. 4, pp. 3358–3363 (2005)
23. Saragih, J., Lucey, S., Cohn, J.: Deformable Model Fitting by Regularized Landmark Mean-Shift. International Journal of Computer Vision 91(2), 200–215 (2011)
24. Weise, T., Bouaziz, S., Li, H., Pauly, M.: Realtime performance-based facial animation. ACM Trans. Graph. 30(4), 77 (2011)
25. Ekman, P., Friesen, W.V.: Facial Action Coding System: A Technique for the Measurement of Facial Movement. Consulting Psychologists Press (1978)
26. Unay, J., Grossman, R.: Hyper-real advanced facial blendshape techniques and tools for production. In: ACM SIGGRAPH 2005 Master Class (2005)
27. Alexander, O., Rogers, M., Lambeth, W., Chiang, M., Debevec, P.: The Digital Emily project: Photoreal facial modeling and animation. In: ACM SIGGRAPH 2009 Courses, New York, NY, USA, pp. 12:1–12:15 (2009)
28. Digital-Tutors, Facial Rigging in Maya, http://www.digitaltutors.com (accessed: May 15, 2009)
29. Boris with Facial GUI - Free Character Rigs Downloads for Maya, http://www.creativecrash.com/maya/downloads/character-rigs/c/boris-with-facial-gui (accessed: November 20, 2013)
30. Lucey, P., Cohn, J.F., Kanade, T., Saragih, J., Ambadar, Z., Matthews, I.: The Extended Cohn-Kanade Dataset (CK+): A complete dataset for action unit and emotion-specified expression. In: 2010 IEEE Computer Society Conference on Computer Vision and Pattern Recognition Workshops (CVPRW), pp. 94–101 (2010)

31. Pantic, M., Valstar, M., Rademaker, R., Maat, L.: Web-based database for facial expression analysis. In: IEEE International Conference on Multimedia and Expo, ICME 2005, p. 5 (2005)
32. BBC - Science & Nature - Human Body and Mind - Spot The Fake Smile, http://www.bbc.co.uk/science/humanbody/mind/surveys/smiles/ (accessed: November 23, 2012)
33. Hoque, M.E., McDuff, D.J., Picard, R.W.: Exploring Temporal Patterns in Classifying Frustrated and Delighted Smiles. IEEE Transactions on Affective Computing 3(3), 323–334 (2012)
34. Dibeklioğlu, H., Salah, A.A., Gevers, T.: Are You Really Smiling at Me? Spontaneous versus Posed Enjoyment Smiles. In: Fitzgibbon, A., Lazebnik, S., Perona, P., Sato, Y., Schmid, C. (eds.) ECCV 2012, Part III. LNCS, vol. 7574, pp. 525–538. Springer, Heidelberg (2012)
35. Petridis, S., Martinez, B., Pantic, M.: The MAHNOB Laughter Database. Image and Vision Computing Journal 31(2), 186–202 (2013)
36. ELAN, http://tla.mpi.nl/tools/tla-tools/elan/ (accessed: January 27, 2014)

Geometric Surface Deformation Based on Trajectories: A New Approach

Manuel González-Hidalgo*, Arnau Mir-Torres, and Pere Palmer-Rodríguez

Departament de Ciències Matemàtiques i Informàtica.
Universitat de les Illes Balears
{manuel.gonzalez,arnau.mir,pere.palmer}@uib.es

Abstract. This paper describes the development of a free-form deformation model (FFD) which is an extension of the *Scodef* model of geometric constraint-based deformations. The deformation is applied to a point over the surface and it is restricted to a region which is limited by a closed B-Spline curve acting as a profile. The main difference from the original model is that in the new one, the conditions to define restrictions with non rectilinear trajectories have been established. These conditions are represented by 4D B-Spline curves. With the proposed solution, the deformed surface is adjusted precisely as described by both B-Spline curves. The model has been called N-Scodef.

Keywords: B-Splines, Free-Form Deformations, Constrained Trajectories, Profile Curves.

1 Introduction

Simple constrained deformations, *Scodef*, can be considered as Free-Form deformations, FFD, [3], [12]. The deformations are applied onto a point of the object and affect an area around this point and, also, more than one deformation can be applied at the same time. The shape changes more o less depending on the distance function:

$$f_i(Q) = B_i \left(\frac{\|Q - C_i\|}{R_i} \right), \tag{1}$$

f_i measures how much the point Q of the object is affected by the constraint C_i. R_i is the influence radius, which determines the area affected by C_i, and B_i is a B-Spline basis function centered at 0 such that $B_i(0) = 1$ and $B_i(1) = 0$. The points which are at a distance from C_i greater than R_i will not be affected by the deformation, and the nearby points will be affected in proportion to their distance to C_i. The *Scodef* model is extended in [3], where a way to apply non-rectilinear constraints is described. The presented paper can be considered as an extension of [4].

* Partially supported by the funds of Govern Balear for competitive research groups, number 28/2011/44, year 2011.

F.J. Perales and J. Santos-Victor (Eds.): AMDO 2014, LNCS 8563, pp. 180–194, 2014.

2   N-Scodef

Based on the notation originally expressed in [2] and then used in [3] defining a simple constraint-based deformations, *Scodef*, the deformation of an object is defined by manipulating the so called constraints; points selected by the user that must have a certain behavior along the deformation process.

From the chosen deformation function and the constraints defined by the user, a projection matrix, M, is calculated. M must guarantee that the constraints are met. The influence zone of a constraint is defined as the region of the original object whose distance to the point where the constraint is applied is less than some value, the influence radius. Obviously, the shape of the zone of influence will change depending on how this distance is calculated and how the radius of influence is determined. Fig. 1 shows some deformations applied over a cylinder. The deformation process has three steps:

1. The user selects the displacements, D_i, the constraints, C_i, the influence zone of each constraint, the selection of the influence radius, R_i, and the formulation of the deformation function, $\mathcal{F}$. In this way, given a point $Q \in \mathbb{R}^n$ it is possible to determine its displacement with respect to the constraints defined by:

$$d(Q) = \sum_{i=1}^{r} M_i \, f_i(Q). \tag{2}$$

   In [12] some variants for (1) are proposed. The equation (2) can be rewritten as $d(Q) = M\mathcal{F}(Q)$ where M is a matrix of n rows and r columns, one for each constraint, $\mathcal{F}(Q)$ is a vector of dimension r composed by the functions f_i of each constraint.

2. Calculation of the projection matrix, M, in a way that the constraints set by the user can be satisfied. That is, solving the lineal system of equations, $d(C_i) = M\mathcal{F}(C_i), 1 \leq i \leq r$, being r the number of constraints and $\mathcal{F} = (f_1, f_2, \ldots, f_r)$. The influence of a constraint over the point of application of the others depends mainly on the shape of the influence region and the radius of influence. If there exists an overlapping with the influence regions, possibly the deformation behavior could be inadequate. In that case an ad hoc solution must be applied, [12], [8], [11], [13], [14], [10].

3. Once the matrix M is obtained, it is possible to proceed to calculate the deformation.

The displacements are expressed as a lineal vector, but they can also be specified with some kind of curve ([13], [14], [1], [7]).

The main goal of this paper is to deform a 4D B-Spline surface, S, following the *Scodef* schema in a way in which the parametric representation of S is maintained after the deformation.

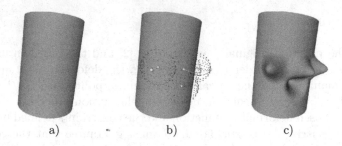

a)   b)   c)

Fig. 1. A *Scodef* deformation. a) The object to deform, a cylinder. b) The constraints are shown as points over the surface and the places where these points have to be displaced, also the influence zone, represented as a sphere of points, is shown. c) The cylinder, after the deformations.

The deformation is expressed in the following way: Let $d : \mathbb{R}^n \longrightarrow \mathbb{R}^n$ (usually $n = 2, 3$ or 4) be the deformation function representing the displacement of the points of S, $d(S(u,v))$ being $(u,v) \in [0,1]^2$. The function has the form:

$$\forall (u,v) \in [0,1] \times [0,1] \quad d(S(u,v)) = \sum_{i=1}^{r} M_i \, f_i(S(u,v)),$$

where

- r is the number of constraints set by the user.
- M_i is the i-th column of the matrix M.
- $\tilde{f}_i : \mathbb{R} \longrightarrow \mathbb{R}$ is a monotonically decreasing scalar function such that $\tilde{f}_i(0) = 1$ and $\tilde{f}_i(x) = 0 \ \forall x : |x| \geq 1$. It is associated to the constraint C_i. This function determines the influence of the constraint over each surface point $S(u,v)$. The function $f_i : \mathbb{R}^n \longrightarrow \mathbb{R}$ depends on the constraints C_i and the influence radius, R_i is defined as follows:

$$f_i(S(u,v)) = \tilde{f}_i \left(\frac{\|S(u,v) - C_i\|}{R_i} \right). \tag{3}$$

So, for each point $Q = S(u,v)$ it is verified that

$$f_i(Q) = \begin{cases} 1, & \text{if } \|Q - C_i\| = 0, \\ 0, & \text{if } \|Q - C_i\| \geq R_i, \\ 0 \leq f_i(Q) \leq 1, \text{ in other case.} \end{cases} \tag{4}$$

To guarantee the continuity of the deformed surface, $\tilde{f}_i$ has to be also continuous. In this case, the function $\mathcal{F} = (f_1, f_2, \ldots, f_r)$ is a vectorial function whose components are continuous functions. Fig. 2 shows the described components. It is possible to define a great variety of deformation functions which satisfy the described conditions. Obviously the shape of each deformation function, $\tilde{f}_i$, directly influences the way in which the object is deformed. In order to offer a

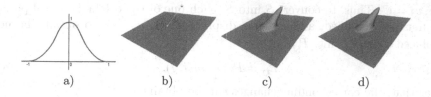

Fig. 2. Elements for a constraint-based deformation and its action over a 4D B-Spline surface. a) The deformation function, b) The constraint (yellow point over the surface) and the displacement, the sphere of points represents the influence zone, c) the deformed surface with the constraint, and d) the resulting deformation.

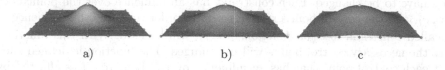

Fig. 3. The effect of the influence radius: a surface B-Splines 4D is deformed with a spherical influence radius, in a) the radius is less and in c) greater

better functionality, it is possible to offer to the user the option to select the desired function from a set of already predefined functions.

The influence radius, as it has been introduced in [3], is very useful in the deformation process. It defines locally the deformations, by the restriction of their spatial influence [14]. The effect of the influence radius can be seen in Fig. 3. It is possible to use non-spherical influence zones, and it is also possible to use non-euclidian distances [12], [13], [14], [5], [7], [4]. Also the influence zones can have an anisotropic shapes.

2.1   Particularities of the 4D B-Spline Implementation

The main drawback of the use of parametric model, as 4D B-Spline, is that the deformation *Scodef* causes the loss of the relationship between the represented object and their structure, as it can be seen in Fig. 3 where the surface changes, but the control points remain unchanged. If the surface has to continue being a 4D B-Spline surface, then the control points have to be modified in a coherent way. If the deformation is lineal, that is, the constrained point is moved directly to another place in the space, then an analogous approach to the described in [6] and in [7] is enough to accomplish that, if it is adapted to a 4D B-Spline representation.

Given a surface 4D B-Spline $S(u, v)$ of degrees p and q and $m \times n$ control points to be deformed, let C be the surface point in which the deformation is applied, and let $\tilde{C}$ be the point where C has to be moved, so $D = \tilde{C} - C$ is the corresponding displacement. The resulting surface $\tilde{S}(u, v)$ will be a 4D B-Spline of degrees p and q with $m \times n$ control points such that if $S(u, v) = C$ then

$\tilde{S}(u, v) = \tilde{C}$. Thus, to convert S into $\tilde{S}$, each one of the original control points, P_{ij} must be modified, adding some displacements, $m(i, j)$, to obtain the new displaced control points $\tilde{P}_{ij}$:

$$\tilde{P}_{ij} = P_{i,j} + m(i, j). \tag{5}$$

After that, the corresponding changes can be obtained

$$D = \sum_{i=0}^{n} \sum_{j=0}^{m} N_{i,p}(u)N_{j,q}(v)m(i, j), \tag{6}$$

where $N_{i,p}$ and $N_{j,q}$ are the B-Spline basis functions. Generally, it is necessary to determine which control points are affected by the constraint, and therefore they have to be changed. Each constraint has an influence over the point $C = S(u, v)$, and the control points related to it. In order to define this influence, a so called *constraint location function*, $\hat{f}(i, j)$, will be used. With this function, only the necessary control points will be changed. The function is defined such that each control point that has an influence over C is more o less affected by the deformation:

$$\hat{f} : \{0, \ldots, n\} \times \{0, \ldots, m\} \longrightarrow \mathbb{R}^{+}. \tag{7}$$

Furthermore, at least some of the changed control points must belong to the convex hull of the point:

$$\exists (i, j) \in \{0, \ldots, n\} \times \{0, \ldots, m\} \mid N_{i,p}(u)N_{j,q}(v)\hat{f}(i, j) \neq 0. \tag{8}$$

In short, $\hat{f}(i, j)$ indicates which control points are affected by a constraint and in what extent they are. Any function satisfying the previous conditions can be used, in [6] some of them are proposed. A simple way to determine the value of this function is to establish that the restriction is defined by the characteristics of the surface to be treated; that is, the basis functions used to express the B-Spline surface are used to determine the location function:

$$\hat{f}(i, j) = N_{i,p}(u)N_{j,q}(v). \tag{9}$$

Combining $\hat{f}$ and D, an expression for $m(i, j)$ is obtained:

$$m(i, j) = \frac{N_{i,p}(u)N_{j,q}(v)}{\sum\limits_{k=0}^{n} \sum\limits_{l=0}^{m} (N_{kp}(u)N_{lq}(v))^2} D. \tag{10}$$

Figure 4 shows some examples of deformations based on the described method. As it can be seen, the constraints can be defined in such a way that coincides with a control point or not, and in both cases the surface, and the control points, are changed coherently. Thus, the control points with a parametric image outside the parametric zone of influence remain unchanged. And those inside the parametric zone will change the more the closer they are to the parametric image of P_{ij} of the parametric space point where the constraint is applied. If there are not enough control points in the parametric zone of influence to perform the deformation, prior to the calculation, it is necessary to proceed to add enough control points to ensure that the deformation can be made correctly.

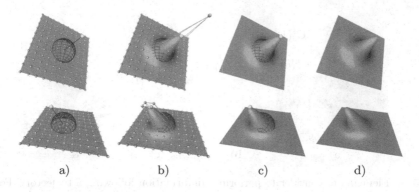

a)   b)   c)   d)

Fig. 4. Two examples of deformation of a surface by applying a linear constraint. a) the surface with a constraint defined; b) the deformation showing the control points and the constraint; c) the deformed surface with the constraint, as it can be seen, the surface always matches the constraint; d) the surface deformed.

2.2 Trajectory Constraints

The definition of a constraint-based deformation of a B-Spline surface, following a trajectory and such that the parametric properties of the deformed surface remain unchanged is a work where it has not been solved yet. In this section an approach to this question is proposed. In order to define a constraint-based deformation following a trajectory, the main elements to consider are:

- The trajectory curve, C^t, which determines the trajectory followed by the deformation. It will be expressed as a 4D B-Spline curve.
- The profile curve, C^p, which determines the contour of the deformation. Instead of defining a zone of influence through some kind of mathematical function, it can be defined by a 4D B-Spline curve, closed in principle, defining the contour of the area to be deformed. This curve can be defined interactively by the user, drawing it directly over the surface, or also it can be previously defined and then applied to the zone to be modified.

The profile curve will follow the path defined by the trajectory curve oriented in the normal plane at each point and scaled by a function analogous to the function of deformation (1), see Fig. 5.a. Therefore the path curve may not be in contact with the surface. The surface point, x, where the constraint is applied will be the surface point with a minimum distance between $C^t(0)$ and S. In order to determine the contour of the deformation, C^p has to be oriented to rest on S and such that the barycenter matches with x.

The size of C^p has to be adjusted using a distance function which determines the surface area to be deformed. This distance represents a scale factor for C^p. Thus, if the radius of influence is r and the distance from x to $C^t(0)$ is l, then the effective distance which determines the scale factor will be $d = \sqrt{r^2 - l^2}$. Therefore, C^p will be inscribed in a circle of radius d centered at x and oriented

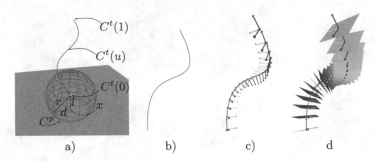

Fig. 5. a) Elements to consider to perform a deformation following a trajectory. For a curve in the space b), at each point it is possible determine what is the tangent vector (in red), the normal vector (in yellow) and the rectifying vector (in blue), c), and it is therefore possible to determine the normal plane at each point, d). Thus it is possible to know the orientation of the curve at each point.

to the rectifying plane of S at x. If l is less than r the surface will not be deformed at all. See Fig. 5.a to view the described elements.

The distance of each points to x will be used to set the place where each point has to be displaced. To do this, functions like (1) will be used. The form adopted by the surface in the deformed area and the way it will do it, remember the technique described in [9] to generate *swept surfaces*.

Swept Surfaces. A swept surface is defined from a trajectory curve, $C^t(v)$, and a profile curve, $C^p(u)$:

$$S(u, v) = C^t(v) + A(v)E(v)C^p(u) \tag{11}$$

where

- $E(v)$ is a scale matrix used to adjust the size of $C^p(u)$ based on v,
- $A(v)$ is a transformation matrix which allows the change from a global reference system to a local one with the convenient orientation.

Obviously, the result depends on the chosen curves. If the twisting or bending of the trajectory curve are too large, the result may not have the desirable continuity. All undesirable effects can be conveniently corrected by changing the parameters of the curves.

The idea is to calculate a series of interpolation curves, $\tilde{C}_i^p(u)$, obtained from $C^p(u)$ and displaced and oriented along $C^t(v)$. The surface $S(u, v)$ will be obtained from the interpolation of the curves $\tilde{C}_i^p(u)$ calculated. To calculate $A(v)$ it is necessary to determine, for each control point of C^t, what its projection over the same C^t is. Thus it is possible to calculate the Frenet Frame for this point. The points of $C^t(v)$ for every curve $\tilde{C}_i^p(u)$ are the points of minimum distance from the curve and the corresponding control point. This is the way (it is the same trajectory curve with its own characteristics) which determines the needed interpolation curves. For each control point P_j^t, $0 \leq j \leq m$, it is necessary to determine the parameter $v_j \in [V_{j-q}, V_{j+1})$ such that:

$$\forall\, v \in [V_{j-q}, V_{j+1})\quad \|P_j^t - C^t(v_j)\| \leq \|P_j^t - C^t(v)\|.$$

Once v_j is known, it is possible to determine the Frenet Frame for the point $C^t(v_j)$, and then it is possible to know the orientation that has to have $\tilde{C}_j^p$. If $T(C(v_j))$, $N(C(v_j))$ and $B(C(v_j))$ are the tangent, the normal and the binormal vectors of the curve C^t at the point v_j respectively, then the value of $A(v_j)$ for $\tilde{C}_j^p(u)$ will be:

$$A(v_j) = \begin{pmatrix} T(v_j)_x & N(v_j)_x & B(v_j)_x & 0 \\ T(v_j)_y & N(v_j)_y & B(v_j)_y & 0 \\ T(v_j)_z & N(v_j)_z & B(v_j)_z & 0 \\ 0 & 0 & 0 & 1 \end{pmatrix}^{-1}. \tag{12}$$

Before its orientation, the control points have to be translated to fit its barycenter with the origin of coordinates. To do this, $E(v)$ can be changed to scale and translate the curve at the same time. If the barycenter is defined as:

$$P_c = \frac{1}{m+1} \sum_{i=0}^{m} P_i^p, \tag{13}$$

then

$$E(v_j) = \begin{pmatrix} S_{j,x} & 0 & 0 & P_{c,x} \\ 0 & S_{j,y} & 0 & P_{c,y} \\ 0 & 0 & Sj, z & P_{c,z} \\ 0 & 0 & 0 & 1 \end{pmatrix}. \tag{14}$$

After their orientation, the control points have to be translated again to put their barycenter in the place of P_j^t. Thus:

$$P_{i,j} = P_j^t + A(v_j) \left(P_i^p - \frac{\sum_{k=0}^{n} P_k^p}{n+1} \right),\quad \begin{matrix} 0 \leq j \leq m, \\ 0 \leq i \leq n. \end{matrix}$$

In Fig. 6 this procedure is described. This method generates smooth surfaces. In Fig. 7 some examples can be seen.

Constraint-based Surface Deformations Following Trajectories.

In order to obtain deformed surfaces with a model based on the swept surfaces, (11), every control point of the trajectory curve has to have an interpolation curve obtained from the profile curve. Now, the surface already exists and has to be changed. In order to obtain a correct result, it is necessary to assure the existence of enough control points in the region to be deformed.

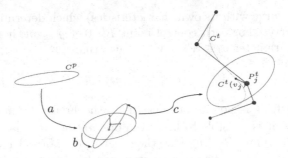

Fig. 6. Orientation of a profile curve. The curve is translated to the origin of coordinates, a. Next, it is oriented upon the calculated values for P_j^t, b. Finally the curve is translated to put the barycenter of the control points to match $C^t(v_j)$, c.

Fig. 7. Swept surfaces examples

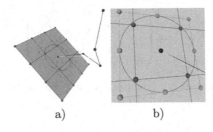

a)   b)

Fig. 8. Constraint applied to a surface. In a) the surface is show, the control points (gray spheres) and a constraint defined by a trajectory curve, in blue, the influence region is defined by a profile curve, in red. In b) clearly there are not enough control points to deform the surface and to adjust them to the trajectory curve.

In Fig. 8, it is shown a 4D B-Spline which has to be deformed. It is also shown the region to be affected, the red circle, which has only 4 control points. It can be observed that the trajectory curve is too complex to be represented with this amount of control points. The procedure to assure the correct amount of control points is iterative. First, the control points needed for the first control point of the trajectory curve are added. After that, it is possible to know how many control points have to be added for the second control point of the trajectory curve, and so on, see Fig 9. This approach has some unexpected effects:

- The control points are obtained via the knot refinement procedure, [9]. In order to maintain the degree, adding a knot requires to add a control point. The surface has to have a regular control point net, so it is necessary to add a whole row or column of control points to maintain the regularity.
- The knot refinement procedure could change the place where several already existing control points are located. This fact has to be taken into account when each control point has to be identified.
- This iterative method described increases considerably the number of control points involved in the deformation. The final amount of these control points may be higher than the expected, so the mapping between the surface control points and the profile curve control points may not exist. This means that it will be necessary to make a knot refinement of the profile curve to assure the matching again. In Fig. 9 the profile curves associated to each step are shown where the number of calculated surface control points grows.

The last control point of the trajectory curve is special because it is the place where this point, where the constraint is defined, has to be moved. The problem is that the place where the last control point to be deformed has to be moved possibly does not match the place where it is located the last control point of the trajectory curve. There exists two possibilities to adjust the surface changing only the last control point and maintaining the shape of the deformed surface:

1. Change the location of the control point putting it away, following the direction defined by the tangent of the trajectory curve at its last point until the surface reaches the desired point. With this solution a suitable outcome is not achieved, since the control points previously calculated exert an influence that it cannot be deleted.

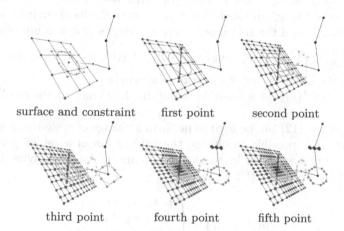

surface and constraint   first point   second point

third point   fourth point   fifth point

Fig. 9. Successive refinements of the control points of a surface. The original control points of the surface are modified in order to have enough control points to satisfy the constraint. This procedure depends on the trajectory and profile curves.

2. Change the weight of the last control point to make its influence much greater than the other control points. If the distance from the last control point to the previous one is high enough, then the shape of last part of the deformed surface could be different from the desired one. Adding a new control point to the trajectory curve close to the last one is a solution for the problem. Empirically it has been estimated that the weight of the last control point has to be, at least:

$$(u, v) \in [U_{k-p}, U_k) \times [V_{l-q}, V_l)$$

$$w_{ij} \geq \sum_{k_1=k-p}^{k} \sum_{l_1=l-q}^{l} w_{k_1 l_1}$$

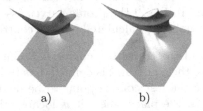

a)   b)

Fig. 10. The extreme of a deformation can be improved if a new control point is added to the trajectory curve. In a) it can be seen a deformation with the trajectory curve unchanged, in b) the same deformation but with the trajectory curve with a new control point added close to the extreme. The b) solution is the smoother one.

Surface Points Orientation. The question of how to place the surface control points is answered by determining, for each control point of C^t, P_i^t, what its parametric image is, u_m. That is: the parametric point such that $C^t(u_m)$ is the closest value of C^t to P_i^t and such that it belongs to the local environment of the control point. Thus, if the trajectory curve has degree p it accomplishes that:

$$\forall\, u \in [U_i^t \ldots U_{i+p+1}^t)\quad p_i^t - C_t(u_m) < p_i^t - C_t(u),\ u_m \in [U_i^t \ldots U_{i+p+1}^t),$$

where U^t is the knots vector of the trajectory curve C^t.

Once known $C^t(u_m)$ it is possible to obtain the Frenet Frame of C^t at point u_m.

The expression (12) can be used to perform a change of system of coordinates. Furthermore, it is possible to change the orientation of a set of points to be aligned with a plane defined by two vectors, v and w, by multiplying the points by a *projection matrix* in $\mathbb{R}^4$:

$$m_o(n, v, w) = \begin{pmatrix} n_x & v_x & w_x & 0 \\ n_y & v_y & w_y & 0 \\ n_z & v_z & w_z & 0 \\ 0 & 0 & 0 & 1 \end{pmatrix}^{-1}, \tag{15}$$

where n is the normal vector to the plane. This expression has the same form of (12). Thus, when a change of basis matrix is created, it is possible to select the place where to put the tangent, normal and binormal vectors. To place the profile curve, C_p on the surface, centered on a point $p = S(u, v)$ it will be necessary to calculate the rectifying plane and the normal vector of the surface at point p, again it is necessary to calculate the Frenet Frame, now for the surface S at point p. The barycenter of the control points will be translated to p and each control point will be rotated and translated into the proper form. Thus, the profile curve $\tilde{C}_p$ oriented and translated to the point p, will be obtained by modifying the control points C_p:

$$\tilde{P}_i = m_o(N_s, B_s, T_s)(P_i - p_c) + p, \tag{16}$$

where p_c represents the coordinates of the barycenter, N_s is the normal vector, B_s is the binormal vector and T_s is the tangent vector.

The Problem of Straight Lines. One of the special cases that can occur with relative ease is when the trajectory curve is actually a straight line, either in its entirety or it is just a part of it, in which case three or more consecutive control points are collinear. The problem arises from the calculation of the normal plane of those control points, because the vectorial product of the first and second derivatives is null, so it is impossible to calculate the Frenet Frame directly. In Fig. 11 the problem, and the solution, are shown. The first solution is to determine an arbitrary vector perpendicular to the tangent vector. The problem now is that the calculated normal and binormal vectors may not have an orientation compatible with the other values calculated in the right way, see 11.c. A better approach is to locate the first control point not collinear and, with it, calculate the first curve point influenced by this control point. Now, it is possible to calculate the Frenet Frame of this point and it is possible to approximate the values for the straight part of C^t, see Fig. 11.d.

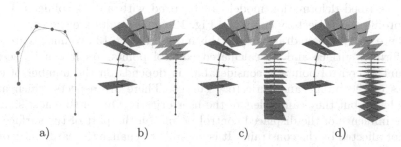

a)   b)   c)   d)

Fig. 11. The tangent problem. When a curve has three o more consecutive control points collinear, a), it is not possible to calculate the Frenet Frame directly, b). A possible solution is to arbitrarily determine a vector perpendicular to the tangent vector, b). But in that case the orientation of this part of the curve may be different to the rest, c). The solution is to locate the first curve segment not collinear, and to calculate the values of the Frenet Frame in that place. d).

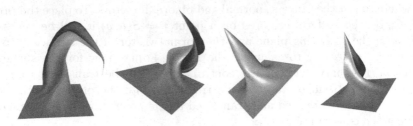

Fig. 12. The proposed model does not impose any limitation on the way the curves are used

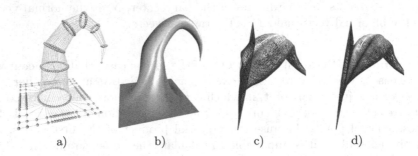

a)   b)   c)   d)

Fig. 13. Some aspects to improve. a) and b) The surface control net can have many control points. Also, depending on the shape of the trajectory curve, it is possible that the deformed surface collapses partially onto itself. In c) no control is established, in d) the first interpolation curve is not oriented along the trajectory curve but it is oriented by the rectifying plane of the surface.

2.3   Results

The described deformation model can be used with any B-Spline surface and any profile and trajectory curves. In Fig. 12 some results are shown.

There are two main drawbacks in this model. In Fig. 13 two images are shown: a deformed surface and its calculated control points. As it can be seen, the amount of control points is considerable, it depends on the number of control points of the profile and trajectory curves. There are aspects which are not considered, but they can be left to the user criteria. One of the most significant is the influence of the displaced control points on the part of the surface which are not affected by the constraint. It is possible to change the cardinality of those control points to reduce their influence. Depending on the trajectory curve, it is possible that the deformed curve collapses partially onto itself; this is due to the curvature and the twist of the trajectory curve and its position respect to the surface, Fig. 13.c. To avoid this effect, the first interpolation curve, $\widetilde{C}_0^p$, can be oriented with respect to the rectifying plane of the surface instead of the normal plane of the trajectory curve. With this modification the corresponding control points are located on the surface, Fig. 13.d.

In short, it is possible to use the model by letting the user to choose the settings to determine the way the deformation will occur.

3   Conclusions

This paper shows a new approach to deform 4D B-Spline surfaces based on a constrained model with trajectories.

As any other geometric model, its application is simple and also computationally very efficient. The model is static, nevertheless it is possible to create animations by interpolating the deformation at different stages. The problem of curve fitting for best results, or, in any case, the results the user wants, is considerably less complex with this model than other FFD models.

It can therefore be concluded that the use of 4D B-Splines together with the deformation model described, based on non-linear constraints is a viable alternative to the deformable objects representation.

References

1. Bechmann, D., Gerber, D.: Arbitrary shaped deformations with DOGME. The Visual Computer 19, 175–186 (2003), http://dx.doi.org/10.1007/s00371-002-0191-x176, 10.1007/s00371-002-0191-x176
2. Borrel, P., Bechmann, D.: Deformation of n–dimensional objects. In: Proceedings of the First ACM Symposium on Solid Modeling Foundations and CAD/CAM Applications, SMA 1991, pp. 351–369. ACM, New York (1991)
3. Borrel, P., Rappoport, A.: Simple constrained deformations for geometric modeling and interactive design. ACM Transactions on Graphics 13(2), 137–155 (1994)
4. Clapés, M., González-Hidalgo, M., Mir-Torres, A., Palmer-Rodríguez, P.A.: Interactive constrained deformations of NURBS surfaces: N-SCODEF. In: Perales, F.J., Fisher, R.B. (eds.) AMDO 2008. LNCS, vol. 5098, pp. 359–369. Springer, Heidelberg (2008), http://www.springerlink.com/content/755x0m42567u22k0/
5. Jin, X., Li, Y., Peng, Q.: General constrained deformations based on generalized metaballs. Computer & Graphics 24, 200 (2000)
6. La Gréca, R.: Approche déclarative de la modélisation de surfaces. Ph.D. thesis. Université de la Méditerranée Aix–Marseille II (2005)
7. La Gréca, R., Raffin, R., Gesquière, G.: Punctual constraint resolution and deformation path on NURBS. In: International Conference on Computer Graphics and Vision, Graphicon 2007 (2007), http://www.graphicon.ru/2007/proceedings/Papers/Paper_38.pdf
8. Lanquetin, S., Raffin, R., Neveu, M.: Generalized SCODEF deformations on subdivision surfaces. In: Perales, F.J., Fisher, R.B. (eds.) AMDO 2006. LNCS, vol. 4069, pp. 132–142. Springer, Heidelberg (2006)
9. Piegl, L., Tiller, W.: The NURBS Book, Monographs in visual communications, 2nd edn. Springer (1997)
10. Brecher, C., Lindemann, D., Merz, M., Wenzel, C., Preuß, W.: Free form deformations or deformations non-constrained by geometries or topologies. In: Brinksmeier, E., Riemer, O., Gläbe, R. (eds.) Fabrication of Complex Optical Components. Lecture Notes in Computational Vision and Biomechanics, vol. 7, pp. 49–74. Springer, Netherlands (2013), http://dx.doi.org/10.1007/978-94-007-5446-1_2

11. Raffin, R., Gesquière, G., La Gréca, R.: Déformations de modèles géométriques. Tech. Rep. LSIS.RR.2007.001, LSIS (2007)
12. Raffin, R., Neveu, M., Derdouri, B.: Constrained deformation for geometric modeling and object reconstruction. In: WSCG 1998 – International Conference in Central Europe on Computer Graphics, Visualization 1998, vol. 2, pp. 299–306 (1998)
13. Raffin, R., Neveu, M., Jaar, F.: Extended constrained deformations: A new sculpturing tool. In: Proceedings of International Conference on Shape Modeling International 1999, pp. 219–224 (March 1999)
14. Raffin, R., Neveu, M., Jaar, F.: Curvilinear displacement of free–form–based deformation. The Visual Computer 16, 38–46 (2000), http://dx.doi.org/10.1007/s003710050005, 10.1007/s003710050005

Author Index